INTEGRATING FAITH AND LEARNING

CASE STUDIES FROM DALLAS BAPTIST UNIVERSITY

EDITED BY
DAVID D. COOK, PH.D., J.D.
AND BRENT A. THOMASON, PH.D.

Integrating Faith and Learning: Case Studies from Dallas Baptist University

Published by D6 Family Ministry
114 Bush Road
Nashville, TN 37217
Visit d6family.com

ISBN: 9781614841715

Printed in the United States of America

What Key Leaders Have to Say About This Book

"Christian higher education faces a crucible at the moment—how do academicians effectively integrate faith with a vast array of disciplines and university services? Quite simply, the need for the integration of faith and learning has never been more urgent. This courageous book urges readers to embrace the concept of 'holistic faith integration' in their approach to Christian higher education. Readers will be inspired by engaging, creative strategies and find their own faith deepened in the process."

—Adam C. Wright, Ph.D., President
Dallas Baptist University

"David Cook and Brent Thomason have done an excellent job editing a much-needed volume to serve the academic leaders of today. By providing best practices that are both practical and inspirational, this resource will soon become a 'must-read' for those striving to integrate faith in every aspect of their campus."

—Cory Hines, Ph.D., President
Howard Payne University

"Dr. David Cook's and Dr. Brent Thomason's case study approach has shown that the integration of faith and learning is not only applicable to the student at a Christian higher education institution, but it is a framework for life-long and life-focused education long after graduation. This research is a helpful cross-discipline reference that encourages integrating faith and learning to enhance and deepen the classroom experience in ways that higher education without the integration of faith in learning cannot. *Integrating Faith and Learning: Case Studies from Dallas Baptist University*, will be a helpful campus resource."

—Shirley V. Hoogstra, J.D., President
Council for Christian Colleges & Universities

"The most important mission for a Christian university is that it would be Christ-centered. During the 28 years that I served as president of Dallas Baptist University, this was my chief aspiration for the institution. At every level, our desire at DBU is to make it known that 'Christ is the reason for this University.' The way we sought to accomplish this goal is by the integration of faith and learning and by the emphasis on servant leadership.

This task has been carried out by many treasured faculty and staff members through the years, and this insightful book contains personal testimonies by many of these dedicated individuals. The editors are to be commended for conceiving the idea of providing this needed and helpful volume. May the Lord bless those who have written these words and provide wisdom for those who read this book."

—Gary Cook, D.Min., Chancellor
Dallas Baptist University

"Producing Christian servant leaders requires a paradigm shift infusing every aspect of the Academy. This read provides *behind the curtain* access to understanding the disposition that begets the 'DBU difference!'"

—Andrea R. Ramirez, MBA, Ph.D.
former Executive Director of the U.S. Department
of Education's Center for Faith & Opportunity Initiatives

"Faith and biblical integration at Christian colleges and universities is a shared responsibility across the campus. *Integrating Faith and Learning* is a must-read for ALL campus leaders. Cook and Thomason have pulled together a comprehensive and practical work that challenges the academic and administrative silos that too often stifle effective integration. Do you want your students to have a seamless faith-integrated experience from the moment they step foot on your campus to when they walk the stage to receive a degree? Start here!"

—Philip E. Dearborn, Ed.D., President
Association for Biblical Higher Education.

Table of Contents

Part 2: Integrating Faith in the Broader Learning Environment of a Christian College

Foreword

As the Provost of Dallas Baptist University, I have the privilege of meeting many full-time and adjunct faculty members and learning about their lives. During interviews with prospective faculty members, we ask them to describe their spiritual journey as a segue into the conversation about the importance DBU places on the integration of faith and learning. These academic colleagues readily describe their credentials, training, and content areas, but some of the most meaningful and significant conversations often revolve around their spiritual journeys. However, since most faculty members have been trained in secular institutions where faith has not been integrated into their studies, we recognize from these conversations that the burden is on us to provide the training necessary for them to integrate biblical faith with their content areas.

DBU's mission and current strategic plan focus on the need to help students integrate faith and learning, and one of the initiatives of our strategic plan in the academic area is to, "Deepen faculty understanding and enhance pedagogy relative to the integration of faith with respective content areas." While we have conducted faculty workshops on the integration of faith and learning, invited speakers to speak on this topic, and pondered ways to be more intentional about this core aspect of our mission, it became clear through our efforts that we had experts among us who were much more adept at these practices and willing to help us train others. The editors of this book are two such experts.

Dr. David Cook has the academic credentials in both law and leadership to assess the institution as a whole and identify the areas where the "living out" of this integration might be more explicit, as well as those areas where it might be more hidden, but no less important. It was his idea to include not only the classroom but also other areas of the campus responsible to integrate Christian faith into those areas. His personal and professional interest in religious liberty also provided a unique perspective from which to encourage evident integration of faith into our campus community.

Dr. Brent Thomason is a biblical scholar, with a particular gift of communicating truths of Scripture in clear and compelling ways. His scholarly, but warm and approachable communication style has drawn countless students into learning how to live out their faith in every aspect of their lives. Brent has also come alongside colleagues to help them understand theological concepts related to their faith. This practical knowledge, combined with his excellent scholarship are evident throughout this text.

The privilege of serving alongside these two scholars, as well as the other gifted contributors to this book, afforded the opportunity to read this text and provide my enthusiastic recommendation. Not only does the work supply theological, philosophical, and practical discussions for professors of various disciplines, it also makes available additional content to support departments all across the campus. Student affairs leaders, physical operations leaders, Title IX leaders, and athletic leaders will find helpful discussions related to integration of faith into their respective areas. The content is representative of the excellent thought and practice from our best leaders and learners at DBU. Other leaders also do a beautiful job of integrating faith, but the investment of time from these very busy scholars to produce this book is an exceptional gift to our campus and, we hope, to other like-minded institutions.

In their book, Learning for the Love of God, Donald Opitz and Derek Melleby acknowledge that:

> . . . integration is a constant challenge to those seeking to be authentic Christian students and scholars. We must continually seek to integrate our beliefs with the testimony of Scripture, our words with our beliefs, our actions with our words, and our academic work with our theology.[1]

---

[1] Donald Opitz and Derek Melleby, *Learning for the Love of God: A Student's Guide to Academic Faithfulness.* (Grand Rapids, MI: Brazos Press, 2014), 57.

Christian colleges and universities recognize the challenges of doing this very thing, but the writers make another statement that helps: "Faithfulness is mostly a matter of inching in the right direction."[2]

Perhaps this text will encourage you and your academic community, along with the faculty and staff at DBU, to inch along in the right direction of integrating faith and learning in the classroom and throughout your campus.

Norma S. Hedin, Ph.D., Provost
Dallas Baptist University

[2] Ibid., 84.

Introduction

Integrating Faith and Learning

By Brent A. Thomason[3]

Rationale for the Book

The book you are holding is one that attempts to explore what it means to truly integrate faith into the totality of the learning environment at a Christian college—not just in a religion class, but in every class, and on the athletic field, in the dorms, and even in the realm of student discipline. In a world that seeks to privatize religion, asking Christians to relegate faith to the backseat of their lives, the concept of holistic faith integration is a radical one. It is one that asks the Christian to see every square inch[4] of their lives as being a missional endeavor where they are part of the grand story of what God is doing to redeem and restore Creation. Rather than bifurcating their lives into the "sacred" and the "secular," faith integration means that God is to be at the forefront of our Mondays just as He is at the forefront of our Sundays. And yet such a concept is quite foreign in a world that does not understand the power of the Gospel message for all areas of life.

It is with this in mind that we are writing this book. We believe Christian colleges play an important role in supplementing the work

[3] Brent A. Thomason serves as Dean of the Graduate School of Ministry and Professor of Biblical Studies at Dallas Baptist University.

[4] Abraham Kuyper, "Sphere Sovereignty: A Public Address Delivered at the Inauguration of the Free University, October 20, 1880," *The Gospel Coalition*, trans. George Kamps, June 2017, https://media.thegospelcoalition.org/wp-content/uploads/2017/06/24130543/SphereSovereignty_English.pdf.

of the local church to transform the minds, hearts, bodies, and souls of young people for Christ. Through the medium of education, a Christian college has the opportunity to shape the lives of young adults at a truly formative stage of their lives. And it is our belief that this job of helping students integrate faith into all aspects of their lives is at the core of why Christian colleges exist in the first place. It is in these faith development laboratories that students can study a discipline in such a way that they become not just a lawyer, but a Christian lawyer, that they become not just a biomedical researcher, but a Christ-like biomedical researcher, that they become not just a businessman, but one who does business for the Lord.

But the process of teaching students to integrate faith into all areas of life is a difficult task. It demands a good deal more than merely teaching a subject: it means teaching the student to see their discipline through the very lens of faith itself. It means we are not merely to relegate faith formation to the chaplain, but to each and every professor and staff member of the University. It is the recognition that faith development may occur just as frequently in campus housing as it does in the classroom, and that therefore every Resident Assistant is a co-laborer alongside every professor in the process of teaching students how to integrate faith. And it means every member of the University family has a role to play in helping students mature into Christ-like adults who are ready to integrate faith into their respective areas of calling and career.

In seeking to examine what it means to truly integrate faith into the whole sphere of the learning environment at a Christian college, therefore, we have a lofty task. This mission is at the core of preparing the next generation to be ready to serve Christ around the world. Christian colleges play a pivotal role in this preparatory mission, and thus our goal in this book is to analyze how such a mission may be accomplished with the utmost care. In analyzing this topic, it certainly could have been useful to survey a broad cross-section of Christian colleges to determine how faith integration is happening. There are, in fact, a variety of other books that have attempted to do just that. But taking such a shotgun approach necessarily means one does not truly understand the deeper context behind the issues at play. Thus, we chose a different route from those that came before us—one that is more laser-focused—in an attempt to tell a more complete story of how one particular Christian college attempts to fulfill this important mission. With that desire in mind, this book provides a unique case study of one Christian college, Dallas Baptist University (DBU), and how it attempts to integrate faith into all aspects of the learning environment.

Our hope is that such a comprehensive, in-depth analysis of one school's efforts will provide rich insights that go deeper than the mere surface of the issue. Case studies naturally provide context-rich descriptions of phenomena, and thus our hope is this particular case study of DBU will illuminate the many facets of this important endeavor. DBU is certainly not perfect, and thus this case study will examine not only what is being done now, but also explore what could be done to enact this mission more fully in the future. In choosing to compile a book that gives a comprehensive view of one university's efforts, our hope is that readers will be able to extrapolate deeper lessons that emerge because of the context-driven focus of the case study method.

An Introduction to the Integration of Faith and Learning at DBU

In looking at this particular missional endeavor, we must first understand a little bit of the context of DBU in general. A good place to start is, of course, the University's official Mission Statement: "The mission of Dallas Baptist University is to provide Christ-centered quality higher education in the arts, sciences, and professional studies at both the undergraduate and graduate levels to traditional age and adult students in order to produce servant leaders who have the ability *to integrate faith and learning* through their respective callings."[5] In the first few years of his leadership, the fifth president of Dallas Baptist University, Dr. Gary Cook led in the drafting of the University Mission Statement. In

[5] "Mission Statement," About DBU, Dallas Baptist University, accessed June 19, 2022, www.dbu.edu/ about /#history.

no uncertain terms, that Mission Statement prioritized the integration of faith and learning. That was 1993.

By 2002, DBU's implementation of faith and learning was wet cement, ready to be poured into every corner of campus life. Then Chair and Professor of Philosophy Dr. David Naugle sunk his palms into faith and learning integration and forever left his handprints on DBU history by authoring the official Commentary on the Mission Statement of DBU.[6] In it he wrote, "DBU's purpose is to produce, not just servant leaders, but Christian servant leaders. This intention largely depends upon instructing students in the task of integrating Christian faith and academic learning…DBU believes that the integration of biblical faith and academic learning is the *raison d'être* of Christian higher education."[7] What Naugle understood as the *raison d'être*, later was coined the "DBU difference."[8] From those early years, integrating faith and learning was what set DBU apart. And it still does!

Since the founding of the mission and the drafting of the commentary, DBU continued to weave faith into the fabric of campus life. In 2004 a new course was created whose sole purpose was to train students in the biblical worldview (DCM 2301 – "Developing a Christian Mind") and was adopted into the undergraduate degrees as a required course. By the time I became a professor in 2014, faculty workshops, plenary seminars, and breakout sessions on integrating faith and learning were a regular rhythm on the academic calendar. Beyond attending many of these events, I have contributed as the workshop speaker or breakout session leader over the years: 2017 (3x), 2019, 2020 (2x), and 2021 (4x). Considering that integrating faith and learning is not only a priority for faculty development, I have also been asked to address the issue to incoming freshmen (2021) and international educational leaders

---

[6] David Naugle, "A Commentary on the Mission Statement of Dallas Baptist University," About DBU, Dallas Baptist University, accessed June 19, 2022, www.dbu.edu/naugle/_documents/mission-commentary.pdf.

[7] Ibid., 7.

[8] "A Holistic Education," The Integration of Faith and Learning, Dallas Baptist University, accessed June 19, 2022, www.dbu.edu/about/integrated-faith.html.

through the International Education and Leadership Forums of DBU's Global Community in 2020 (2x) and again in 2022.

From the examples above, you might conclude that faith and learning integration is emphasized at DBU. Let me be the first to say, it is not. It is more—so much more! Faculty disciplines and staff departments are the two complementary strands that make up our double helix, while faith and learning are the linked bases held together by integration. As you can see, far from being emphasized, faith and learning are imbedded in DBU's DNA.[9] Since this topic is so integral to who we are at DBU, we desire this book to be a resource to brothers and sisters in Christ who are seeking examples of how to practically integrate faith and learning into every aspect of University life on their own campuses.

---

[9] In his commentary on the DBU Mission Statement, Naugle outlines criteria for professors, students, and administrators in order to achieve a holistic integration of faith and learning on campus: "DBU professors must (1) have a pre-requisite and substantive understanding of Scripture, biblical theology, and even the rudiments of philosophy (since all academic disciplines are shaped by certain pre-theoretical commitments), (2) possess a comprehensive and in-depth knowledge of their own area of academic specialization, (3) develop the competency of being able to understand, appreciate, critique, and develop their disciplines through the lens of biblical faith and philosophical commitments, and (4) learn how to communicate a Christian perspective on their disciplines to students and teach them how they might undertake the work of integration for themselves as a lifelong learners. Students, to begin with, must be eager to learn, value education as a gift from God, be curious about creation and human culture, recognize the importance and develop a love for books and ideas, and be an eager participant in the 'Great Conversation' that has shaped the Western and Christian minds. They, too, must be about the business of developing a comprehensive biblical worldview as the grid through which they approach life, and pursue their educational goals and personal callings. Their ambition is to be, while at the University, not just students who are Christians, but distinctively Christian students who are animated by a biblical vision of human greatness, and who are preparing themselves for lifetimes of leadership and service in the Church and in the world. Administrators are not primarily concerned as professors are with the theoretical task of integrating faith and learning, but are challenged and charged with the duty of demonstrating practically on a day to day basis how they have thought through the implications of Christian faith on their work, and how they are integrating biblical principles in their very vocations as servant leaders, especially in the management of people, in economic stewardship, and in the execution of power. They, perhaps more than any other group on campus, have the opportunity to manifest in their daily lives the finished product of Christian higher education before an observant student body who wishes and needs to learn from them as well." Naugle, "Commentary," 9–10.

Defining the Terms

Before we get too far ahead, let us decelerate to define some terms: faith, learning, worldview, and integration. First, in reference to integrating faith and learning, faith can be defined as "a set of rational assumptions about life and truth embraced by personal trust."[10] To label them "assumptions" we are not saying these are only things "hoped for" driven by emotional feelings. Rather, the assumptions form a rational "way of organizing all of the available knowledge."[11] In the context of DBU, the rational assumptions are based upon Scripture and Christian tradition. That is not to say that both carry equal weight, but certainly both inform our beliefs. When talking about the integration of faith and learning, faith carries with it the connotation of the Christian faith, biblical doctrine, systematic theology, the character of God, and other similar concepts as used throughout the book.

With reference to the integration of faith and learning, learning refers to the assimilation of information. For the Christian college campus, what the student is learning relates to general and special revelation of God. We understand the knowledge gained from Scripture to be special revelation while the knowledge gained through other academic disciplines pertains to general revelation. This acquisition and comprehension of revelation takes place both in the classroom and in the other co-curricular environments at DBU among students, faculty, and staff alike.

A worldview, simply put, is a framework through which we view the world. This framework is built upon a set of beliefs. Consequently, a worldview shapes one's perception and interpretation of reality. A worldview can be exposed by asking some basic questions such as, "What is the nature of man?" "Does God exist?" "What happens when a person dies?" "What is the meaning of history?" "How do we know what is right and wrong?" etc. Of course, for DBU this set of beliefs is derived

[10] Jane Beers and Stephen Beers, "Integration of Faith and Learning," in *The Soul of a Christian University: A Field Guide for Educators*, ed. Stephen Beers (Abilene, TX: ACU Press, 2008), 55.
[11] Ibid.

from Scripture, so we talk about a biblical worldview. This worldview is molded and shaped through religion courses, chapel, Baptist Student Ministries, mission trips, philosophy courses, and other experiences on campus. As it relates to the integration of faith and learning, worldview permeates the entire process.[12]

Integration is the infusion of faith at the deepest level of the academic discipline and in the learning environment. It is a process that is integral, not auxiliary, to the study of the subject matter. It is not placing faith alongside learning. That only reinforces a dualistic view of life. While faith and learning may interact in that scenario, they do not integrate.[13] Rather, integration is approaching the data from a position of faith. It is wedding the curriculum to the character of God, and using His truth as the lens through which we view the world. It is taking a spiritual syringe and vaccinating the curriculum with faith in order to inoculate it against secularism, humanism, or any other kind of "ism" that removes God from the picture. Integration is a fusion of the two, and it flows over not only from the classroom, but into the whole sphere of the learning environment itself. It is not just a way of teaching stu-

---

[12] Naugle explains the great need of integrating the biblical worldview into curriculum at DBU: "Hence, DBU aspires to do more than just promote a Christianity which flanks academics. Given the fundamental religious nature of human persons, DBU recognizes that education is not undertaken in an unbiased, objective manner, but is always governed by the previous commitments and control beliefs embraced by the scholarly community. DBU asserts that there is no such thing as presuppositionless scholarship, teaching, or learning. If education is not pursued on Christian grounds, then other religious and philosophic systems will provide the foundation. Consequently, DBU believes that the distinguishing feature of a Christian university is found not only in its external religious environment (Christian proclamation and practice), but also in its commitment to pursuing the academic enterprise on the basis of Christian concepts which penetrate to its very core. The roots of the tree of knowledge must be grounded in biblical soil." Naugle, "Commentary," 8.

[13] Warning about shortfalls to full integration of faith and learning, Naugle writes: "And DBU is equally concerned to provide invaluable training and experience for students through various opportunities for Christian service. While these activities make invaluable contributions to the lives of students and to the campus environment, they do not constitute the integration of faith and learning per se, but might be described as the 'interaction of faith alongside learning.' Oftentimes at Christian colleges and universities, the proclamation and practice of Christian faith merely accompanies academics without necessarily being integrated with them. If that is the understanding and extent of the integration process, then it is incomplete, and the actual activity of education and scholarship most likely proceeds on a foundation other than a Christian one." Ibid., 7–8.

dents how to view a discipline through the lens of faith, but how to view all of life from the lens of faith.

Cosgrove's Four Models

With this orientation of terms in mind, we turn to discuss how faith *relates* to learning, before exploring practical approaches to integrate faith and learning. The seminal work by H. Richard Niebuhr, *Christ and Culture*, codified the discussion on this relation. There he outlined five ways throughout history that Christianity has sought to relate to civilization: (1) Christ *against* Culture, (2) Christ *of* Culture, (3) Christ *above* Culture, (4) Christ *and* Culture, and (5) Christ *transformer of* Culture.[14] The Christ *against* Culture type positions the church in rejection to society. Loyalty to the Lord means condemning the culture. On the other hand, Christ *of* Culture is on the opposite end of the spectrum. According to this type, there is a tensionless relationship between Christians and society since Jesus fulfills the hopes of civilization. Christ is seen as culture's great teacher, enlightener, and moral guide, but nothing more. Christ *above* Culture attempts to synthesize the two prior views by explaining that the tension exists between God and humanity, not God and culture. Consequently, this model is viewed as Christ validating the best parts of culture. Similarly, Christ *and* Culture is the dualistic version of the former. Since the tension between God and humanity is ever present, man lives with a foot in two realms: "Grace is in God, and sin is in man."[15] Christ *transformer of* Culture is the conversionist approach of the former. It views the perverted and corrupted parts of culture as fertile ground for redemption. What can be affirmed in culture is; what cannot is transformed.

More recently, the conversation has shifted from the culture to the classroom.[16] Building upon Niebuhr, Mark Cosgrove proposes four models of how Christ relates to the academic arenas, or more common-

[14] Richard Niebuhr, *Christ and Culture* (Grand Rapids, MI: Eerdmans, 1951), 45–229.

[15] Ibid., 151.

[16] Cf. John D. Carter and Bruce Narramore, *The Integration of Psychology and Theology* (Grand Rapids, MI: Zondervan, 1979).

ly, how faith relates to learning.[17] These models are (1) Sole Authority Model: Faith *against* Learning; (2) Separate Authorities Model: Faith *and* Learning; (3) Equal Authorities Model: Faith *plus* Learning; and (4) Foundational Authority Model: Faith *supports* Learning. In the Sole Authority Model, faith and learning exist in antagonistic relationship. Because the world and humanity are fallen, even the brightest minds err in logic and refuse to accept clear truths from God. The Bible is the only source of truth and authority. Therefore, learning "is considered nonessential, may be in error, and much of the time is simply not worth the effort."[18] Contrary, the Separate Authorities Model views faith and learning as parallel sources of authority. Spiritual truth can be learned from the Bible while natural truths can be gleaned from the academic disciplines. They are akin to the two rails of a train track and consequently, do not overlap. Similar to the former, the Equal Authorities Model admits that the Bible and academic disciplines carry the same weight of authority. But the view espouses that they should overlap in order that the combined weight of the two might create still more truth.

The aforementioned models approach the question of Christ in relation to the classroom from a high view of Scripture. They believe the claims of the Bible are trustworthy. For this, they are to be commended. However, each fall short in their own way to account fully for what can and cannot be learned from nature alone, the Bible alone, or the combination thereof. That is why DBU aligns with the fourth model, Foundational Authority Model. This is often referred to as the worldview model because the Bible creates the framework from which we observe, collect, and interpret the world around us. Admittedly, there is no unbiased learning; worldview always comes to bear in some way on the learning process. Consequently, this model does not jettison what can be learned from the academic disciplines; rather it acknowledges that a biblical foundation aides in the correct interpretation of what is learned in the academy. Tracking in step with Niebuhr's Christ *trans-*

---

[17] Mark P. Cosgrove, *Foundations of Christian Thought: Faith, Learning, and the Christian Worldview* (Grand Rapids, MI: Kregel, 2006).

[18] Ibid., 55.

former of Culture, Cosgrove claims this fourth model "seeks to transform culture and ideas rather than reject, ignore, or just mix with culture and ideas."[19]

Holmes's Four Approaches

Having established how Christ relates to the classroom, we now turn to pragmatic ways of integrating faith and learning not only in the traditional classroom itself, but also in the broader "classroom" of the living and learning environment at a Christian college. While much of the literature on faith and learning integration focuses on the traditional classroom itself, one of the aims of this book is to highlight how integration of faith and learning can occur in a much more holistic way if it is woven into the fabric of all areas of campus life. From the dorm to the gym, from chapel to the dining hall, there is an opportunity to demonstrate how faith touches all areas of life.

In his work, *The Idea of a Christian College*, Arthur Holmes proposes four approaches for faith integration: (1) the Attitudinal Approach, (2) the Ethical Approach; (3) the Foundational Approach; and (4) the Worldview Approach.[20] From the outset, we need to recognize that these approaches are ongoing. These are not static tasks to be completed and crossed off the list, as if one can move on to the next approach and accomplish it as well. To claim that would be tantamount to claiming integration is a position, rather than a process. Additionally, each approach achieves varying degrees of successful integration contingent on the academic discipline or area of daily living. Moreover, we do not investigate these approaches here to form a list of pros and cons, nor do we believe one approach is superior to another. Rather, we understand that collectively the four approaches work in tandem to infuse faith holistically into the learning process.

Likely, the student's first contact with the process of integrating faith and learning comes via the Attitudinal Approach. As the professor

---

[19] Ibid., 58.

[20] Arthur F. Holmes, *The Idea of a Christian College* (Grand Rapids, MI: Eerdmans, 1975), 45–60.

walks into the lecture hall or lab or the Resident Director greets her residents, their positive attitude communicates to the student a desirable affinity toward living and learning. This attitude stems from the faculty or staff member's own Christian commitment: all truth is God's truth, whether in the classroom or the dorm room. On the faculty side, Elton Trueblood claims that the Christian scholar is likely the best scholar: "Every good investigator wants to learn the truth, if he can, but the committed Christian has the added motive in that his intellectual task is a sacred task because it is God's truth that he is trying to learn."[21] Thus, every new discovery is charting new territory on the map of God's character. Every new insight peels back another layer of the *imago Dei*. Likewise, every coach, RA, or student success staffer at the university has the opportunity to display an attitude that radiates the very light of Christ. The Attitudinal Approach is infectious, motivating students to conduct quality research, be excellent neighbors in the dorms, and compete to their highest ability in sports. Why? Trueblood explains: "The Christian faith, when it understands itself, is the sworn enemy of all intellectual dishonesty and shoddiness."[22] Hence, attitude and motivation comprise the first task of integrating faith and learning.

Next is the Ethical Approach. There is no shortage of ethical issues on a college campus. They surface inside and outside the classroom, from cheating on exams to Title IX situations, from plagiarism to admissions processes, from research involving human subjects to financial aid distribution, to name a few. The Ethical Approach identifies the moral dilemma of the moment and raises questions relevant to our fallen world. It engages students in critical thinking about values and principles in conjunction with their relationship to the (a or im)moral predicament. Regardless of whether the predicament presents itself from the curriculum studied or the situation encountered, these discussions are an opportune time to introduce Christian values into the ethical equation. As a result, the Christian faith is integrated in learning via the Ethical Approach.

[21] Elton Trueblood, *The Idea of a College* (New York, NY: Harper, 1959), 19.
[22] Ibid.

The Foundational Approach considers the historical, philosophical, and theological underpinnings of the academic discipline. The "foundations" of that discipline, as testified by course titles that bear their name, stem from one of these underpinnings, or a combination thereof. True integration here encompasses more than the study of facts and figures within that discipline. It explores the ideals and the philosophical, theological, or historical context out of which that discipline arose. For instance, in the study of any academic subject there is a particular philosophy behind it, whether a philosophy of psychology or critical theory or education or science. Exploring the philosophy behind the discipline points to the Foundational Approach. In that exploration, time can be taken to highlight the Christian ideals or historical Christian thinkers who participated in the advancement of that discipline, or the exploration of that field. This type of foundational, interdisciplinary approach will inevitably lead to the bigger theological questions of the next approach. But suffice it to say here, investigating the substrata of any academic discipline will open the pathway to discuss the Divine and His interaction with the mortal, permitting the professor to integrate faith in the learning process. In much the same way, each area of campus has a history of underlying assumptions—a philosophical, theological, and historical foundation upon which it is built. Thus, for instance, as the Title IX department or Dean of Students engages in student discipline, they are building on a foundation of justice that emanates from God's own call for justice in the Bible. Similarly, as the Resident Director prepares for his residents to arrive, he is building on a tradition of living and learning that can be seen in Christ's own model of living with and teaching His disciples. Both in the classroom and beyond, the university faculty and staff have a sacred opportunity to show students the very foundations of faith and learning in all areas of life.

The Worldview Approach to the integration of faith and learning is holistic, exploratory, pluralistic, and perspectival. Let us unpack each. This approach swims against the tide of academic life that is fragmented by siloed departments. Rather it views each academic subject in light of the whole and cross-pollinates with other fields; ergo it is holistic. It views the Registrar's Office and Library as an integrated part of the whole framework of the Christian university, seeing the work done in these areas as a significant part of the student's overall experience of growing in Christ. But it is also exploratory. The Worldview Approach is not a static system but an evolving engine. That is to say, it is always expanding as it learns new data and always operating to process older information. It is an endless cycle, not a closed system, ever exploring God's natural and supernatural revelation. Accordingly, it is likely pluralistic providing for a diversity of perspectives of interpreting the data, though still within the same Christian tradition. Lastly, it is perspectival, looking within the discipline or department for relationships among data points while simultaneously looking without for its relevance in other arenas of the student experience. This all-encompassing approach to integration provides ample opportunity to bring Christian beliefs to bear on the subject. It approaches learning from a position of belief while simultaneously pointing back to the belief from the midst of the data itself. Faith supersaturates the subject matter of the classroom, the locker room, or the dorm room through the Worldview Approach.[23]

Overview and Outline

With Holmes's approaches in mind, what follows is an in-depth, comprehensive look at the integration of faith and learning through case-studies written by faculty and staff at DBU. To ensure a comprehensive investigation of the integration of faith and learning at DBU, the book has been divided into two parts reflective of a student's campus life experience: academic and co-curricular. Part One examines the integration of faith and learning in a variety of academic disciplines.

---

[23] Explaining the permeation of faith integration through the Worldview Approach, Naugle writes: "Thus, for DBU, the phrase 'integrating faith and learning' refers to the scholarly activity in which the fundamental doctrines of the Christian faith—God, creation, humanity, sin, and redemption—serve as the theological and philosophical starting points by which the various disciplines are studied, appreciated, critiqued, and developed. The integration of faith and learning, which may be better termed 'the integration of Christian theology and learning,' is the pursuit of academic study within the framework of the assumptions and presuppositions of the biblical worldview. It is a 'critical-appreciative dialogue' with the various academic disciplines informed by Christian faith." Naugle, "Commentary," 8.

The disciplines have been chosen to reflect a range of subjects within each college, where possible, with each college represented: College of Humanities and Social Sciences (History, Legal Studies, Psychology/Counseling), College of Business (Business, Entrepreneurship, Business as Mission), College of Natural Sciences and Mathematics (Science, Mathematics), College of Fine Arts (Music, Art), College of Education (Education), College of Christian Faith (Religion), and Cook School of Leadership (Leadership). Part Two of the book focuses on the co-curricular experiences at DBU. Here staff write about the integration of faith and learning in their specific department. Again, departments have been selected as representative of University life and part of the student experience: Student Affairs, Athletics, Title IX, Physical Operations, and International Affairs.

Both faculty and staff approach their respective area from Cosgrove's Foundational Authority Model in which faith *supports* learning. But it is Holmes's Four Approaches that surface in each chapter, providing practical ways that faith is integrated into the discipline or department. Resultantly, the Approaches anchor the book and provide consistency across chapters. Collectively, these chapters illuminate the impact that holistic integration of faith in the learning environment can have on students at a Christian college. Soli Deo gloria!

Part 1

Integrating Faith and Learning Within Selected Academic Disciplines

Chapter 1

Integrating Faith in Legal Studies

By David D. Cook[1] and Cicely Jefferson[2]

Introduction

By virtue of the profession, lawyers are many times seen as leaders in society. From the very beginning of our nation, 25 of the 56 signers of the Declaration of Independence, and 32 of the 55 framers of the Constitution were lawyers or had received significant legal training.[3] To this day, more than half of all U.S. Presidents have been from the legal profession,[4] and roughly 40% of the members of Congress in the 2000s have been attorneys.[5] As John Adams famously noted, America is a land of "laws, and not of men,"[6] and thus lawyers play an important role in such a society. As Gene Veith noted, the law is a "culture-making profession."[7]

---

[1] David D. Cook serves as the Senior Legal Counsel to the President, Dean of Global Studies and Pre-Professional Programs, and Professor of Leadership at Dallas Baptist University.

[2] Cicely Jefferson serves as Assistant Professor of Business Law and as the Assistant Dean of the College of Business at Dallas Baptist University.

[3] "How Many of the Founding Fathers were Lawyers," *State Bar of Michigan Law Blog*, July 4, 2011, https://sbmblog.typepad.com/sbm-blog/2011/07/how-many-of-the-founding-fathers-were-lawyers.html.

[4] Norman Gross, "Presidential Bar Leaders: Fascinating Facts About America's Lawyer-Presidents," *Bar Leader* 34, no. 3 (January–February 2010): 1, https://www.americanbar.org/groups/bar-leadership/publications/bar_ leader/2009_10/january_february/presidential/.

[5] Nick Robinson, "Declining Dominance: Lawyers in the U. S. Congress," *The Practice: Lawyers in Politics* 2, no. 1 (November 2015): 1, https://thepractice.law.harvard.edu/article/declining-dominance/.

[6] John Adams, "Thoughts on Government, April 1776," Founders Online, accessed November 27, 2023, https://founders.archives.gov/documents/Adams/06-04-02-0026-0004.

[7] Gene Veith, *God at Work* (Wheaton, IL: Crossway, 2002), 67.

But equally true is that a large portion of society does not believe lawyers are trustworthy. A Gallup poll spanning almost 50 years has consistently shown that only around 19% of Americans rate lawyers as high or very high in terms of honesty and ethical standards.[8] This is a level that is below even the level of auto mechanics and is only a few percentage points above the level of trust in insurance salespeople. Sadly, many in society see lawyers as manipulative, conniving, and deceitful, and this has led to the general distrust that is documented in the Gallup poll results above. Colloquially, many people liken lawyers to sharks, always lurking for unsuspecting prey. As William Shakespeare famously noted in terms of dealing with these problems, which were already emblematic in 16th century England, "The first thing we do, let's kill all the lawyers."[9]

With these concerns in mind, the deep distrust of lawyers in society has led many to wonder: can a lawyer truly be a Christian?[10] This chapter will argue the answer to that question is a resounding "yes," and that is why the integration of faith into legal studies is so very vital. Our role as Christian legal studies educators is one that carries a great responsibility for developing the next generation of attorneys who can swim against the tide by being honest, ethical, and Christ-like representations of justice in society. As Mike Schutt, a Christian law professor, notes:

> If God is redeeming the law and the legal institutions in which we operate we may help bring them, slowly and uncertainly, under his authority as a means to liberate captives, vindicate the rights of victims, exercise stewardship, punish wrongdoers, and do justice...Our calling is humbly to love and serve our neighbors...[11]

With such a lofty goal in mind, this chapter will explore why this endeavor is so important in light of the biblical mandate for justice and

[8] "Lawyers," Honesty/Ethics in Professions, Gallup Poll, accessed November 17, 2023, https://news.gallup. com/poll/1654/honesty-ethics-professions.aspx.

[9] William Shakespeare, *Henry VI*, part 2, act IV, scene 2.

[10] Michael P. Schutt, *Redeeming Law: Christian Calling and the Legal Profession* (Downers Grove, IL: IVP, 2007), 16.

[11] Ibid., 22.

how Dallas Baptist University uniquely engages in the process of integrating faith into this discipline of legal studies.

Theological Underpinnings for the Integration of Faith Into Legal Studies

As Christians, the character of God provides a starting point for our understanding of faith and law. Throughout the Bible, God reveals that He is a God of justice (e.g., Isaiah 30:18 (NIV): "For the LORD is a God of justice"). As Psalm 9:8 notes, "He rules the world in righteousness and judges the peoples with equity" (NIV). As the biblical narrative unfolds throughout the Old Testament, God reiterates His desire for justice again and again to His people and provides them with laws that will help to order their relationships to Him and to others. The most significant example of God providing laws that serve as a foundation for justice is, of course, when God gives Moses the Ten Commandments.[12] These commandments provided a glimpse into God's own character as a God of justice and gave the Israelites an understanding of what it meant to relate to God and others in a just way.

One of the most famous iterations of God's call for justice amongst His people is found in Micah 6:8, where the prophet notes: "He has shown you, O mortal, what is good. And what does the LORD require of you? To act justly and to love mercy and to walk humbly with your God" (NIV). It is clear that, just as God acts justly, He calls His people to walk in a similar fashion. This admonition to act justly is not merely a minor part of God's call to His people; as King Solomon himself noted in Proverbs 21:3, "To do what is right and just is more acceptable to the LORD than sacrifice" (NIV).

While the Ten Commandments, Levitical laws, and admonitions such as Micah 6:8 served as a cornerstone for a system of justice, God also provided a variety of other laws and commands to His people throughout their history as a way to help them order their society in a just way. Thus, we see that God cared deeply about economic justice

[12] Exod. 20:1–17; Deut. 5:6–21.

when He created rules for redemption and the Year of Jubilee.[13] He likewise showed His deep desire to see justice for the oppressed when He instructed His people concerning gleaning laws and commands on how to relate to orphans and widows.[14] A correlation to this can be seen in the racial justice He demanded as He held His people to high standards in their treatment of sojourners, foreigners, and immigrants who were ethnically distinct from the Israelites.[15] Similarly, He held the people's leaders to high standards of legal and political justice, as evidenced by His commands to use just weights and measures[16] and continued admonitions against corruption amongst officials.[17] Finally, we see God demanding the leaders of His people exhibit justice in shepherding His people and leading with God's own justice in mind.[18]

Likewise, throughout Scripture, we see that God invests government officials, judges, and civic leaders with the responsibility to bring justice to their people. In 1 Peter 2:13–15, Christians are commanded to be subject to government officials since they are "sent by him to punish those who do evil and to praise those who do good" (ESV). Such a double-edged role—to punish evil and promote good—was one of the key functions God demanded of rulers and government officials throughout the biblical narrative. Paul echoes this exhortation in Romans 13:1–5 when he instructs Christ-followers to be "subject to the governing authorities...For the one in authority is God's servant for your good...They are God's servants, agents of wrath to bring punishment on the wrongdoer" (NIV).

As we have seen from this brief review of Scriptures relating to justice, there is a consistent call throughout the Bible for God's people to

---

[13] Lev. 25.

[14] Exod. 22:21–24; Lev. 19:9–10; 23:22; Deut. 24:19–21; Ruth 2:1–23; Isa. 1:17; Ps. 82:3; James 1:27. The "gleaning" laws, in particular, provided a unique mechanism for feeding the poor by mandating that landowners leave some of the edges of their fields and crops unharvested so the poor could gather enough grain to help feed themselves. Such a system made individual landowners agents of God's justice by giving them the responsibility to help their community out of their abundance.

[15] Lev. 19:33–34; Deut. 27:19; Zech. 7:9–10; Mal. 3:5.

[16] Lev. 19:35–36; Deut. 25:15; Prov. 11:1; 20:10; Ezek. 45:10.

[17] Prov. 16:12; 28:15; 29:4; Isa. 1:23; Jer. 23:1–4.

[18] Ezek. 34:1–16; John 10:1–18.

be just, as God Himself is just. Yet despite this mandate, the biblical narrative is riddled with examples of injustices done by ruler after ruler (e.g., the Egyptian Pharaoh in Exodus, the Assyrian kings in Isaiah, the Babylonian leaders in Habakkuk, and the Roman rulers mentioned throughout the Gospels). Yet God consistently calls leaders to stand in the gap and bring justice to His people. Figures such as Moses, Joseph, David, and Daniel provide strong examples of those in governing offices who sought to bring justice for their people in God's name.

Similarly, in our modern society, lawyers, judges, and legislators have a comparable mandate from God to bring justice to the people they represent. If, as Romans 13 reminds us, these leaders in the legal profession are truly "God's servants," then there is a unique need for Christian colleges and law schools to be preparing future lawyers, judges, and legislators who will have a holistic, biblical view of justice and service to God and man. The remainder of this chapter will look at how we attempt at Dallas Baptist University to do just that by training future lawyers to be "God's servants" in the legal profession.

Practically Integrating Faith Into Legal Studies at DBU

Attitudinal Approach

A good starting point in understanding how professors can integrate faith into legal studies is Arthur Holmes's Attitudinal Approach. Under this approach, our idea is to guide future lawyers to see their work as a calling, to have a mindset of stewardship, to strive for excellence in all they do, and to see their profession through a lens of service. If we are truly to prepare a future generation of lawyers who will be "God's servants" in the legal field, we must start with the idea of transforming their minds. Paul admonishes us in Romans 12:2 to "…not conform to the pattern of this world, but be transformed by the renewing of your mind. Then you will be able to test and approve what God's will is—his good, pleasing and perfect will" (NIV).

The true starting point in this endeavor is to help students discern their calling to the legal profession. We believe the best place to start in helping them discern calling is to assemble a faculty who first model that calling to the legal profession. Thus, a key criterion in the selection of faculty in legal studies is their demonstrated commitment to integrating faith into their previous legal practice. The integration of faith in this area is a natural one for our professors because they can attest to a "sense of calling" to the legal profession and the desire to participate in God's restorative work in humankind. Each of our DBU Pre-Law professors had significant experience in private practice before coming to DBU, and thus they are able to share with students what it really means to live as a Christian lawyer in a secular environment. As professors share personal stories in the classroom with students, they help students to avoid the pitfall of viewing the legal profession as just a job or career, or their educational experience as merely job training.[19] Instead, they are able to share stories in which they personally were able to serve as God's "hands and feet" to people with legal needs. One professor noted that: "I tell my students that, as a Christian lawyer, you will be able to speak into the lives of hundreds or thousands of people who would never darken the doorstep of a church. You may be the only glimpse of Jesus they see."

Likewise, we ask our faculty to actively mentor students as they determine whether God is calling them to the legal profession. This manifests itself in meetings with students during office hours, discussions over coffee, or investing in their lives while sharing a meal. One professor noted that a Pre-Law student joined him every week for two years for one-on-one discipleship sessions to discuss faith, calling, and his future in life. Another DBU Pre-Law graduate noted:

> Mentorship is the overarching theme of how I would define the role DBU professors played in encouraging me to grow in my faith as I was considering, and then heading into, law school. There was never a time that I had a professor who was unwilling to discuss not only my career ambitions, but my day-to-day life and walk with God. And

[19] Cornelius Plantinga, Jr., *Engaging God's World: A Christian Vision of Faith, Learning, and Living* (Grand Rapids, MI: Eerdmans, 2002), 114–15.

> never were these conversations separate: They were always about my life and how law, or any other area of academia that I enjoyed, related to my walk with Christ. It was almost always the case that professors reached out to me first, which was very encouraging as a student who sometimes needed a push to reach out for help.

A key component of integrating faith in legal studies is modeling the appropriate behavior inside and outside of the classroom. Being available to pray for students, listen to them, and provide guidance are integral in helping students to rely on their faith to direct them in all areas of life. Integrating faith in legal studies can show up in a myriad of ways as students make choices about their future. Faith shows up in the conversation about a student's future as she wrestles with what's next after graduation, or as students share their struggles with serious physical and mental health issues. Faculty members who are Christians lead alongside God in these conversations, and they provide wisdom and guidance that only comes from Him. In addition to conversations, students are encouraged when they know that their professors are praying for them and are willing to support them in other areas of their life. Faculty and staff at Dallas Baptist University have the unique privilege of impacting lives simply by living their lives in a way that brings glory to God.

This also plays out in the way professors demand excellence of themselves and their students as they prepare to be "salt and light" in the world. A student stated that "the strongest witness for Christ in my life were people who clearly chased the Lord and pursued excellence in the things He had given them to do." Professors in legal studies share how important it is that students understand the profession of law can be a dark place, but God can give them the courage to be "salt and light."[20] This can only be done if the lawyer is first excellent at what they do and respected for the excellence of their work. Thus, professors remind students that Christian lawyers must be excellent because they are working "as for the Lord."[21] One professor recalled that when she

[20] Matt. 5:13–16.

[21] Col. 3:23.

began working in "Big Law" she thought it was incompatible with being a Christian until she understood that God had called her to be a light in a dark place. Consequently, during class discussions, she encourages students to be bold in their faith and not to be ashamed of what they believe or how God can use them to impact others in their field.[22]

Ethical Approach

Just as it is important to train students to see the study and practice of the law as a "calling" to model excellence, it is also quite important to teach them to be ethical in all they do. Unfortunately, there is no shortage of examples that the law is in need of the type of values and morals Christians can provide.[23] Furthermore, it is widely known that many Americans outside and inside of the legal profession view attorneys in a negative light.[24] The reckless actions of a few have tainted the reputation of the profession.[25] In addition to not faring well in society, lawyers also had a difficult time consistently reading the Bible and drawing strength from it for their spiritual life because they tried to "test" Jesus.[26]

The successful integration of faith in legal studies requires that we teach students how to intertwine Christianity and the law.[27] Faculty and staff must set high expectations for students and provide them with the tools to meet those expectations. The sin of greed is a real problem in the legal profession because a significant number of legal professionals have been indicted for various crimes and misconduct.[28] It is important to teach students that they are not just accountable to the organization in which they work, but they are accountable to God, and this empha-

---

[22] Phil. 1:20.

[23] R. Garrett Rice, "Can a Christian Be a Corporate Lawyer? Tracing Corporate Law's Religious Roots and Identifying How We Can Integrate Our Faith and Work," *The Journal of the Legal Profession* 143, no. 2 (Spring 2019): 154.

[24] Ibid., 155.

[25] Ibid., 156. Cf. Bruce Nash and Allan Zullo eds., *Lawyer's Wit and Wisdom* (Philadelphia, PA: Running Press, 1995), 164, quoting Alan Dershowitz, "Any profession that suffers from so foul a reputation must, in some way, provoke it."

[26] Kenneth Starr, "Christian Life in the Law," in *Can a Good Christian Be a Good Lawyer? Homilies, Witnesses, and Reflections*, eds. Timothy Floyd and Thomas Baker (Notre Dame, IN: University of Notre Dame Press, 1998), 47; Luke 10:25–29; Matt. 22:35–36.

[27] Rice, "Can a Christian," 164.

[28] Ibid., 164–71.

sis fits well with Holmes's Ethical Approach to integration. This faith integration directs the students to view their actions through the lens of biblical ethics, rather than simply based on whether an action is legal. One former student, who is now in law school, reiterated that he had received deep personal mentoring by DBU faculty, and that these interactions had helped prepare him to have an unwavering faith even in a secular environment.

Professors also share real-life examples of their successes and failures as it relates to the struggles that arise when Christian values come into conflict with the values, or lack thereof, in the legal profession. Students are reminded they are believers first, and legal professionals second. Cultivating this type of "Christian community" in legal studies provides an opportunity for students to live out their calling so they "naturally do what's right."[29] One professor describes it as a mutual exchange in which students are involved in exploring the ethical issues that arise in the legal profession using Scriptures to define what is acceptable behavior according to God's standards. This exploration is brought to life as students present devotionals from a devotional series published by the Christian Legal Society. In another class, emphasis is placed on the Bible as the ultimate authority using hypotheticals to help students discern the difference between what is legal versus what is biblical and ethical. Laws and regulations may dictate what is legal, but they often fall short on what is moral or ethical according to the Bible.[30] Some professors play devil's advocate to help students think critically about both sides of an issue. One former student who is currently in law school spoke of his time at DBU as follows: "I wasn't being told *what* to think; I was told instead to challenge and think critically about the world."

Thus, one of the hallmarks of integrating faith into legal studies is that DBU professors and students learn to grapple together with challenging ethical issues. Whether this be discussing how to engage ethically in the cross-examination of a witness, how to be honest in contract negotiations, or how to apply biblical principles to "gray" areas of the

[29] Plantinga, Jr., *Engaging God's World,* 115, 131.
[30] Rice, "Can a Christian," 149.

law, DBU students are encouraged to discern how Christian ethics play out in real-world scenarios. As several DBU alumni in law school noted, these types of exercises were so important in preparing them for the "hostile" environment of law school and the legal world. One former student summed it up well:

> My years at DBU were well spent and well timed—my faith was encouraged, strengthened, and solidified at DBU. Thus, when it was then exposed to a more hostile environment, the foundation had already been laid for me to continue to live out my faith and to view my new surroundings as a blessing...

Foundational Approach

Another area of focus for DBU professors in integrating faith into legal studies is giving students a sense of the philosophical and historical foundations for a Christian approach to the law. In many ways, understanding *why* we engage in this field of study and *how* that has played out in the biblical narrative and in history provides a strong cornerstone for students to see their small part in a broader history of thousands of years of Christians engaging with the law. Thus, just as Holmes's Attitudinal Approach and Ethical Approach to integration are vital, DBU Pre-Law professors also seek to incorporate this Foundational Approach, as well.

This starts with discussions in a variety of classes about why students should study the law and prepare themselves for careers in the legal field. Thus, in a required course titled "A Christian Worldview for Business, Politics, and the Law," students are exposed to biblical texts about justice as a basis for understanding what their role is in bringing justice to the world around them in God's name. Students learn about the names of God found in the Old Testament and what these names tell us about His nature and the type of character He asks of His followers. Students then engage in a class exercise where they split into groups, read a variety of biblical texts about justice, and are challenged to create a summary statement of what it means to enact justice in society. Students in one section of this class crafted the following summary statement as part of this exercise:

> Biblical justice means standing up for our neighbors (including even the poor, the oppressed, the brokenhearted, and the sojourners) in God's name and with His love by giving people voice, advocating on their behalf, treating them equitably, and holding their oppressors accountable.

Likewise, in several classes, professors focus on the philosophical underpinnings for understanding the law from a missional perspective. Students are shown how the Bible provides a grand narrative of God's mission of restoration, and then discuss how they can play a part in enacting His mission through the field of law. As one student said: "DBU has equipped me to see my life, my calling, and my career as missions. My whole life should be devoted to advancing the kingdom of God, and if I can do that through the pursuit of law, so be it." Another current student put it this way:

> With being taught how to be a believer and a lawyer at the same time it has shown that we can do missionary work without being a missionary. We can lead by example in a world that doesn't encourage what we are called to do and be a source of love in a field that shuts it out.

As a part of this philosophical justification for why Christians should study the law, we believe it is important for Christian lawyers to build a foundation that results in an undivided life in which their faith works in tandem with the practice of law.[31] This requires an intentional commitment to ensuring that core Christian beliefs become an integral part of practicing law and the way lawyers express themselves in all areas of life.[32] Lawyers must avoid the path of the "hired gun" who is willing to take any action to please the client without giving thought to whether

[31] Rice, "Can a Christian," 171, citing Helen J. Alford and Michael J. Naughton, "Managing as if Faith Mattered: Christian Social Principles in the Modern Organization," *Theology Today* 60, no. 3 (October 2003): 412.

[32] Ibid., 171. Cf. Peggy Noonan, "Wisdom of a Non-Idiot Billionaire," *Wall Street Journal*, May 10, 2018, https://www.wsj.com/articles/wisdom-of-a-non-idiot-billionaire-1525992653, when discussing Home Depot Founder Ken Langone's autobiography and noting that it "doesn't offer rules for living but you can discern some between the lines. 1. Take your religious faith seriously."

those actions align with Christian values and beliefs.[33] Faculty and staff can assist students with developing a foundation for their identity that is deeply rooted in Christ, rather than the opinions of their clients and colleagues. Regardless of the profession, a Christian works for the Lord.[34] Lawyers, however, must take great care to ensure that this work does not become an idol and that they do not seek glory for themselves.[35] Unfortunately, many lawyers have based their self-worth on their salaries, client lists, and courtroom record.[36] Therefore, it is important to teach aspiring lawyers to build their career on altruistic acts such as providing pro bono legal services to the poor, serving at their local church, treating coworkers and fellow attorneys with dignity and respect, and using the gifts God has given them to make a difference in this world.[37]

While Americans in general may find it difficult to integrate their faith and work,[38] it is critical for students to understand that at its core, a lawyer's work presents many opportunities to display Christian character. For example, lawyers often serve as peacemakers by helping to resolve disputes through non-adversarial processes and as gatekeepers by serving as the corporate conscience to prevent behavior that could have a negative impact on society. Moreover, lawyers often serve as counselors to their clients, which gives them the opportunity to exert positive influence over the client's decisions. Christian lawyers have a unique opportunity to set the example for what it means to integrate faith and the law.

---

[33] Ibid., 172–73.

[34] Ibid., 172; Col. 3:23; 1 Cor. 12:5–6: "There are different kinds of service, but the same Lord. There are different kinds of working, but in all of them and in everyone it is the same God at work" (NIV).

[35] Rice, "Can a Christian," 179, 181. Cf. Schutt, *Redeeming Law*, 60.

[36] Ibid., 179. Cf. Patrick J. Schlitz, "On Being a Happy, Healthy, and Ethical Member of an Unhappy, Unhealthy and Unethical Profession," *Vanderbilt Law Review* 52, no. 4 (1999): 915, 951, observing that "an ethical lawyer is to act ethically in your work, even when you aren't required to do so by any rule."

[37] Ibid., 181–83.

[38] Ibid., 185. Cf. "Importance of Religion and Religious Beliefs," U.S. Public Becoming Less Religious, Pew Research Center, November 3, 2015, http://www.pewforum.org/2015/11/03/chapter-1-importance-of-religion-and-religious-beliefs/.

In addition to this philosophical *why* for the practice of law, DBU Pre-Law professors seek to provide a broad view of *how* this has historically been accomplished. One professor focuses on how the Ten Commandments, Levitical laws, Sermon on the Mount, and passages such as Romans 13 provide historical examples for the role of judges and lawyers who are tasked by God with enacting justice. In a Mock Trial class, students discuss how the modern jury system and trial procedures such as cross-examination of witnesses provide mechanisms for exploring the truth, and how these procedures have foundations in biblical legal methodologies. Additionally, in multiple classes, students focus on the U.S. Constitution and discuss clauses such as the First Amendment and how those laws help to promote a just society for all people. Professors focus on how, as Christian lawyers, we have a role to play in defending freedom of religion and other basic freedoms for Christians and non-Christians alike, and how this has been accomplished historically in our country through caselaw. Additionally, students are taught they are "stewards" of God's justice, and that Christian lawyers through the centuries have played a large role in shaping the bedrock values of our society through bringing biblical concepts of justice to their interactions with the law.

Throughout students' time at DBU, the goal is to give them a deeper sense of why they are studying the law and how they can be a part of God's restorative mission of justice in the world. As one student said, it was a "blessing" to know that we are "stewards of God's creation." Likewise, several former students noted that, in the highly competitive environment of law school, it was helpful to have already gained a foundation at DBU for their mission and that their identity is rooted in Christ. The hope is that these future lawyers will walk away from DBU with a deep understanding of how they fit into God's broader restorative mission of justice in the world around them.

Worldview Approach

Once the foundation has been built for students to see the law as an opportunity to serve God through the infusion of their faith into the application of legal principles, they can "live their whole life in a way that extends the reach of Jesus Christ."[39] It is through the four approaches outlined by Arthur Holmes that faculty shape the attitudes, ethics, foundation, and worldview of students by building on God as the foundation for all knowledge, which allows students to "see all things in relationship to God as their Creator, Redeemer, and Lord."[40] This development will only occur if there are intentional efforts by faculty and staff to create an environment that teaches the "mind of Christ" in such a way that students adopt the "mind of Christ" as their own.[41] This is especially important because the "mind of Christ" is one devoted to serving others, especially the marginalized in our society.[42]

Moreover, professors and staff intentionally place more emphasis on the type of person the student is becoming rather than the type of job they will hold.[43] One former student who is currently in law school recalled that her professors did not limit their discussions to her career ambitions, but they were always interested in her "day-to-day life and walk with God." She stated that these "conversations were never separate," but they revolved around life, law, and her spiritual development. She further described her experience as "holistic" mentorship, which stressed that Christ was before academics.

The goal is to teach students the importance of protecting themselves from being influenced by secular views, while also becoming an influencer for Christ through their actions. One way we do this at DBU is by requiring all Pre-Law students to take a special course titled "A Christian Worldview for Business, Politics, and the Law." In this course, students grapple with divisive social issues from culture and learn how to apply a Christian worldview to those issues. Professors show them how the character of God, as evidenced in His names and attributes throughout Scripture, provide a basis for understanding not only the Ten Commandments and Levitical laws, but also modern-day situa-

[39] Plantinga, Jr., *Engaging God's World,* 93.

[40] Holmes, *The Idea of a Christian College,* 45–60.

[41] Plantinga, Jr., *Engaging God's World,* 94.

[42] Ibid.

[43] Ibid., 115.

tions that affect our culture. Students are tasked with a variety of papers, presentations, and in-class exercises that ask them to apply biblical principles to modern problems in a way that brings the *shalom* of God[44] into the world around them. A current Pre-Law student shared that this course gave him the "tools to approach issues with a biblical worldview" and that it helped him understand how "my faith should be integrated into every area of my life."

In discussing his time at DBU, another former student shared that the foundation for his faith was laid during his undergraduate years on campus and now he continues to live out his faith on his law school campus. He noted that he views his current environment as a "blessing—an open field to harvest the Gospel." He recalled that he did not have a faith-based worldview when he arrived on campus, but through the Christ-centered education, his faith was "ignited and nourished," which gave him the confidence to be a witness to others. Another student described himself as having two missions while in law school: "to finish and to share the Gospel with those who do not know Christ."

The legal profession can be a very competitive field, but students are reminded that God does not call them to be in competition with one another, but rather to serve in humility.[45] When faith is taught as the center of one's life, it assists in the development of a Christian worldview that invades every aspect of life. It is important for students to understand that their faith and vocational calling should coexist in the same sphere and should not be compartmentalized.[46] After experiencing a faith-based education on our campus, a student shared that his education has taught him that: "Faith is something that should show

[44] Matt. 5:9; Cf. David Cook, "Bonhoeffer as a Prophetic Leader," in *Dietrich Bonhoeffer: Perspectives on Costly Leadership*, ed. Jay Harley (Nashville, TN: Randall House, 2021), 91, saying, "Jesus tells his disciples that 'blessed are the peacemakers…' this verse echoes Mic. 5:5, which foretold the coming of Christ, who would be the peace that the world so desperately needed. His peace was all-encompassing, not merely denoting the absence of strife, but true *shalom*. This Jewish concept of *shalom* encompassed a much broader concept of wholeness—of having a singular focus on God that caused one to emanate God's justice, integrity, holiness, peace, and righteousness to the world around them."

[45] Phil. 2:3–4.

[46] Rice, "Can a Christian," 146.

through in everything that one does—certainly in those endeavors relating to education and vocation."

As students graduate, it is important for professors to help them to develop a Christian community in their career by connecting them to outside resources to find other Christians in the legal field with whom they can find encouragement and support. Developing Christian lawyers "who work for the Lord"[47] is no small task, but Christian colleges and universities are uniquely positioned for this great work. Nurturing a new generation of legal professionals who pursue the virtues of honesty, integrity, and steadfastness is the solution to improving, and ultimately changing the reputation of the legal profession. The Christian lawyer is one who treats coworkers and opponents with sincere respect and kindness, and one who seeks and carefully handles the truth.[48] When demands are high and the pressure is mounting, the words of Scripture provide a healing and calming balm for the legal practitioner that cannot be found in any other source.[49] Developing a generation of legal professionals who are equipped to successfully integrate their faith into their practice is not only a great idea, but it is a necessary priority if society is to reach its fullest potential.

Conclusion

This chapter has attempted to provide at least a starting point for understanding what it means to integrate faith into the realm of legal studies. This weighty task must be at the forefront of the minds of every Christian educator in legal studies. Lawyers who integrate their faith into the practice of law are in short supply, therefore, it is imperative that Christian educators accept the responsibility of producing legal professionals who carry the mission of Christ forward in their pursuit of justice. We have a lofty calling: to train the next generation of Christian lawyers to be instruments of God's justice in the broken world around them.

---

[47] Col. 3:23–24.

[48] Starr, "Christian Life in the Law," 48.

[49] Ibid., 49.

Chapter 2

Integrating Faith in Psychology

By Parnell Ryan[1] and Harry Beverly[2]

Introduction

The task of faith-learning is to bring insights of a particular discipline into constructive dialogue with the Christian faith. Some areas of the integration of faith and learning seem to come naturally and even intuitively, but the integration of faith into the field of psychology brings with it apprehension and debate. In writing on the integration of psychology and the Christian faith, Santrac noted this is a "daunting task because of the divergent approaches of these academic disciplines."[3] In the early 1950s, Fritz Kunkle first applied the term "integration" to describe the early attempts of dialogue between the study of psychology and religion.[4] Since then, the integration movement has grown significantly with the rise of masters and doctorate-level programs that provide a framework for training in counseling and clinical psychology at Christian universities and seminaries. Biola University's Rosemead School of Psychology has been operating since 1973 and publishes

---

[1] Parnell Ryan serves as Assistant Professor of Psychology and the Program Director for the MA in Psychology.

[2] Harry Beverly serves as Assistant Professor of Counseling and Psychology.

[3] Aleksandar S. Santrac, "Towards the Possible Integration of Psychology and Christian Faith: Faculties of Human Personality and the Lordship of Christ," *Die Skriflig* 50, no.1 (May 2016): 1, accessed November 28, 2023, http://dx.doi.org/10.4102/ids.v50i1.1908.

[4] Brad D. Strawn, Earl D. Bland, and Paul S. Flores, "Learning Clinical Integration: A Case Study Approach," *Journal of Psychology and Theology* 46, no. 2 (April 2018): 85–97, https://journals.sagepub.com/doi/pdf/10.1177/0091647118767976.

original integrative research in their *Journal of Psychology and Theology*. Similarly, beginning in 1956 and continuing today, the Christian Association for Psychological Studies (CAPS), which was founded for the benefit of Christians in the mental health fields, publishes integrative research in their *Journal of Psychology and Christianity*. The Minirth-Meier Clinics based in Richardson, Texas opened in the 1970s and became a nationally known psychiatric center that treated patients from an integrative perspective. In 1991, the American Association of Christian Counselors was formed to equip the "community of care" of licensed professionals, pastors, and lay church members, and now boasts some 50,000 members. Even the American Psychological Association created its own Division 36, entitled the Society for the Psychology of Religion and Spirituality, which:

> promotes the application of psychological research methods and interpretive frameworks to diverse forms of religion and spirituality encourages the incorporation of the results of such work into clinical and other applied settings; and fosters constructive dialogue and interchange between psychological study and practice on the one hand and between religious perspectives and institutions on the other.[5]

Fraser Watts writes that "the dialogue between theology and science is notoriously one-sided. Theology is much more interested in science than science is in theology."[6] Thus the pursuit of the integration of Psychology and Christianity consists mostly of evangelicals who have shown a growing interest in the fields of psychology and counseling and believe the fields together bring a value-added benefit not only to the Christian community but all people in general. Consequently, this chapter will explore the value of an integrated approach to the study of psychology while offering examples of how DBU integrates the Christian Faith in the field of psychology and counseling.

---

[5] "Society for Psychology of Religion and Spirituality," Divisions of APA, American Psychological Association, accessed November 27, 2023, https://www.apa.org/about/division/div36.

[6] Fraser Watts, "Doing Theology in Dialogue with Psychology," *Journal of Psychology and Theology* 40, no.1 (March 2012): 45–50.

History of Faith and Psychology Integration

In 2018 Strawn, Bland, and Flores[7] elaborated on Worthington's[8] *waves* or periods of development within the integration conversation. Wave 1 (prior to 1975) was identified as the *apologetic wave*,[9] in which the debate was on "should we or should we not" be integrating psychology and Christianity in the first place. This quickly led to Wave 2 (1975–1985), the *models wave,* in which people began to take sides on the issue and to spell out their position. The *models wave* saw the development of models that defined the unique framework for how both disciplines relate to one another. For example, Carter (1997)[10] developed his four-model paradigm with the first three having a secular and sacred version (see also Brian Eck's "Integrating the Integrators" organization of 27 integration models).[11] First, the *against model* (or Crabb's "nothing buttery")[12] holds to the idea that Psychology and Christianity are "enemies" in that they are incompatible and fundamentally opposed to one another, rejecting any dialogue between the two. Jay Adams' biblical or nouthetic model[13] represents the sacred side of the against model. In the past, a great deal of tension was observed between the biblical counselors and the integrationists as they battled over "turf wars." Biblical counselors tend to see psychology as the "Trojan Horse" that is subversively bringing man's wisdom into the church. Philip Monroe summed up the different perspectives: "Biblical counselors are narrow minded and treat the Bible as a textbook for counseling and Christian psychologist have replaced sanctification with therapy."[14] This tension

7 Strawn, Bland, and Flores, "Learning Clinical Integration," 86–87.

8 Everett L. Worthington, Jr., "A Blueprint for Intradisciplinary Integration," *Journal of Psychology and Theology* 22, no. 2 (June 1994): 79–86.

9 Strawn, Bland, Flores, "Learning Clinical Integration," 86.

10 John D. Carter, "Secular and Sacred Models of Psychology and Religion," *Journal of Psychology and Theology* 5, no. 3 (June 1977): 197–208.

11 Brian E. Eck, "Integrating the Integrators: An Organizing Framework for a Multifaceted Process of Integration," *Journal of Psychology and Christianity* 15, no. 2 (Summer 1996): 101–115.

12 Larry Crabb, *Effective Biblical Counseling: A Model for Helping Caring Christians Become Capable Counselors* (Grand Rapids, MI: Zondervan, 1977), 40.

13 Jay E. Adams, *Competent to Counsel* (Grand Rapids, MI: Baker, 1970).

14 Philip Monroe, "Building Bridges with Biblical Counselors," *Journal of Psychology and Theology* 25, no.1 (January 1997): 28–37.

has mostly been in private and has diminished some as biblical counselors and integrationists have come to respect and understand each other.

Second, the *of model*, specifically Entwistle's manipulative model,[15] represents the psychology of Religion. In this model there is an open exchange between psychology and religion. It proposes that common ground can be found between the two, but there is no effort to work toward a broader unifying principle. Third is the *parallel model* (Crabb's "separate but equal")[16] where the focus is on distinctives and each discipline having its "rightful place." In other words, if one has a psychological problem he would see a psychologist, or if one has a spiritual problem she would see a pastor. While there is mutual respect for each discipline, there is no effort to come to a broader unifying principle. The parallel model is a "safe" model because keeping the disciples in their own compartments generally leads to less conflict between the two. Fourth is the *integrate model*, which sees psychology and Christianity as "allies" (Crabb's "Spoiling the Egyptians")[17] in which God is the author of all truth so there must be one set of explanatory hypotheses. The *integrate model* proposes that "reason, revelation, and the scientific method all are seen as playing a vital role in the search for truth."[18] The *integrate model* allows for a direct interchange between the two fields in hopes that as they challenge and inform one another; this will lead to congruent findings.

Wave 3 (mid-1980s), the *empirical wave,* brought the focus on the experimental science of the psychology of religion. Here, for example, researchers study the impact of religious and spiritual traditions or practices on the psychological health of people.[19] The difficulty with this wave was that the traditions and practices of religious people were very difficult to quantify while also not taking into consideration the supernatural aspects of people's behavior. Strawn et al. have identified

---

[15] David N. Entwistle, *Integrative Approaches to Psychology and Christianity* (Eugene, OR: Cascade Books, 2021), 204.

[16] Crabb, *Effective Biblical Counseling,* 33.

[17] Ibid., 47.

[18] Carter, "Secular and Sacred Models," 103.

[19] Strawn, Bland, and Flores, "Learning Clinical Integration," 87.

a fourth wave, *clinical integration*, in which the current trend is "Don't just tell us what we are supposed to do, show us."[20] Neff et al. found that students in advanced degree programs desired to "have more awareness of how to concretely apply and conceptualize integration within the clinical setting."[21] Clinical integration brings to the forefront what Christian counselors and psychologists actually do in the counseling room in diverse clinical settings.

Rationale for Integrative Work

At DBU, we see the value that the integrated approach brings to the study of psychology. First, Christianity and Psychology are interested in the same subject matter—the human being. They place a high value on understanding people in relationship to themselves, others and to God. Matthew 10:30–31 tells us that "even the hairs of your head are all numbered...you are of more value than many sparrows" (ESV). Second, they have the same objective, which is to help people live more fulfilling lives. In John 10:10 Christ states that He has "come that they may have life, and have it to the full" (NIV). Third, Christianity and Psychology both challenge people toward maturity and growth. Freud identified the *ego* as the part of the human psyche that was to be responsible and realistic. Christian psychologists and counselors encourage people not only to mature psychologically but also spiritually with the development of spiritual disciplines. Fourth, Psychology and Christianity at their best are depth disciplines. They move beyond the naïve and superficial attempts to put "band-aids" on the hurts and challenges of life. For example, Psalm 6 is a Psalm of David in which he is lamenting to God the richness of his pain in his current situation. Fifth, Christianity and Psychology uniquely explore human constructs (those things we know to be true but are not directly observable) that enable us to understand ourselves and one another more effectively. In Luke

[20] Ibid., 89.

[21] Megan A. Neff, et al., "Re-imagining integration: Student and Faculty Perspectives on Integration Training at Christian Doctoral Programs," *Journal of Psychology and Theology* 49, no. 1 (January 2021): 67–84.

10:25–37, Jesus tells the parable of the Good Samaritan after having been prompted by a lawyer's question, "Who is my neighbor?" After the parable is complete the lawyer says that a "neighbor" is defined as one who has mercy or compassion for others and then does the right thing. So, a "neighbor" is not just someone who lives next door, it is a "construct" for how God would have us treat all people we meet so we can share the love of Christ with them. Sixth, since the creation of humanity, we have been trying to understand *why we do what we do,* which today is commonly called the field of psychology. For example, the story of Cain and Abel (Genesis 4:1–16) is the first great "case study" in human behavior. Cain brought offerings to God with questionable motives, he felt rejected by God, responded with anger and resentment toward God, experienced jealousy toward his brother Abel, and then devised a plan to remove the competition for God's acceptance. He did this while God was warning him all along what was about to happen, and thus, we have a microcosm of human behavior that has not changed much since the beginning of time. Lastly, the dominance of secular mental-health practitioners in the helping professions motivates us to develop compassionate and competent Christian practitioners who can be "salt and light" (Matthew 5:13–16) to those Christians and non-Christians in need of soul care.

The Two Book View

In 1605 Francis Bacon famously quipped, "God has, in fact, written two books not just one. Of course, we are familiar with the first book he wrote, namely Scripture. But he has written a second book called creation."[22] The resulting premise then is the divine truths found in either special revelation through God's Word or through general revelation in God's creation will ultimately be reconcilable.[23] Carter and Narramore state, "Given this unity of truth, it is possible to integrate truth arrived

---

[22] William L. Hathaway and Mark A. Yarhouse, *The Integration of Psychology and Christianity: A Domain-Based Approach* (Downers Grove, IL: IVP, 2021), 23.

[23] Ibid.

at from different sources and different methodologies."[24] Paul, in the book of Colossians, writes, "For in him all things were created: things in heaven and on earth, visible and invisible, whether thrones or powers or rulers or authorities; all things have been created through him and for him."[25] Most integrationists view the apparent potential conflicts between peer-reviewed psychological science and that of Christian understanding as a "productive moment of tension…forming a more biblical understanding."[26]

Psychology is most often defined simply as the scientific study of the mind and behavior. When people in general consider the field of psychology, they often tend to think in the narrowest terms such as theory or technique. Integrationists though embrace a broad view of psychology as a profession and of psychological science which examines the biological, cognitive, developmental, social, and mental aspects of the human condition. Take for example, a Christian man or woman struggling with general anxiety with a panic disorder. Would we not have the trained Christian therapist explain to the client about the autonomic nervous system (fight or flight response) in dysregulation mode in which the sympathetic nervous symptom is triggered in some people under stress? The physiological changes they are experiencing during an anxiety attack can be debilitating and lead to questions of *where is God in these moments*? The biological knowledge allows the therapist to help the client understand that God has made the human body in remarkable ways and that the dysregulation they are experiencing has a cause and there is hope for healing. A Bible only approach could not consider this possibility and would potentially leave clients in a hopeless situation. Thus, the Two Book View guides our integration of faith in the study of psychology at DBU.

[24] Carter and Narramore, *The Integration of Psychology and Theology*, 13.
[25] Col. 1:16 (NIV).
[26] Hathaway and Yarhouse, *The Integration of Psychology and Christianity*, 27.

Task of Integration

In 2015, Sandage and Brown, in their article on *Relational Integration,* pointed out that "disciplines don't integrate, people do."[27] Although this seems to be obvious, most people's perception of integration as "integrating abstract bodies of knowledge"[28] misses the point of the interpersonal or relational dynamics involved in the integrative journey. Psychologist and pastor Siang-Yang Tan proposed three components to effective integration for the counselor/psychologist. Consider it a three-legged stool in which each leg is crucial to the stability and development of the integrator. First is *principled integration,*[29] in which the integrationist must do the work of applying the truths of God (His Word and world) into effective practice, as 2 Timothy 3:16–17 states: "All Scripture is God-breathed and is useful for teaching, rebuking, correcting and training in righteousness, so that the servant of God may be thoroughly equipped for every good work" (NIV). For the young, and even seasoned psychologists, doing the "work" or the process of being "equipped" in integrating psychology and Christianity into an effective whole appears daunting. They are often fearful that in the integration process they will misquote or misapply biblical truths with psychological principles. This often results in them "falling back" into the against, of, or parallel models, not always by conscious choice but inaction. For most Christian professionals, though, this is an untenable position and so they work on returning to the integration journey. The principled integrationist also takes both the science and practice of psychology and the Christian foundations and faith seriously. The integrationist will keep the Scriptures as the ultimate standard and reject areas of psychology that contradict it, especially morally and ethically.

---

[27] Steven J. Sandage and Jeannine K. Brown, "Relational Integration, Part 1: Differentiated Relationality Between Psychology and Theology," *Journal of Psychology and Theology* 43, no. 3 (September 2015): 165–78.

[28] Ibid., 165.

[29] Siang-Yang Tan, "Integration and Beyond: Principled, Professional, and Personal," *Journal of Psychology and Christianity* 20, no. 1 (Spring 2001): 18–28.

Second is *Professional Integration*[30] which entails all that is involved in the process of the clinical practice of psychology or counseling. The Christian counselor or psychologist in practice lives out the words of 2 Timothy 2:15, which says, “Do your best to present yourself to God as one approved, a worker who has no need to be ashamed, rightly handling the word of truth” (ESV). The Christian professional needs to be prepared to practice in a variety of clinical settings while being true to their core Christian convictions. Tan sees *Intentional Integration* as “the ‘key’ to professional practice: prayerfully depending on the Holy Spirit to lead and guide the therapeutic session, using implicit or explicit integration or both in a professionally competent, ethically responsible and clinically sensitive way for the benefit and growth of the client.”[31] *Implicit Integration* “refers to a more covert approach that does not initiate the discussion of religious or spiritual issues and does not openly, directly, or systematically use spiritual resources.”[32] Of course, the key here is the word *initiate*, which gives the professional the option to address the issues if the client brings it up. The implicit approach though is still substantial in that the therapist is able to use their own spiritual resources such as prayer and reliance upon the Holy Spirit for wisdom and guidance. *Explicit Integration* “refers to a more overt approach that directly and systematically deals with the spiritual or religious issues in therapy and uses spiritual resources like prayer, Scripture, sacred texts.”[33] Tan writes that the therapist will “move along the continuum between explicit and implicit integration depending on the needs and problems of the client,”[34] regardless of the setting they are in.

Lastly is *Personal* or *Intrapersonal Integration,* which is the most foundational aspect of integration—a person’s own appropriation of faith and integration of psychological and spiritual experiences.[35] The degree to

[30] Ibid., 199.
[31] Ibid.
[32] Ibid.
[33] Ibid.
[34] Ibid.
[35] Ibid., 200.

which a person is a follower of Christ will have a significant impact on their ability to do integration. Paul, in the book of Ephesians, writes:

> That according to the riches of his glory he may grant you to be strengthened with power through his Spirit in your inner being, so that Christ may dwell in your hearts through faith—that you, being rooted and grounded in love, may have strength to comprehend with all the saints what is the breadth and length and height and depth, and to know the love of Christ that surpasses knowledge, that you may be filled with all the fullness of God.[36]

The importance of one's appropriation of faith, personal godliness, and spiritual disciples leads to a congruent and effective helper.

Integrating Faith and Learning Within the Classroom at DBU

The training up of Christ-centered servant leaders begins with an approachable attitude. Our full-time and adjunct psychology faculty are not only highly qualified academically but are also licensed practitioners who have been in the helping fields and have clinical experience enabling them to show students how to integrate their faith within the field of psychological theory and practice. The faculty recognize the relational aspect of the helping fields and thus seek to build relational capital with students through approachableness, humility, and self-disclosure. Our faculty communicate the importance of life-long learning (continuing education is a requirement for licensure) and perspective about the integrative process. Our faculty help our students refine their calling into the helping fields, recognizing their calling is more than the desire to "help people" but a commitment to showing the love of Christ to all who are suffering. Lamentations 3:21–23 says: "Yet this I call to mind and therefore I have hope: because of the LORD's great love we are not consumed, for his compassions never fail. They are new every morning; great is your faithfulness" (NIV). Our desire is to instill in our students that the hope they are sharing with their clients is not just in

[36] Eph. 3:16–19 (ESV).

helping them resolve their conflicts with others, for example, but in a lasting hope that is found in the person of Jesus Christ.

The second focus of training up Christ-centered servant leaders for the helping professions is in the area of ethics. The field of psychology holds its professionals to the highest standards of ethical principles and codes of conduct that the Christian practitioner is uniquely qualified to maintain. We model the overall ethic of Micah 6:8: "He has shown you, O mortal, what is good. And what does the LORD require of you? To act justly and to love mercy and to walk humbly with your God" (NIV). This text challenges the Christian to act with integrity and principle when it comes to following the codes of conduct of the license they practice under. The Christian uses mercy and humility whenever a particular standard, code, or principle potentially conflicts with Christian values or ethics making every attempt to resolve the conflict in a productive way. The higher standard the Christian acts with is that their ethical behavior reflects not only themselves but also of Christ. Case studies are used to help students resolve the potential ethical conflicts from both a biblical and professional basis. Students can role-play potential ethical conflicts so they can understand how best to resolve them psychologically and biblically.

The next focus of training up Christ-centered servant leaders for the helping professions is in the area of Holmes's Foundational and Worldview Approaches. Throughout its history, the church has been more of a contributor than an obstacle to meeting the needs of the soul and human suffering. DBU psychology faculty live out 2 Corinthians 1:3–7—as God the Father comforts us and is compassionate to us, we in turn share that same comfort and compassion to others during times of need and suffering. We recognize the human being as created in the image of God (Genesis 1:27) with each person having great worth. God created humans in His likeness and thus they are intellectual, emotional, creative, free, relational, and full of potential. Yet the other side of the coin is that man through his rebellion and disobedience fell from grace and dwells in sin, resulting in a "likeness" that is imperfect and "fallen" (Genesis 3:1–24). This duality of human nature as "fallen" is where the theory of personality begins for the Christian. In all we do, this is the framework for working with people that have incredible worth and need a Savior. DBU emphasizes the importance of students understanding the Christian/biblical view of anthropology, epistemology, and metaphysics and how this varies from the psychological/humanistic/naturalist view. Using implicit integration DBU students learn how to be professional and competent helpers in any therapeutic setting be it secular or sacred.

Student Experiences

The integration of psychology and theology experiences at DBU are importantly revealed in the perceptions and thoughts of students. One DBU student noted:

> I wanted to be in an environment where I could process questions I had about my Christian faith as it relates to the field. DBU met that expectation by encouraging the professors to share about the way they have learned to integrate faith and work through devotions and explicit teaching. I also had a number of specific assignments that encouraged my critical thinking of faith and counseling.

Another student revealed the impact on her biblical worldview:

> The professors at DBU do an excellent job showing every student that every calling, if surrendered to the Lord, can be a missional endeavor. Specifically, the professors in the counseling program have shown me what it looks like to extend the love, compassion, and gentleness of Christ as counselors. Jesus describes His heart as "gentle and lowly" (Matthew 11:29 [ESV]). DBU teaches students to draw on the bottomless ocean of the empathy and tenderness of the Creator and Sustainer of the universe. They have shown me that divine calling extends far beyond the world of ministry. The Lord needs willing, obedient, faithful servants not just in the church but also in the office building, at the investment firm, in the hospital, and in many other places—including the counseling room.

It appears the integration of this academic discipline and biblical faith inspires purpose, confidence, and hope in the learner rather than confusion, despair, and disregard for the psychological topic. These same students reveal personal insights:

> I have learned to view counseling as a prayerful endeavor in which I seek to partner with the Holy Spirit's work in the client's life. I believe that sin has marred us personally, socially, and environmentally, but that nothing is beyond redemption. Therapy is a common grace that engages with psychological and neurological processes of healing that God created. At its core, counseling is confessional. I, as a counselor, get to bear witness, promote safety, extend compassion, and help clients consider what making amends/changing course/repentance might look like. I have found that this is the case whether the client is a Christian or not and whether they know this is a Christian concept or not.

The DBU learner who attempts to integrate Christian faith and psychology has the challenging opportunity of knowing and following God's instruction along with analyzing and synthesizing the field of psychology in light of Scripture. One student wrote:

> As a Christian entering the world of counseling, I often find myself stretching and straining to bridge the chasm that has developed between psychological science and the Christian faith. As I seek to reconcile psychological science and biblical truth, I rely on the old adage that all truth is God's truth. Psalm 127 tells me that "Unless the Lord builds the house, those who build it labor in vain" [ESV]. In the same way, I believe unless the Holy Spirit works through me as the number one counselor in that room, I counsel in vain.

The above students' viewpoints seem to emphasize the value of incorporating biblical principles within the career of psychology along with enhancing discipleship within oneself.

Conclusion

There is so much potential for Christians to step into the discipline of psychology and make a difference. As this chapter has discussed, our faith provides a rich framework for understanding the human condition and how we, as Christians, can help serve others. At DBU, we have seen great fruit from integrating faith not only into the classroom experience for students, but into all aspects of their whole-person development.

Chapter 3

Integrating Faith in Business

By Jeff Johnson,[1] Justin Gandy,[2] and Ross O'Brien[3]

Introduction

At a Christ-centered university, the integration of faith and learning lies within the realm and responsibility of both the professor and the student. As faculty, we strive to teach from an integrated perspective and demonstrate to our students what it means to view our discipline through the lens of Scripture; but we also desire our students to do the same. Consequently, it is both our responsibility *and* theirs. We can demonstrate the integration of faith and learning while even encouraging it, but we cannot do it for them. When we see them integrate their faith with their own learning, it is perhaps one of the most rewarding experiences we can have as faculty.

Consider the testimony of Mary:[4]

> I am currently a senior at Dallas Baptist University, but the past three years of my undergrad were spent at the University of State. While attending the University of State, I came to know the Word of God, and I accepted Christ as my Savior.

[1] At the time of writing this chapter, Jeff Johnson was Dean of the College of Business at Dallas Baptist University. He is now President and CEO of Coram Deo Academy.

[2] Justin Gandy is the Senior Associate Dean of the College of Business and Professor of Management at Dallas Baptist University.

[3] Ross O'Brien is the Director of the Master of Business Administration program, Director of the Center of Business as Mission, and Professor of Management at Dallas Baptist University.

[4] Mary's name and university have been changed to honor her privacy.

> I was not raised in a Christian home, so coming to know the Lord completely turned my life right-side up. My desires changed, my motivation shifted, and my life was no longer my own. I ended up withdrawing from my senior year in order to complete a biblical training program because I wanted to lean into Scripture deeper than before. At this program, I was alongside many DBU alumni as well as other people who received an education based on faith integration. After talking with them, I knew this is how I wanted to finish my college experience.
>
> Before Christ, the reason for my work was solely to find success within myself. I had so much confidence in all the wrong things. Now, worship is the extent of my work. Faith integration allows me to experience the glorification of God by worshiping Him through my education. Coming from a secular college, I can see the difference in the students' posture. What an immaculate blessing it is to proclaim the Gospel through the education of business, music, sports management, and so on. By having faith integrated into our education we are being equipped with eyes to see Him through our daily processes.
>
> Imagine how all of our students can change the workplace, and the world, because we have been taught to have outward eyes instead of focusing on ourselves. We are having this displayed to us by the faculty and the immersion that we experience in our classroom settings.

Mary said it was an "immersion," and we agree. It is an immersion that we require faculty to demonstrate and that we pray students will adopt. The College of Business at DBU has no desire to be anything other than a Christ-centered institution of higher education.

Christ Is the Core of the College of Business (What?)

In that regard, the faculty of the College of Business at Dallas Baptist University views our calling and values through the lens of our personal relationship with Jesus Christ, which serves as our foundation for our entire life,[5] including our business teaching. Grounded in our faith, we understand we are called by Christ to be excellent in all things. As Christian educators, students, businesspeople, alumni, and administrators, the College of Business desires to proclaim the excellence of Christ Jesus (1 Peter 2:9) who called us to His own glory and excellence (2 Peter 1:3). In other words, He calls us to be excellent for Him.

In 2 Peter 1:5–7, Peter identifies eight qualities that produce excellence. These qualities include faith, virtue, knowledge, self-control, steadfastness, godliness, brotherly affection, and love (ESV). We are to practice these qualities (v. 10) and to see them grow and increase in our lives, so that we are effective and fruitful in our daily actions and activities (v. 8). These qualities define godly excellence. Further, the qualities Peter outlines build on themselves, beginning with faith and ending with godly love. We, as a College of Business, will grow in excellence for Christ as we grow in faith, virtue, knowledge, self-control, steadfastness, godliness, brotherly affection, and love. These qualities should define who we are and what excellence looks like in our lives as Christians in the workforce, in the halls of the academy, and in our personal lives.

The vision of the College of Business at DBU is to honor God by becoming a leader in Christ-centered business education. Basically, we aim to bring Christ into every classroom—that in everything, He might be preeminent.[6] We are striving to become the best business school possible through the direction and grace of our Lord Jesus Christ, so God the Father's name is made famous, and our lives and work are useful for His purposes in the marketplace and in academia. In short, we strive to do good works so others will see them and glorify the name of God.[7]

This vision of the DBU College of Business is unusual in the context of a business education today, as so many business schools have stopped teaching from a Christian or faith-centered approach. Surprisingly, many of the elite business schools in the U.S. are still associated with

[5] 1 Cor. 3:11.

[6] Col. 1:18.

[7] Matt. 5:16.

Christian denominations or came from a historic Christian university, yet they have drifted away from this connection and any scriptural, or even values-based, teaching philosophy. This drift from their original beliefs is almost counterintuitive, as so many businesses are seeking employees and leaders with Christian values and a mentality of service and servanthood.

As an example of this longstanding values drift, one of our professors noted while attending a well-known business school at a mainline denominational university in the 1980s, not one graduate class that was taught at this renowned school ever mentioned Christ or His teachings. The Christian ethic and value system was not an integral part of the business school's teaching or even what they were communicating to prospective students—it just was not who they were trying to be. This is a tragic development that mimics the significant drift of many of the faith-oriented universities over the last century as well.[8] This is not the vision of the DBU College of Business.

Building on the vision of the College of Business, the mission of the college is to produce exemplary servant leaders and followers who blend Kingdom wisdom and market knowledge for the glory of God. Our great hope is that they can serve, and in fact transform, their organizations and communities. This Christian business education integrates faith and business to equip the college's servant leaders, which includes not only current students, but also our alumni, faculty, and staff, with a Christ-centered worldview. The students, alumni, faculty, and staff of our college should be capable of the highest level of problem solving and effective application, thereby becoming transformative in each organization and community.[9]

The first of three strategic goals of the College of Business is to deepen our Christian faith and commitment. We are encouraged by what the Apostle Paul wrote in Romans: "that we may be mutually encouraged by each other's faith…as it is written, 'The righteous shall live by

[8] Cf. Peter Greer and Chris Horst, *Mission Drift: The Unspoken Crisis Facing Leaders, Charities, and Churches* (Bloomington, MN: Bethany House, 2014).

[9] 2 Chron. 15:7; Matt. 5:13–16.

faith.'"[10] The College of Business is a Christ-centered school that exists to glorify God through business education. It is our firm belief that to properly fulfill this calling, a consistent emphasis on godliness, Christian faithfulness, and being a channel of biblical truth must be at the center of each academic endeavor. The fear of the Lord is the foundation of true knowledge (Proverbs 1:7), and the College of Business desires to train up our students in this way (Proverbs 22:6). True knowledge, wisdom, and discipline are admirable goals for graduates of the College of Business, and we attempt to instill this holy reverence, honor, and obedience to our Lord as foundational and fundamental in each classroom.

The College of Business faculty are also attempting to strengthen our academic rigor as we raise the visibility of the college in the business community in Dallas and Fort Worth as well as in Texas and nationally and internationally. We seek, as Paul instructed, to "destroy arguments and every lofty opinion raised against the knowledge of God, and take every thought captive to obey Christ."[11] Furthermore, we follow Christ's teaching that we "let our light shine before others, so that they may see our good works and give glory to our Father who is in heaven."[12] In this way, we build on the rich history and steadfastness of the college's vision and mission while working to provide outstanding, transformative business education.

Objections to Faith Integration in Business Education (Why?)

In contemplating the integration of faith and business, some might object to the idea itself. Perhaps you have pondered some of the following questions: Is not the very idea of a Christian business education unreasonable? Is not the idea of Christian business an oxymoron? Is not a person's faith a more personal, private matter while business is a more social and public enterprise? Are not biblical principles and business

[10] Rom. 1:12, 17 (ESV).
[11] 2 Cor. 10:5 (ESV).
[12] Matt. 5:16 (ESV) pronoun updated to *our* from *your*.

objectives in conflict with each other? Profit versus salvation? Success over people? Short-term, quarterly focus versus eternity?

Christ taught often about matters of wealth, money, possessions, and business. Randy Alcorn stated in his book, *The Treasure Principle*, that "15 percent of everything Christ said relate[d] to this topic—more than His teachings on Heaven and Hell combined."[13] Christ told several business-focused parables, including that of the talents and the treasure of great price, and often interacted with businesspeople, including Zacchaeus, and even several of His disciples. His teaching covered farming, purchasing real-estate, building, dealing with employees, and debt. In fact, more than half of all of Jesus' parables dealt in some way with business. This teaching of moral business was important to Christ and should be just as important to a student's education today.

In this regard, should we not leave the teaching of Christian principles to the "experts," like pastors or seminarians? If religion is taught at the college level, perhaps the department of religion is better qualified to teach these matters, and not the College of Business? To the contrary, if Christ utilized business and its concepts in His teaching, we also should do the same in our business teaching. As Paul wrote to Timothy, "Do your best to present yourself to God as one approved, a worker who has no need to be ashamed, rightly handling the word of truth."[14] In the College of Business we need to know and teach God's Word as it is so very important to God as well as to the proper administration of business and a complete business career. Jesus and His values need to be taught in every business class.

One might wonder, since business is a global activity, and companies interact with people from all over the world who have or are influenced by a variety of belief systems that are not Christian, should we impose our Christian views on these students? Should international students or even American students who come from a different religious traditions or no religious tradition at all be taught from a Christian perspective? There are several ways to think about this question, and it

---

[13] Randy Alcorn, *The Treasure Principle* (New York, NY: Multnomah, 2001), 3.

[14] 2 Tim. 2:15 (ESV).

begins with who we represent ourselves to be. We are very clear with prospective students that we are unapologetically Christ-centered. It is the focus of our vision and the first pillar in the DBU Strategic Plan 2019–2024.

Secondly, we would argue every college of business teaches from the perspective of a certain worldview. We have merely been overt at identifying and embracing a biblical one.[15] Finally, although most businesses in the world are not specifically Christian, most would like their employees and leaders to practice many of the values that are taught or lived out in the Christian faith. Values like honesty, integrity, loyalty, hard work, humility, servanthood, virtue, self-control, steadfastness, joy, peace, patience, kindness, all combined in a love for others should be what businesspeople desire. These virtues are taught in the College of Business at DBU and lead to advancement of the Kingdom of God as their deeper purpose, while also advancing the student's academic career and ultimately each business career. This moral teaching is good for every student, no matter their background or country of origin.

We believe Jesus came to restore all things that are broken. In this regard, much of what is in business is broken and needs Christ's healing work—work He often looks to His people to accomplish for Him. To that end, Paul instructed Timothy to teach the wealthy to live a different life, one that is not self-focused but instead altruistic. Paul said:

> As for the rich in this present age, charge them not to be haughty, nor to set their hopes on the uncertainty of riches, but on God, who richly provides us with everything to enjoy. They are to do good, to be rich in good works, to be generous and ready to share, thus storing up treasure for themselves as a good foundation for the future, so that they may take hold of that which is truly life."[16]

This instruction is the transformative work the College of Business is attempting to produce each day in every course taught. Our vision makes

---

[15] Cf. Brian J. Walsh and J. Richard Middleton, *The Transforming Vision: Shaping a Christian World View* (Downers Grover, IL: IVP, 1984), 35.

[16] 1 Tim. 6:17–19 (ESV).

clear the end goal, but it begs the question of how. The following section will explore how the College of Business practices the integration of faith and learning using the framework developed by Arthur Holmes.[17] It begins with hiring the right kind of professors.

Holmes's Framework (How?)

For our professors to integrate faith and learning, they must be people of faith. Organizations can easily begin to drift from their mission by hiring people who do not share the same values and beliefs. Both full-time and adjunct business professors must demonstrate active involvement in a local, evangelical church, and they must present a letter of endorsement from their pastor. Faith integration is part of the interview process; it is outlined in the faculty handbook, and each professor is encouraged to read a commentary on the DBU Mission Statement written by the late David Naugle.[18] Faith integration is not only emphasized during the hiring process, it is also part of the evaluation process for all faculty members. At the end of each semester, we ask students how effectively the professor integrated faith with the course content, and we also ask how well the professor exemplified the concept of a servant leader throughout the semester. The overt emphasis on faith integration in both the hiring and evaluation of faculty helps generate a more cohesive culture through the attraction, selection, attrition model.[19]

The process of faith integration begins with hiring Christ-centered faculty, but those faculty must do something to actually integrate their faith. Before looking at four specific ways to integrate faith, perhaps it would be prudent to pause for a minute to think about the objective of integrating faith with learning.

---

[17] Holmes, *The Idea of a Christian College,* 45–60.

[18] Naugle, "Commentary."

[19] Cf. D. Brent Smith, *The People Make the Place: Dynamic Linkages Between Individuals and Organizations* (New York, NY: Psychology Press, 2012), on this topic for further clarification.

While there is certainly a bevy of works written on the topic of integrating faith and learning,[20] we believe a simple way to understand this concept is through a simple illustration involving the brewing of sweet tea. In the southern states, many people drink sweet tea, and when making sweet tea, everyone knows you have to stir the sugar into the tea or else it will just sit in a lump on the bottom of the glass.[21] Faith integration is like adding sugar to cold tea; it tends to just sit at the bottom unless you stir it around. Many people will try to add faith to their lives, but it ends up just sitting in a pile in one part of their life without ever really affecting the rest of their life. In a classroom setting, this could look like reading a devotional or offering a prayer at the beginning of class and then carrying on with business as usual. For faith to be truly integrated, it (the sugar) must be stirred around so every part of the education (the tea) is affected by it. It may look the same to the casual observer, but it definitely does not taste the same. The goal of faith integration is that every part of our lives—including our learning—would be impacted and changed by our faith. Our faith must not merely be an additional component in our lives.

In his chapter "Integrating Faith and Learning," Arthur Holmes describes faith integration in a bit more sophisticated manner and focuses on how it might be accomplished by Christian professors. He acknowledges the challenge of true integration of faith and learning for both the professor and student, and he proposes four unique approaches—or frameworks—that help avoid indoctrination or mere interaction and move us toward integration. In the following sections, we consider these approaches and how they are lived out in the halls of the College of Business at DBU.

---

[20] For additional reading, see David S. Dockery and Gregory A. Thornbury, *Shaping a Christian Worldview: The Foundation of Christian Higher Education* (Nashville, TN: B&H, 2002); Plantinga, Jr. *Engaging God's World*; Tawa J. Anderson, W. Michael Clark, and David Naugle, *An Introduction to Christian Worldview: Pursuing God's Perspective in a Pluralistic World* (Downers Grove, IL: IVP, 2017); Rick Ostrander, *Why College Matters to God: A Student's Introduction to the Christian College Experience* (Abilene, TX: ACU Press, 2009), specifically focuses on faith integration in a college setting.

[21] Actually, the best way to make sweet tea is by adding the sugar to the hot tea just after it has been brewed, but hopefully this illustration still serves the point.

Attitudinal Approach

According to Holmes, an initial point of faith integration is in "the attitude of the teacher or student."[22] This is especially true in those areas when the content itself is focused on a particular set of skills such as in statistics, accounting, or finance. This is not to say those disciplines have no other options for faith integration, but sometimes faculty in skills-based areas wonder how they are supposed to integrate their faith when they are teaching through formulas and equations. One place to start is in our attitude toward education.

Holmes laments, "A positive attitude toward liberal learning is not always evident among Christians."[23] Paul admonishes us to have the same attitude as Christ, and we should endeavor to display that attitude in all circumstances. For our faculty, a faith-infused attitude will push us to see our vocation as a calling from God and not simply a job. A right attitude will keep us from becoming complacent and treating our work as a means to an end—a paycheck.

We also need an attitude of desperation for wisdom. The Book of Proverbs admonishes us to seek wisdom more than gold or silver because of its surpassing worth (16:16). We should eagerly seek wisdom in all facets of life, which includes staying current in our disciplines. Our students should see in us an excitement to learn. Holmes concludes his section on attitude by stating, "The most important single factor in the teacher is the attitude towards learning."[24]

Visit with faculty in the College of Business—both full-time and adjunct—and you will hear a sense of amazement and gratitude regarding God's call to our work. We get to conduct research, exploring the foundations and branches of our disciplines and then building upon them, contributing to the body of knowledge in our fields. With further excitement, our colleagues share that we get to pass on this knowledge to students, investing not only facts and figures but also a curiosity to explore, learn, and grow. This same sense of gratitude is heard in ac-

[22] Holmes, *The Idea of a Christian College*, 47.

[23] Ibid.

[24] Ibid., 50.

ademic halls all over the world; yet at Christ-centered universities, the calling goes beyond this because we understand that work is a part of God's great design. When we utilize the gifts and abilities God has given us in the places to which He has called us, we have the great privilege of co-laboring with Christ in his redemptive work; we demonstrate love for God and for neighbor in deep and meaningful ways.

In doing so, we support students in their academic growth as well as their personal and spiritual growth both in the classroom and outside the classroom. Holmes expresses the importance of passion, discipline, and intellectual curiosity in the role of the professor. Not only does this make us more effective in our craft, but it also has a more lasting and holistic impact on the lives of our students. As one College of Business alumni stated, "Generally, what I recall is the humility expressed by each one of my professors who acknowledged God as sovereign over all things."

For students, a Christ-like attitude will show in how they approach their homework and in how they think about their classes in general—especially those classes outside their major. In the College of Business, we often hear students mumble about an English class or a fine arts class as they wonder why they are necessary. We can help them see their faith should compel them to think about education differently and to have an attitude of intellectual excellence marked by diligence, integrity, and motivation. "The scholar's love of truth becomes an expression of love for God."[25] We can help students adopt an attitude of love for truth and a desire to seek wisdom. A student stated, "During my time at DBU, I recall professors challenging us to do everything with excellence by working hard and diligently as for the Lord and not for men." The professor must have a love and reverence for God demonstrated in our partnership with Him in restoring creation. In word and in deed, we instruct our students. As a result, students recognize their studies are a part of their spiritual calling from God. They are more likely to take

[25] Ibid., 48.

upon themselves the example of curiosity, discipline, and integrity they see in their professors.

Another way the College of Business continues to encourage a Christ-like attitude in its professors is by hosting a weekly prayer time. Both adjunct and full-time faculty have been meeting weekly for the past several years to think about, discuss, and examine various aspects of Christian thought and belief. We encourage one another, pray for one another, and challenge one another to think more biblically about our lives and various subject areas. Holmes states, "The first task of integration is at the personal level of attitude and motivation,"[26] and this is true for both faculty and students.

Ethical Approach

Holmes's Ethical Approach addresses how faculty ground their academic discipline and instruction in the excellence and integrity of the Lord, encourage respect for all people including their laws and customs, and support the values of freedom and justice. The study of business must be established in an awareness of ethical theory and practice. The idea that business education—or any other for that matter—is value-neutral is both limited and short-sighted.[27] Faith integration must include an exploration of the ethical issues within a discipline especially with a focus on how those issues lead to certain value judgments. The entire curriculum of a Christ-centered business school must holistically prepare students for the life of a Christian engaged in business. Holmes says of the Christian professor that her values will show themselves in her work, and "it had better be conscious and well reasoned rather than unconscious and unreasoned, or else it will likely appear dishonest and be confused."[28] For the College of Business, particular attention must be paid to ethical issues within every discipline, but specific attention is given to business ethics as a whole.

---

[26] Arthur F. Holmes, *The Idea of a Christian College* (Grand Rapids, MI: Eerdmans, 1975), 49.

[27] Ibid., 51.

[28] Ibid.

Because business is ubiquitous in society, examples of unethical practices in business, especially in large corporations, come to light in the press and have given rise to public sentiment against business. The fact that Ken Lay and Bernie Ebbers and the companies they directed are household names illustrates this point. Rutherford, et. al claim academic research and the mainstream media "share a common belief that business schools need to increase the level of attention they pay to business ethics in their curricula."[29]

In fact, we have seen an increase in the number of ethics classes and programs in business schools over the past three decades. Even so, Rutherford, et al. point out the number of undergraduate programs that require business ethics as a component of their core curriculum is small. Yet simply offering or even requiring business ethics courses in universities does not necessarily mean we will see a reduction in unethical practices in the business world. Research suggests the development of moral understanding and moral identity begin in childhood and develop in adolescence.[30] Can we expect, then, that a single college course in business ethics will change the values of young adults? The focus of these courses then should be to make students aware of the ethical issues businesspeople face and provide them with tools in the form of ethical theories and decision-making frameworks they can use when addressing these ethical dilemmas.

For example, professors introduce students to the ethics pyramid (see below). Students are encouraged to see ethics as the individual decisions made in a particular time and place for a specific circumstance; however, those ethics are built upon morals established from principles that come from our beliefs, which *should* be grounded upon ultimate truth. The second version of the pyramid illustrates that when our beliefs are not founded upon truth, it will ultimately lead to ethics that have no solid footing and will finally topple over. After discussion, even

[29] Matthew A. Rutherford, et al., "Required Course: Investigating the Factors Impacting the Decision to Require Ethics in Undergraduate Business Core Curriculum," *Academy of Management Learning and Education* 11, no. 2 (June 2012): 174–86.

[30] Sam A. Hardy and Gustavo Carlo, "Moral Identity: What Is It, How Does It Develop, and Is It Linked to Moral Action?" *Child Development Perspectives* 5, no. 3 (September 2011): 212–18.

students who are not Christ-followers understand the need to pursue objective truth. To be ethical, we must be seekers of truth, and we uphold Jesus as the Truth.

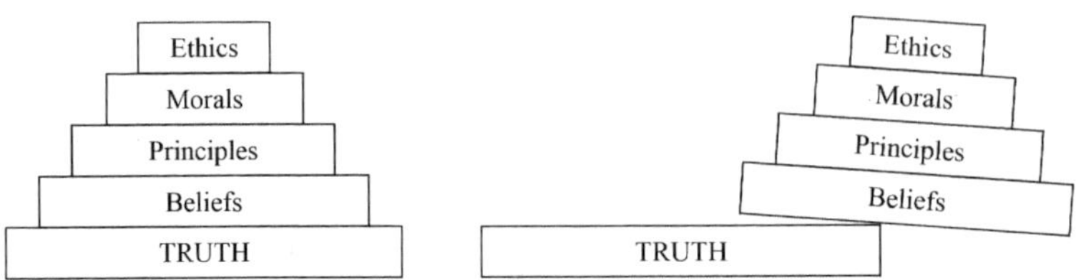

Foundational Approach

The word "business" dates back to an Old English word *bisignes* from the 14th century, but we know people engaged in business long before that. In the New Testament, we read about Joseph as a carpenter and Paul as a tentmaker; and in the Old Testament, there are stories of shepherds, bakers, cupbearers, and prison guards among others. So, where did the idea for business come from, and where did the concept for a College of Business originate? Holmes suggests asking questions such as these is another way to integrate faith and learning. He proposes Christian colleges look at the historical, philosophical, and theological roots of a discipline.

For Christians, the very beginning of business is when God gave Adam the job of naming all the animals and then followed it up with the directive that all mankind should cultivate the earth.[31] Whelchel writes, "And so from the very beginning our purpose has been bound up with our identity."[32] God gave us work to do but not just because He wanted to keep us busy or keep us from being bored, but because we were made in His image. He is a creative God, and He has asked us to join Him in that endeavor.

In Exodus, we also see that God intends for each of us to have unique skills and abilities related to our work. God tells Moses to get

[31] Gen. 1:28 is often referred to as the creation or cultural mandate.

[32] Hugh Whelchel, *How Then Should We Work* (Bloomington, IN: WestBow Press, 2012), 14.

Bezalel and Oholiab "and every skillful person in whom the LORD has put skill and understanding to know how to perform all the work...."[33] We share these verses and stories with our students to help them see business is not something Wall Street created. From a theological perspective, we see God has been involved with and concerned about business from the very beginning.

From a historical and philosophical perspective, successful businesses exist to solve problems and add value. Likewise, business schools emerged to solve the problems that businesses experienced in training managers to carry out their work effectively in changing environments. While business education in Europe proceeded the development of business schools in the U.S., the introduction of mechanical technologies during the second industrial revolution along with the access to land, labor, and capital in the U.S. resulted in significant growth in industries such as steel, oil, and railroads. As companies in these and other industries grew in both size and complexity in the late 19th century, they needed managers trained to oversee people, processes, and money in multidivisional firms. Thus, schools like the Wharton School at the University of Pennsylvania and the Haas School of Business at the University of California were borne, and with them came a new social class of managers trained in finance, accounting, operations, and human resources who arose to oversee these corporations.

The growth of these businesses created the potential for advances in transportation, infrastructure, communication, medicine, and many other areas. Even in the late 1800s, Carnegie could accurately state, "The poor enjoy what the rich could not before afford. What were the luxuries have become the necessaries of life."[34] Even more so today we see the benefits of business and free market economics in the reduction of global poverty rates, improvements in life expectancy, and access to goods and services that enrich life.

To accomplish this work, faculty in Christ-centered business schools like DBU engage students in the critical conversations of our discipline.

[33] Exod. 36:2 (NASB).

[34] Andrew Carnegie, "Wealth," *The North American Review* 148, no. 391 (June 1889): 654.

In the field of economics, two of our professors[35] challenge students to think deeply about the current rhetoric espousing socialist "solutions" to recognize that a 2000-year-old book still speaks with relevance and truth to the way we view wealth, money, and resources of all kinds. In macroeconomics, students are challenged to think about the role of taxes in a society and propose an argument for a specific tax system that would be consistent with biblical teaching.

To do so, faculty leverage their own work as well as that of academics, practitioners, and pastors. For example, students in a business ethics course answer the fundamental question, "What is the purpose of business in society?" From a Christian worldview the answer to this question includes glorifying God and working with Him to promote human flourishing. The answer to that question informs discussions regarding the stakeholder vs. stockholder debate, corporate social responsibility, fiduciary responsibilities of the manager, care for employees and the environment, and more.

Worldview Approach

Holmes suggested the Worldview Approach to faith integration is the "most embracing contact"[36] between faith and learning. It is a focus on the whole rather than the parts and how the God of the universe relates to that whole. Ostrander states it this way: "The difference between a Christian university and other institutions of higher education is this: a Christian college weaves a Christian worldview into the entire fabric of the institution, including academic life."[37]

Unfortunately, this comprehensive Worldview Approach is not often evident in business. Even among those businessmen and women who are Christ-followers, there is often a dualistic mindset and a false separation of faith and business. At its worst, the church only sees the businessperson as a source of income, and the businessperson only sees

---

[35] For more information, see the book, Dave Arnott and Sergiy Saydometov, *Biblical Economic Policy: Ten Scriptural Truths for Fiscal and Monetary Decision-Making* (Sisters, OR: Deep River Books, 2021).

[36] Holmes, *The Idea of a Christian College,* 57.

[37] Ostrander, *Why College Matters to God,* 17.

his faith in terms of how much he gives. Our goal as faculty in the College of Business is to help our students see how fundamental and comprehensive their faith is to their chosen vocation. One student captured this thought well with the statement: "It was made very clear that every aspect of business and marketing should be done with integrity and faith at the forefront."

For us, a holistic Worldview Approach to business begins with how we conceptualize work. It begins with a foundational look at work as mentioned above, but it must go beyond that to look at the nature and purpose of our work. Often, work is seen as a necessary evil in the world, and many people cannot wait to retire so they can start enjoying life. God's view of work, however, is quite different. Work is good, work is given by God, and work is a joint venture with God to spread His kingdom. We want our students to see their major is not just a way to make money; it is a way they can join God in advancing His kingdom. We want our students to get great jobs when they graduate, and we prepare them with the skills and abilities they need to be the very best, but we strive to help them see how that job fits into God's overall view of His plan for us in this world. This way of looking at work emphasizes two of the characteristics Holmes suggests are part of a Worldview Approach—one that is holistic and one that is confessional. "The church needs to be teaching lawyers, doctors, construction workers, and mothers homeschooling their children how to carry out their vocational calling from a truly Christian perspective."[38]

In addition to the concept of work, we also strive to present a holistic, biblically based view of money. A worldview is a lens through which we see things, and just as glasses alter everything viewed through them, our biblical worldview will and should alter everything we see through it—especially money. The message of the world is to get rich so you can live a comfortable and carefree life, but the Bible has a warning about placing trust in wealth:

[38] Whelchel, *How Then Should We Work*, 4.

> As for the rich in this present age, charge them not to be haughty, nor to set their hopes on the uncertainty of riches, but on God, who richly provides us with everything to enjoy. They are to do good, to be rich in good works, to be generous and ready to share, thus storing up treasure for themselves as a good foundation for the future, so that they may take hold of that which is truly life (1 Timothy 6:17–19 [ESV]).

As a Christ-centered college of business, we must help our students "see" money the way God sees money.

For example, students in our Corporate Finance class discuss the goals of financial management and wealth maximization in conjunction with biblical teachings on wealth and money. In the field of business ethics, professors encourage students to think critically about topics such as the stockholder-stakeholder debate and corporate social responsibility, moving away from zero-sum arguments toward an acknowledgment of our role as steward of God's businesses and resources. Students are introduced to concepts like triple-bottom-line and quadruple-bottom-line[39] and asked to think about them from the worldview of Scripture.

Holmes suggests another characteristic of a Worldview Approach to faith integration is that it will likely be exploratory. He states the task of completely understanding every discipline from a biblical worldview "would require the omniscience of God"[40] Himself. We are on this journey along with our students, and we must be open to God's guidance as we seek to understand these concepts. We want our students to develop the habit of exploring every topic they encounter through the lens of Scripture. They may not understand everything at first, but we must be committed to the journey of discovery and the enlightenment of the Holy Spirit.

---

[39] Triple-bottom-line is often summarized as people, profit, and planet; and while there is some debate regarding a quadruple-bottom-line, it generally involves adding a spiritual, cultural, or purpose element.

[40] Holmes, *The Idea of a Christian College*, 59.

Benefits to Stakeholders (So What?)

So, what are the benefits of integration of faith and learning and how does this integration impact all involved, including the students, the employers, the faculty, and the alumni? As has been outlined earlier in the chapter, there are a great number of benefits derived by these constituents and they can be understood as follows:

For Students, faith integration does the following:

- Helps them see how God has gifted them and how He wants to use them in this world.
- It helps gives them a sense of purpose.
- They feel cared for and loved as an individual, not just a number.

In this regard, a student stated:

> I have felt as though [the] professor took the time to pour into me with no strings attached. She cares deeply about my faith and future; I could have often been found in her office weighing life's decisions. As a graduating senior, I had no idea what direction I was to go in. [The] professor took the time to sit down with me, outside of the two classes I was taking from her, and go over my job opportunities and counsel me through my next journey. I am certain that she is one of the greatest cheerleaders and prayer warriors most students will ever encounter.

For Employers, faith integration does the following:

- Students they hire have deep values and morals as well as a good cultural fit. One employer that hires DBU graduates recently stated, "As we recruit talent, we seek those who find our vision and mission compelling…DBU students and those who have a business oriented and Christian-based education tend to be a great cultural fit for us."
- Students have a strong work ethic and desire to serve others. This same employer said, "Those who have had a servant-leader mindset instilled in their formal development have been

well-prepared to serve [here] and find it to be a place where they can grow their faith, skillset, and career."

For Faculty, faith integration does the following:

- There is a sense of meaning and purpose in our work and fulfillment in doing what God has called us to do.
- The personal relationships with students are rewarding and lifelong friendships can be made.

For Alumni, faith integration does the following:

- Provides an opportunity to pour back into students through mentoring, guest lectures, etc.
- Creates an interest in hiring DBU business school graduates.
- Instills a desire to give back to their college.

There are numerous examples of committed adjunct faculty as well. Those who felt called by God to teach at DBU and brought with them not only their business experience and knowledge of their subject matter, but also their personal walk with God. We often see in these adjunct faculty members a service to their students, the College of Business, and to God that does not end in the classroom. This manifests itself in activities such as meeting with students outside class for hours each week, helping them with the academic content of the course, and mentoring them in their professional preparation and discipling them in their walk with Jesus, etc. One alumnus recently stated, "I was fortunate to have several professors as mentors who have been a resource to me throughout my career."

Conclusion

We live in a fallen world and the effects of sin remain. Every area of life and creation is broken in need of God's restoring work. In His wisdom, God enlists His followers to join in this restorative work. Some He gifts with skills, abilities, and interests in the field of business; and it is critical that students with this gifting and calling receive the education they need to lead effectively in business. These future business leaders must have a knowledge of their fields, a sense of curiosity and ability to solve problems, to add value in the work they do and to see their calling as an act of worship and as part of God's restoring work. In the DBU College of Business, our great hope is that we are fulfilling our mission in a deeply meaningful way by producing exemplary servant leaders and followers who blend Kingdom wisdom and market knowledge for the glory of God.

Chapter 4

Integrating Faith in the Study of Business as Mission

By Ross O'Brien[1]

Introduction

In the early months of 2020, as COVID-19 made its way toward the scale of global pandemic, one of my graduate students studying business as mission (BAM) found himself stuck in the Philippines where he had been serving on a short-term mission trip. Given shelter by a remote farming family, he sought to put his studies into practice. The family with whom Roberto was staying, like many others dealing with the effects of quarantine, found the daily sales of their produce dwindling. Pre-pandemic daily sales ranged from 500–1,000 Philippine pesos, approximately $10–20 a day.

In an effort to assist the kind family who had taken him in, Roberto began helping to harvest the produce. However, an increase in supply does not necessarily result in an increase in sales if demand drops. Markets in and around the village were closed due to fear of the virus gaining a foothold in the country, resulting in a significant drop in business for this family. Already living at subsistence levels, the family feared what might happen.

[1] Ross O'Brien is the Director of the Master of Business Administration program, Director of the Center of Business as Mission, and Professor of Management at Dallas Baptist University.

That's when Roberto reports, "after reading the documents and sessions that you sent me, I got an idea to apply BAM and help them to create an online market with delivery. I was saying to myself 'I have to help my brothers to make a profit.'"

With limited access to the Internet, Roberto used the one resource available in the village, the famer's cell phone, which had Facebook access. With this he created a Facebook page promoting the farm's produce, connecting with buyers, and coordinating delivery in a safe way. This creative solution rocketed the family's sales to 15,000–25,000 pesos daily, a huge increase to their pre-COVID-19 daily sales. This story illustrates the power of seeing business as a platform for promoting flourishing in a Gospel-centered way.

This chapter will examine the importance of a strong biblical foundation and integration of Christian values in business in general, and specifically in the work of businesses established to expand the Kingdom of God in holistic and sustainable ways. The chapter will begin by addressing some possible objections to the concept and practice of business as mission (BAM). Next, the framework developed by Arthur Holmes on integrating faith and learning will be utilized to examine the concept of business as mission from a Worldview, Foundational, Attitudinal, and Ethical Approach. Within each of these approaches, examples from faculty, students, and external stakeholders provide insight into the means of integrating faith and learning as well as outcomes of this process.

Objections to Faith Integration in Business as Mission

Business as mission (BAM) involves sustainable, for-profit businesses run by followers of Jesus who seek to join God in His work of holistically restoring creation and fostering flourishing with an intentional focus on making disciples who faithfully walk with and obey Jesus. BAM businesses are one model of a Christian faith orientation in business. Other definitions and other models will be discussed later in the chapter. But first, some obvious objections arise from the idea and practice of BAM that have relevance regarding the instruction of BAM in a Christ-centered university.

Objection 1: Is business in and of itself too tainted to be used for missional purposes?

Response: The media presents the free market and business as driven by greed. The question then arises whether one can mix the holy calling of missions with such a tainted practice? After all, to propose "drug dealing as mission" or "human trafficking as mission" would be anathema. Can we, then, propose the combination of business activity and God's call to make disciples among all nations?

This criticism has an element of truth to it but also a fundamental misunderstanding of the nature of free markets and business. Critics correctly suggest we are inclined toward greed. The truth is that we are fallen creatures. God gave the tenth commandment about not coveting our neighbor because He knew in our fallen nature, we are given to envy. We become greedy for what others have. Some research even suggests we are willing to lose some percentage of value if it means others lose even more.[2] He and others suggest that not only do people seek their own self-interest, but they do so in ways that set themselves against others, and these tendencies must be accounted for when a firm considers the costs of doing business both inside and outside their own organization.

Greed, then, is the desire to gain more than others, to amass wealth even at the expense of others. This tendency is real in all people, not just businesspeople. If we suggested business is an unworthy instrument for missions because of this tendency then we would have to eliminate every other organizational form, as well, since fallen people engage in every human institution, including mission organizations and even the local church.

The misunderstanding about the nature of free markets and business comes from a faulty interpretation of Adam Smith's description of the role of self-interest in free markets. In their article on the distinction

[2] Daniel J. Zizzo and Andrew J. Oswald, "Are People Willing to Pay to Reduce Others' Incomes?" *Annales d'Économie et de Statistique*, no. 63/64 (July-December 2001): 39–65.

between greed and self-interest, Jay Richards and Ann Bradley state, "Self-interest is different. Every time you take a breath, eat a meal, or brush your teeth, you act in your self-interest."[3] Business owners and managers benefit themselves when they benefit their customers, suppliers, employees, and other stakeholders. When they act only in their self-interest to the detriment of others, their businesses fail. The free market actually mitigates the risk of greed because greed diminishes self-interest over time. In serving our employees, customers, suppliers, and other stakeholders well, we also serve our self-interest. While this distinction does not address the motivation to act in others' interest or our own interest, it does illustrate the point that unethical business behavior, rather than the norm, is a condition of the fallenness of people and not of the system of business or free market economics.

Objection 2: Is not using business as a vehicle for missions just a ruse to get past immigration offices and gain entry into countries that would otherwise not want Christians evangelizing their people? Is not there a lack of integrity when you say you are in the country for one reason but are truly there for another?

Response: Unfortunately, in the early days of BAM some mission agencies and missionaries fell into this practice. With good intentions they realized that the traditional means for missionaries to gain access into countries, with a missionary or religious worker visa, was no longer possible. Given their passion to see all people reached with the gospel, missionaries and mission agencies set up shell corporations that only served to gain access into these closed countries. Little or no actual business was conducted. This dishonest practice continues today, but not as frequently. It does not honor God and is not true BAM. As defined above, BAM businesses are for-profit companies. A company must make a profit to remain in business, and to do so it must deliver products or services of value in efficient and effective ways.

---

[3] Jay W. Richards and Ann Bradley, "Goldman Sachs, Greed and Self-Interest," *Washington Times*, March 16, 2012, https://www.washingtontimes.com/news/2012/mar/16/goldman-sachs-greed-and-self-interest.

The reality is that an entrepreneur starting a coffee shop (or any business) in Dallas, Texas has mixed objectives. She might have a passion for coffee that drives her to open a shop. She must remain profitable to stay in business. She might also have a desire to build community in the city in which she operates. She might want to use her business as a haven for those who have escaped human trafficking. In this one hypothetical business, four different motivations drive the entrepreneur. Likewise, a BAM business does exist to spread the good news of Jesus, but also must deliver an exceptional product or service and meet the needs of employees, suppliers, and others while also making a profit. There is no lack of integrity in this model, simply an intentionality behind the multiple motives and goals of the business.

Objection 3: This brings up the third objection. The three bottom lines of a social businesses (financial, social, environmental) are challenging enough. Is it wise or even feasible to add a spiritual bottom line to the responsibilities of the business?

Response: Certainly, social enterprises and BAM businesses must balance multiple objectives. We see the same challenges with any business engaging in corporate social responsibility (CSR). Research in the field of CSR reveals the complexity of the relationship between CSR and firm performance.[4] In general, findings demonstrate a positive relationship between the two variables[5] but the relationship is not unambiguous. Beyond philanthropy, Minna Halme and Juha Laurila suggest that businesses that integrate and innovate their CSR initiatives into

[4] Elisabet Garriga and Domènec Melé, "Corporate Social Responsibility Theories: Mapping the Territory," *Journal of Business Ethics* 53, no. 1–2 (August 2004): 51–57; Joshua D. Margolis and James P. Walsh, "Misery Loves Company: Rethinking Social Initiatives by Business," *Administrative Science Quarterly* 48, no. 2 (June 2003); Michael E. Porter and Mark R. Kramer, "Strategy and Society: The Link Between Competitive Advantage and Corporate Social Responsibility," *Harvard Business Review* 84, no. 12 (December 2006).

[5] For examples, see Charles Kang, Frank Germann, and Rajdeep Grewal, "Washing Away Your Sins? Corporate Social Responsibility, Corporate Social Responsibility, and Firm Performance," *Journal of Marketing* 80, no. 2 (March 2016); Marc Orlitzky, Frank L. Schmidt, and Sara L. Rynes, "Corporate Social and Financial Performance: A Meta-Analysis," *Organization Studies* 24, no. 3 (March 2003); Zia Ur Rehman, Asad Khan, and Asim Rahman, "Corporate Social Responsibility's Influence on Firm Risk and Firm Performance: The Mediating Role of Firm Reputation," *Corporate Social Responsibility and Environmental Management* 27, no. 6 (August 2020).

the practice of their business are more successful financially as well as in terms of their social objectives.[6] For example, a company might give a percentage of their profits to a non-profit organization. If the business is honest, they acknowledge that the goal of this charitable act is twofold: to serve the greater good of society and to promote the brand in the eyes of consumers. This is a philanthropic CSR strategy. On the other hand, a company like Nguvu Dairy in Uganda uses an integration CSR strategy. They seek to employ survivors of trauma such as former child soldiers, formerly trafficked persons, and refugees. Nguvu realizes these employees benefit from counseling and partners with a non-profit to arrange for trauma counseling. The financial investment in this social cause helps their employees on a personal level but also benefits the company because the employee is more capable to work effectively and demonstrates loyalty to the business. This integration CSR strategy benefits both the company and the greater social good. While the primary motivation behind the social commitments of companies like Nguvu Dairy in Uganda and Sunshine Nut Company in Mozambique and others like them is others-centric, there is a genuine and significant positive business outcome, as well.

As far as adding a fourth, spiritual objective, perhaps a better perspective than seeing the spiritual as a fourth objective is to understand the spiritual nature of the financial, social, and environmental impact of the company. By caring for the environment, we show faithful spiritual stewardship of God's creation. By loving employees, customers, and other stakeholders we demonstrate God's love. By generating profits through honest means, we act as faithful stewards of God's business. Like the two stewards given the three and five talents in Jesus' parable of the talents in Matthew 25, we want to create a solid return on the investment on behalf of our master. The spiritual nature of the financial, social, and environmental outcomes of a business reflects a Kuyperian understanding of the lordship of Christ over every domain. Applying

[6] Minna Halme and Juha Laurila, "Philanthropy, Integration or Innovation? Exploring the Financial and Societal Outcomes of Different Types of Corporate Responsibility," *Journal of Business Ethics*, no. 84 (February 2009): 325–39.

Abraham Kuyper's declaration of Jesus' lordship to the field of business we can say, "There is not a square inch in the whole domain of (business) over which Christ, who is Sovereign over all, does not cry: 'Mine!'" He was, after all, making this statement at the opening of a new university, making the claim that Christ's lordship encompasses every field of study.[7]

Holmes's Framework

In keeping with the use of Arthur Holmes's framework for integrating faith and learning, we next examine Holmes's four approaches to the challenge of this integration. In the following section, the teaching of business as mission in a Christian university is addressed from a Worldview, Foundational, Attitudinal, and Ethical Approach along with examples and outcomes of this work.

Worldview Approach

Many students who attend Christian universities come from a faith background in which they have taken part in various ministries and perhaps even mission trips. They often carry with them a sense of obligation or "oughtness" to enroll in studies of Christian ministry or missions. Some of these students also have a genuine interest in or curiosity about business. The idea that God might have gifted them for business so they can engage a lost world with the good news of Jesus has never dawned on them. For example, a recent MBA graduate shared her experience. "I always thought I was going to have to give up ministry or limit it to Sundays when I decided to pursue a career in business. But through the integration of faith in my business classes, not only did I discover a whole new world, but I found the calling that I had been looking for many years."

Unfortunately, it is not only students who have not made this conceptual leap. It reflects a bifurcated worldview that places the sacred above the secular, the spiritual above the material and even the Great Commission above the Great Commandment. The professor in

[7] Roger Henderson, "Kuyper's Inch," *Pro Rege* 36, no. 3 (March 2008): 12–14.

a Christ-centered business school must help students understand and adopt a more accurate and more complete worldview that destroys these false distinctions and forms a holistic perspective of life, gifting, and calling.

Students arrive at college with this false hierarchy of sacred/secular because it is what they have heard in their churches and homes.[8] When business leaders are mentioned from the pulpit, it is usually as an example of greed or, when they are praised, it is for their financial generosity to the church or their leadership on committees, as teachers or deacons. Seldom do pastors support, encourage, or challenge their members who work in the business world to see their work as their God-given ministry. Seldom do businesspeople recognize their vocation as their calling by God. As Os Guinness[9] points out in *The Call*, all Christians are called first to a personal relationship with God through Jesus Christ and second to work that utilizes our God-given gifts to co-labor with Him in restoring creation. Authors like Andy Crouch[10] and Tom Nelson[11] reflect in modern terms what Luther made clear centuries ago, that all work is important to God. In fact, not only is this true theologically, but as Wade Myers of Boldmore Growth Partners and Eagle Venture Fund points out, from a pragmatic perspective, business leaders in the workplace have over 8,000 times greater potential for influence on the lost in the workplace than does the average pastor.

Teaching the theory and practice of BAM in the university provides an important bridge between these two worldviews. As will be discussed later in this chapter, BAM is just one expression of faith integration in business. While other forms of business can be equally "spiritual," BAM, with its distinct mission to make disciples in holistic ways, might serve as a first step in the transition from the worldview that embraces the sacred/secular divide to a more biblical worldview of faith and work as calling.

---

[8] Mats Tunehag, "God Means Business: An Introduction to Business as Mission, BAM," Business as Mission, April 2008, https://businessasmission.com/resources/god-means-business.

[9] Os Guinness, *The Call* (Nashville, TN: Thomas Nelson, 1997).

[10] Andy Crouch, *Culture Making* (Westmont, IL: IVP, 2008).

[11] Tom Nelson, *Work Matters* (Wheaton, IL: Crossway, 2011).

Further, teaching BAM in the Christian university helps students understand and appreciate the varying views on what it means to act as a Christian in business. Students will be familiar with many examples including Chick-fil-A closing its doors on Sundays and In-N-Out Burger printing Scripture references on the bottom of their drink cups, but are probably not familiar with ways businesses alleviate poverty, prevent trafficking, and restore those trapped in trafficking, and in many other ways foster human flourishing. In his book *Created in God's Image*, Hoekema states, "God has created us in his image, so that we may carry out a task, fulfill a mission, pursue a calling."[12] God has uniquely created each person (Psalm 139) and set aside work for us to do in the name of Christ Jesus (Ephesians 2:8–10). In that work, we demonstrate love for God and love for neighbor, expressed in service (Matthew 25:35–40) as we do these things "for one of the least of these brothers and sisters of mine" (NIV). In addition, as disciples of Jesus, we are commanded and authorized to make disciples among all nations (Matthew 28). Followers of Jesus do not have the option of selecting one of these commandments but are empowered to fulfill all of these through our work. We express our God-given talents by stewarding His creation well. We meet social needs by producing products and services that add value to life, by employing, developing, and paying employees for their work, by reflecting God's integrity and excellence in the way we handle money, issues of quality control, and all activities of business. We strive to bring the good news of Jesus as we build relationships with others in the workplace and the market, demonstrating in word and in deed the fullness of life in Christ.

Gen-Z students, as a group, desire to work in impactful, meaningful roles and organizations. The challenge, then, is to help them understand they can have a more holistic impact by addressing both social and spiritual needs, the here-and-now as well as the eternal. In teaching BAM in the Christian business school, we have the opportunity to help

[12] Anthony A. Hoekema, *Created in God's Image* (Grand Rapids, MI: Eerdmans, 1994), 73.

students develop a biblically based, holistic worldview regarding their calling by God into business.

Foundational Approach

As Mats Tunehag suggests, while BAM is a relatively new term, the integration of business and God's work of restoring creation is not a new concept or practice. We see examples of business and mission combined in the New Testament such as Lydia's support of Paul's work and the new church in Philippi with resources earned from her textile trade. Paul himself used business as a means of supporting his ministry financially but also as an entrée into a new community, engaging and building relationships with customers and other tentmakers. Many of Jesus' teachings took place in the marketplace or in reference to market principles.

Throughout history, we see similar examples. William Carey, considered the father of modern missions, believed missionaries should be self-supporting. Likewise, missionaries from the Moravian Mission Movement launched their global mission strategy using businesses as a means of financial support as well as a way to engage the people to whom they were sent.[13] Business has played a role in the spread of the gospel for centuries. However, BAM as a movement is a new development in missions and a BAM ecosystem has only developed in the past three decades.

Still, BAM is only one model of faith integration in business. The following is not intended as a comprehensive description of these, but rather as an introduction to some of the ways in which businesspeople partner with God in His work of restoring creation including tentmaking, Kingdom business, business as mission, and business for transformation.

While the apostle Paul literally made tents as a means of supporting himself financially and to meet people, modern tentmaking involves Christians taking jobs in foreign countries where they can live out their

---

[13] William J. Danker, *Profit for the Lord* (Eugene, OR: Wipf and Stock, 1971).

faith among people who do not know Jesus.[14] The companies in which tentmakers find employment often do not have a faith-orientation. For this reason, tentmakers must balance their role as faithful employee with their role as missionary.

Tentmaking is sometimes characterized as "job taking" since the tentmaker takes a job within an existing company. On the other hand, BAM involves "job making." Mats Tunehag, a leading spokesperson for the BAM movement, describes BAM as "real, viable, sustainable and profitable businesses; with a Kingdom of God purpose, perspective and impact; leading to transformation of people and societies spiritually, economically, socially and environmentally—to the greater glory of God."[15] In a BAM business, the missionary/entrepreneur creates businesses that add value to society, are financially sustainable, operate on biblical principles and reflect the character of Christ with a goal of making disciples among those who do not know Jesus.

Similar to BAM, B4T or business for transformation involves sustainable, for-profit business that operate in countries with little access to the Gospel of Jesus with the goal of transformation of individuals, families, and society resulting in discipleship and church planting.[16] The primary distinction between BAM and B4T is the emphasis on transformation at the individual, group, and community levels as well as on disciple-making and church planting. BAM has these goals also, but the OPEN Network of Patrick Lai places greater emphasis upon this transformational work.

BAM and B4T businesses are a subset of what we might call Kingdom companies. Similar to the former, Kingdom companies are run by Christians, deliver value to the communities in which they exist and seek to operate in ways that honor God and follow biblical principles. In general, these businesses do not exist for the purpose of making disciples or planting churches. Chick-fil-A, Hobby Lobby, and similar well-known businesses fall into this category. These Kingdom companies are

[14] Patrick Lai, *Tentmaking: The Life and Work of Business as Missions* (Westmont, IL: IVP, 2006).
[15] Tunehag, "God Means Business," 8.
[16] Patrick Lai, *Business for Transformation* (Pasadena, CA: William Carey Library, 2015).

not opposed to disciple making but it is not usually a primary objective nor a metric the business tracks to evaluate its performance. It is important to keep in mind there is not a hierarchy of spirituality among these models of faith integration. Each follower of Jesus must seek to honor and obey God using the business skills, knowledge, and experience God has given to glorify Him through work.

In addition to these businesses, a broader ecosystem has emerged supporting BAM, B4T, and Kingdom companies. Marketplace ministry organizations such as C12, Convene, and Marketplace Chaplains support the work of Christian business leaders who seek to operate their businesses on biblical principles. Angel investment networks and venture capital firms with a focus on Kingdom business and BAM provide financial support and mentoring for entrepreneurs. Some Christian universities now offer classes in BAM, travel study, or other means of informing and inspiring their students regarding the integration of their business gifting with an awareness of God's call to all Christians to serve Him through their vocations.

At DBU, we strive to meet this need in various ways. Every faculty member at DBU engages actively in their local church and seeks to integrate their faith in the content of their courses and in the interaction with their students. In other words, our call to teach at DBU is a spiritual calling and flows from our personal walk with Jesus. Beyond the student-faculty engagement, DBU's College of Business partners with North Texas C12 groups to connect C12 members with DBU students for a year-long mentoring program.

Travel study courses provide students an opportunity to learn about business practices in other countries. At DBU, we utilize this learning opportunity to also explore how a faith-oriented business can love God and love neighbor in particular contexts. For example, one travel study course to South Asia examined the micro-finance industry (MFI) in general and worked with one particular MFI that included a faith component that sought not only to meet financial needs but spiritual needs, as well.

Each spring, DBU is privileged to host the Lion's Den DFW, an annual pitch event that brings Christian entrepreneurs together with Christian investors. Companies from around the world pitch to an audience of over one hundred accredited investors who seek to honor God and generate a healthy return on investment (ROI) with their investments. Students attend and take part in various ways, learning from the event and building their professional network for future internships or jobs. One DBU student was surprised and inspired by what she saw. "Businesses like that exist, and faith driven entrepreneurs and investors are real and they are making real changes."

Through these and other ways, DBU seeks to prepare students to be effective and faithful in their future calling. In Matthew 9:38, Jesus instructs His disciples to "ask the Lord of the harvest, therefore, to send out workers into his harvest field" (NIV). College students represent a powerful labor pool for missions. Faculty, staff, and administrators at Christian universities must pray for our students and work to prepare them academically and spiritually as they go out into the fields ripe for harvest.

Attitudinal Approach

Providing wonderful curricular, co-curricular, and extracurricular activities for students to learn the fundamentals of business disciplines is necessary but insufficient in the work of equipping them to co-labor with Christ in restoring creation through business. Enthusiastic, informed, and engaged Christian faculty act as the catalyst that brings the content to life.

These faculty must set a high bar academically. We serve an excellent God and should strive for excellence in our own work while motivating students to work with excellence. We serve a purposeful and effective God and should likewise strive to prepare our students to be effective in their vocational callings, being effective ourselves in doing so. Our own intellectual curiosity should be contagious, prompting students to go beyond memorization of facts to discover a deeper level of learning and engagement with God's Word and creation. And our personal walk with Jesus should overflow in the fruit of the Spirit, "modeling the way" for our young disciples (to borrow a concept from Kouzes and Posner).[17]

Including BAM concepts, courses, co-curricular, and extra-curricular activities in a business curriculum provides a fertile ground for the integration of faith and learning in a Christian university. As Holmes points out, in some academic disciplines faculty and students struggle to identify the salient differences Christianity plays. Hopefully this chapter demonstrates many ways that our faith integrates with the content of business in general and BAM in particular. But content without the personal impact that a professor makes inside and outside the classroom does not have the same result in the lives and development of our students. One DBU student recalls the enthusiasm and passion demonstrated by the professor. "I remember what I learned in the classroom. Work is worship. When we work to worship the Lord something fundamental changes in the perspective of what we are meant to create. I remember my professor asking, 'what is God up to in the world? We get to partner with Him in this!'"

BAM's social, spiritual, and environmental impact make it easy for faculty to engage students, especially the Gen Z student population. This rising generation desires purposefulness in the companies from which they make purchases as well as the jobs to which they aspire.[18] BAM's goal of quadruple bottom-line results inspires these students. Yet faculty must motivate students to go beyond a feel-good enthusiasm and promote the discipline required to have a lasting social, spiritual, and environmental impact while also creating and maintaining profitable businesses. The work of BAM businesses is purposeful but it is also incredibly difficult.

[17] James M. Kouzes and Barry Z. Posner, *The Leadership Challenge* (San Francisco, CA: Jossey-Bass, 2017).

[18] Jeff Fromm and Angie Read, *Marketing to Gen Z* (New York, NY: AMACOM, 2018).

Ethical Approach

Holmes's Ethical Approach addresses how faculty ground their academic discipline and instruction in the excellence and integrity of the Lord, respect for all people including their laws and customs, and supporting the values of freedom and justice. The study of BAM provides a ready avenue for these discussions. As already mentioned, BAM involves businesses that reflect the excellence and integrity of God. Operating within the framework of God's law and also man's law is a part of this work. But observing the law is only the entry point to ethical behavior. BAM businesses also serve the goals of human rights, justice, and freedom.

While not all BAM businesses operate among the least reached people of the world, there is a heightened awareness of the needs in these locations and the potential for business to have an impact there. The great majority of people who never have an opportunity to hear the good news of Jesus Christ live in a region called the 10/40 Window. "The 10/40 Window is the rectangular area of North Africa, the Middle East and Asia approximately between 10 degrees north and 40 degrees north latitude."[19] Almost 70% of the people groups living in this region are considered unreached, meaning well over 3 billion people in these countries have little or no Scripture in their heart language, few or no churches or Christians among them, and many have no Christian mission work among them at all.

In this 10/40 Window we also find some of the poorest nations with unemployment rates ranging from 30–70%. High rates of human trafficking, infant mortality, illiteracy, and other social challenges accompany this poverty. Surely the good news of Jesus and the *shalom* that it promises are needed in these regions. In these regions, injustice, a lack of freedom and human rights, and a sense of hopelessness will continue unless transformation occurs.

[19] "What is the 10/40 Window?" Joshua Project, accessed June 11, 2022, https://joshuaproject.net/resources/articles/10_40_window.

The *Poverty Cure* film series points out that the best poverty reduction program involves employing people.[20] As has already been suggested, BAM businesses are job makers, not just for the BAM founders but also for others living in the regions where BAM businesses operate. Companies like Joyya (formerly Freeset) provide jobs for girls and women who had previously been trapped in the sex trade in India. Employment at Joyya provides safe and meaningful work for hundreds of women and young girls, learning a new trade as well as fundamental educational skills like reading, writing, and basic mathematics.

BAM businesses also set the example of honesty and integrity. One accounting firm in the Middle East refuses to assist clients in hiding money or misrepresenting financial reports. Their policy means they lose some business but as their reputation for integrity grows many banks recognize the value of their third-party audits resulting in more client opportunities. In addition, accountants who move from other accounting practice to this BAM accounting firm appreciate the fact they can use sound accounting practices and are not forced to falsify reports. A construction firm in South Asia is known as the company that does not take or pay bribes. Their bids for projects might be higher than competitors because they use quality materials and strive to deliver projects on time and budget. Other firms lie to gain a client's business then use inferior materials and overrun budgets. Again, their policies make it difficult to compete on the front end but pay off in many ways. The integrity of this BAM construction company became visible when an earthquake struck the region where they work. A building they constructed was the only one remaining amidst the rubble of buildings that collapsed during the quake.

The goal of BAM businesses is to co-labor with Christ in restoring creation. The examples above illustrate how they work ethically and strive to promote justice, freedom, and maintain their integrity in very challenging environments. To cut corners or misrepresent themselves would not glorify God. Most business ethics classes encourage students

[20] *Poverty Cure*, directed by Simon Scionka, featuring Michael M. Miller (Acton Institute, 2013).

to avoid certain unethical behaviors, not committing sins of commission in the workplace, so to speak. These BAM businesses go beyond this rudimentary definition of ethics by promoting *shalom*, flourishing for all stakeholders.

In the sections above, we have seen how teaching about business as mission provides an effective way to help students recognize how their faith in Jesus plays a fundamental role in shaping the understanding of and commitment to their vocational call. What evidence do we have, then, that this attempt at integrating faith and learning in a college of business makes a difference?

Evidence of Value Added

Students

Teaching business as mission as a course or simply as components in other business courses adds significant value in the life of a Christian student. At DBU, we meet freshmen business students who hear about business as mission for the first time express an excitement about their major. While they have had an interest in business coming into college, some communicate this is the first time they have heard about God calling people to business, adding a sense of purposefulness that was sadly missing. As has already been mentioned, many Gen-Z students desire purposefulness. What greater purpose can a Christian have than to use the gifts God has given them to work alongside Him in restoring creation!

External Stakeholders

In our work to build mentoring relationships between our students and external stakeholders, we anticipated and received positive feedback from the students. The time and intentionality provided by the mentors has had life-impacting effect. However, we were surprised and excited to hear the mentors share how the experience has positive impact on their lives, as well. As busy as these executives and business owners are, they look forward to the time with their student and feel blessed to have the privilege of being a part of the shaping process in the student's life.

Likewise, the Lion's Den DFW core team has actively engaged in the lives of DBU students, speaking in classes, providing internship opportunities, and even allowing students to serve as judges in the annual pitch event. They expect quality work, but also provide coaching and mentoring to help prepare the students. Beyond Angels, a nation-wide, faith-oriented angel network, provides internship opportunities for DBU students who are interested in learning about private equity and investment in startup businesses. Angels in the network mentor student as they work together to conduct the due diligence on startups seeking investments. These organizations follow the example of the Apostle Paul who spent time and energy equipping young disciples who would carry on the work after he was gone.

Employers such as Turas Group, Amplio Recruiting, and others continue to return to DBU seeking candidates for open positions. They do this because they see the quality of the character, capabilities, and knowledge of the students in the program. But they have also communicated that DBU has prepared students with a worldview of faith and business integration that many other universities miss.

Conclusion

All universities recognize their responsibility to equip students with the knowledge, skills, and abilities (KSAs) to do good work in their chosen vocations. Some universities seek to build character development upon that academic foundation. However, few universities understand that a student's educational foundation must be established in their personal relationship with Jesus Christ. The Apostle Paul pointed out that,

> no one can lay any foundation other than the one we already have—Jesus Christ. Anyone who builds on that foundation may use a variety of materials—gold, silver, jewels, wood, hay, or straw. But on the judgment day, fire

> will reveal what kind of work each builder has done. The fire will show if a person's work has any value.[21]

Upon this foundation, character is developed and KSAs are taught. By using concepts and practices of business as mission in curricular and co-curricular activities, students learn how to leverage what they have learned to work with God more effectively as He restores creation.

[21] 1 Cor. 3:11–13 (NLT).

Chapter 5

Integrating Faith in Leadership Studies

By Mark Cook[1]

Introduction

I remember coming across the title of Sharon Daloz Parks' 2005 book *Leadership* Can *Be Taught* and having a good laugh. I instinctively knew that she got it. Here was someone who had clearly been in the trenches, and knew that teaching leadership can seem at times like a Sisyphean task. Parks' manifesto was based primarily on the case-in-point method that she saw legendary Harvard professor Ronald Heifetz use to great effect in his courses, which reminded me that even in the upper-echelons of the academy the vexations of teaching leadership still exists.[2] As this volume surveys the integration of Christian faith and learning in a variety of campus settings, I will in this particular chapter explore what that weighty idea might mean in the domain of leadership studies. To set the context, though, it is worth naming the challenges of teaching leadership in more detail, beginning first with the obvious and then moving on to the more obscure.

The obvious challenges begin with the fact that leadership studies draw on a multiplicity of disciplines. In J. Thomas Wren's chapter in *The Quest for a General Theory of Leadership*, he recalls the various scholars present at a 2001 attempt to formally articulate a more unified approach

[1] Mark Cook serves as Associate Professor of Leadership in the Gary Cook School of Leadership at Dallas Baptist University.

[2] Sharon Daloz Parks, *Leadership Can Be Taught: A Bold Approach for a Complex World* (Boston, MA: Harvard Business School, 2005), 6–8.

to leadership studies. In his list were political scientists, historians, philosophers, and psychologists, among others.[3] However the field also draws from religion, literature, business, and the sciences in dizzying ways. For example, consider Peter Senge's use of biology in his exploration of leadership,[4] or Margaret Wheatley's use of quantum physics in hers.[5] This inter-disciplinary diversity is what makes the field so rich, but is also what creates such problems for unity to emerge. It also poses a problem to student and teacher alike in terms of the boundaries of content mastery. To borrow an agricultural metaphor, it can seem at times there is no defined "fence" around the field, and thus there are endless fields to plow.

When one comes to grips with the multidisciplinary approach, however, a new challenge emerges, which is that the field of leadership has both theoretical and practical components to it. While this is of course a reality for nearly every other academic discipline, the highly public and consequential nature of leadership on daily life means there is always a bias toward the practical. While scholars of leadership have tried to counteract the often arbitrary and subjective nature of the practical side of the field with a deeper focus on the theoretical, Joanne Ciulla's depressing conclusion to her afterward of *The Quest for a General Theory of Leadership* does not seem to offer hope that there is any possibility for consensus there, either:

> These chapters are not perfect or all encompassing expositions but, taken as a whole, they demonstrate that the real problem with leadership studies is not that it is too lightweight, but that it is too heavy. It takes more than one scholar, discipline, or theoretical approach to understand leadership. The study of leadership forces us to tackle universal questions about human nature and destiny. For

[3] George Goethals and Georgia L. J. Sorenson, *The Quest for a General Theory of Leadership* (Northampton, UK: Edward Elgar, 2006), 1.

[4] Peter Senge, *The Fifth Discipline: The Art and Practice of the Learning Organization* (New York, NY: Doubleday, 2006), 68–70.

[5] Margaret Wheatley, *Leadership and the New Science* (Oakland, CA: Berrett-Koehler, 1992), xvii.

> those questions, there will probably never be a general theory.[6]

If a passionately committed group of scholars who set out to articulate a unifying theory of leadership cannot, after years, do so, and whose representative then says that by the end she does not even think it is possible, is it not obvious why so many scholars and practitioners of leadership retreat toward the practical aspects of the discipline?

These two obvious challenges to leadership, however, are not what I want to focus on with the rest of this chapter. I will describe some of the less obvious challenges to teaching leadership that will directly lead us into a more fruitful way of seeing how a Christian approach to teaching leadership can offer greater stability overall. I will first describe these less obvious challenges, and will eventually return to each of them in my conclusion. In between I will offer what I hope is a fresh vision for integrating faith and learning in the field of leadership studies. This major section will set forth the Christian theological foundations of leadership by focusing on the doctrine of the Trinity, before moving into an application of how Trinitarian theology should frame the teaching and study of leadership. My central thesis about the vital role of the integration of faith and learning in the field of leadership is this: Our perspective on leadership was always meant to be intimately, deeply, and fundamentally connected to the supreme reality of the Trinitarian God.

Challenges of Teaching Leadership

When I first started teaching leadership, I was not fully aware of the extent to which the field is saturated by a human-centered perspective. In the process of my journey of studying leadership through the formal academic program of a doctorate in leadership, I had been blessed to be guided by a program that holds a God-centered perspective on leadership. But after finishing my formal studies and taking in the wider

[6] Joanne B. Ciulla, "What We Learned Along the Way: A Commentary," in *The Quest for a General Theory of Leadership*, ed. George Goethals and Georgia L. J. Sorenson (Northampton, UK: Edward Elgar, 2006), 233.

breadth of the field of leadership as I prepared for a new phase of teaching leadership, I began to realize the pervasiveness of the human-centered approach. What I mean in distinguishing a God-centered from a human-centered approach to leadership is to highlight the latter's relativity and plurality towards truth in general, but more specifically to point out the metaphysical presupposition that the starting point for leadership is humans rather than something outside of humans. The easiest way I can think to explain this is to peruse any general textbook on leadership studies. In the table of contents of Northouse's, for instance, discussion is divided into chapters on the Trait Approach, Skills Approach, Style Approach, and Situational Approach, before shifting toward a theory-based focus including Transformational, Servant, and Authentic leadership, to name just a few.[7] Absent from this type of presentation of leadership is the Christian understanding that leadership exists in reference to the Trinitarian God. Some texts will lump the Christian approach to leadership along with the other major world religions into a vague moniker like "spiritual leadership," but this term leaves much to be desired.

Leadership study that only takes into account the human aspect is limited by its own set of parameters. It can easily lead into another of the less obvious challenges I have encountered in teaching leadership, which is that many leadership development programs approach leadership as something that can be mastered rather than a life-long process of development and growth. Perhaps the reason for the emergence of this focus is related to the task or situational focus of much recent leadership theory, where the leader and the leadership situation are conceived of in similar fashion to purchasing disposable cups, plates, and cutlery for a party. The focus narrows to the utility and pragmatic aspects of the situation, which cuts out the long-term aspect of both the leader and the rest of the group or organization. It reminds me of an analogy I ran across when reading Ashley Woodiwiss's fine "From Tourists to Pilgrim," where she makes the prescient observation that modern ed-

[7] Peter Northouse, *Leadership: Theory and Practice* (Los Angeles, CA: Sage, 2019).

ucation both encourages and produces students who are more akin to tourists of knowledge than pilgrims on a long-term journey of growth.[8]

Going along with the emphasis on short-term leadership situations, the final challenge to teaching leadership that I began to notice is how leadership material and curricula is heavily skill-centric rather than character-centric. James M. Burns, probably the most influential scholar in the two decades when leadership truly emerged as a discipline, bemoaned this phenomenon in a provocatively titled question to one of the last chapters of his book *Leadership*: "Teaching Leadership or Manipulation?" In this section he says: "The vogue of the 'how to' manual still thrives today: How to gain power. How to influence people. How to win office. How to take over an organization. How to organize a people's movement."[9] But while not dismissing the approach altogether, he ends his paragraph with pointed disapproval: "Situation-specific, they are directed so intensively at concrete circumstances that they may positively handicap persons who wish to advance beyond those circumstances."[10] What Burns noticed and that I have observed now running rampant in leadership training materials is the detrimental long-term consequences that take place when the hard work of character development is not undertaken as a primary objective of leadership study.

In summarizing the three less obvious challenges that I have noticed as I have taught leadership, they together have led me to perceive that the contemporary field of leadership studies feels dis-integrated. There does not seem to be any center that holds the whole endeavor together. Students and teachers alike are left to sift through the various disparate theories, programs, and personalities, and are encouraged to formulate their own understanding of leadership from the rubble. It appears to me that the field of leadership is in desperate need of rediscovering a more integrated approach that has clearer definitions, aims, and purposes than the human-centric model has offered. Burns' vocabulary of

---

[8] Ashley Woodiwiss, "From Tourists to Pilgrims: Christian Practices and the First-Year Experience," in *Teaching and Christian Practices: Reshaping Faith and Learning*, ed. David I. Smith and James K. A. Smith (Grand Rapids, MI: Eerdmans, 2011), 123.

[9] James M. Burns, *Leadership* (New York, NY: Harper, 2010), 446.

[10] Ibid.

"moral values and ethical norms," or what has since become the amorphous approach to leadership termed the "values-based approach," while commendable, has done little to clarify what those essential values and norms should be.[11] Leadership is challenging to think about, challenging to practice, and certainly challenging to teach. However, I believe that a more integrated approach to leadership, starting with the theological foundation of the Trinitarian God, can offer the field a sturdier foundation.

Theological Foundation For Leadership: The Trinity

Instead of burying the lede, let me put a finer point on the thesis statement I provided earlier: a Christian understanding of leadership begins with God the Trinity, not with humanity. This is a fundamental distinction, and one worthy of exploring in greater depth. It has always surprised me that so much of our own discussion of leadership as Christians has perhaps postulated something similar to what I just offered, but has neglected to actually connect the corresponding dots that eventually lead to the more popular formulations as lead like Jesus.[12] The problem with neglecting to start with the Trinitarian reality of God is that what often results is a distorted and/or incomplete picture of Christian leadership that does not offer a sharp enough contrast with non-Christian understandings.

Basic Tour of Philosophical Distinctions

The problem forces us to go back to beginnings, and to do that we need to understand a bit of philosophy. I have hardly ever heard the branches of metaphysics and epistemology in reference to leadership, yet they have an astounding impact on how one works through the thorny questions of leadership. Most modern leadership theory only deals with issues of anthropology, which is far downstream of metaphysics and epistemology. It of course *does* have answers to the basic metaphysical

[11] James M. Burns, "Afterward," in *The Quest for a General Theory of Leadership*, ed. George Goethals and Georgia L. J. Sorenson (Northampton, UK: Edward Elgar, 2006), 235.

[12] Ken Blanchard and Phil Hodges, *Lead Like Jesus: Lessons From the Greatest Leadership Role Model of All Time* (Nashville, TN: Thomas Nelson, 2008).

and epistemological questions, but does not usually openly admit its presuppositions. To start with anthropology and eventually work down toward ethics, as most leadership theories do, without setting forth what metaphysical and epistemological presuppositions undergird the entire program, is as preposterous as a farmer not wanting to deal with the conditions of the soil but rather "just get on with planting the seed." But I am getting ahead of myself.

Metaphysics is of course the branch that deals with first principles, or as J. P. Moreland defines it: "the philosophical study of the nature of being or reality and the ultimate categories or kinds of things that are real."[13] While that may sound like too much philosophical jargon to some, as a sort of navel-gazing posture that is not to be cultivated by active, decisive, visionary leaders, the truth is that what one counts as most real will determine everything else they believe about life, and, correspondingly, leadership.

C. S. Lewis has my favorite pithy summarization of Christian metaphysics in his book *Miracles*: "God is basic Fact or Actuality, the source of all other facthood."[14] In other words, the Trinitarian God is the foundation of everything we see in the material universe. Now, this is rooted in what Dallas Willard labels metaphysical realism, which includes two important points. First, that there is a mind-independent world, and "it and the entities within it are what they are independent of our thinking about them. That means that invisible things such as soul, spirit, the Trinity, and the kingdom of God are as much a part of reality as apples, chairs, and snowflakes."[15] Secondly, "the physical, sense-perceptible world is not all there is."[16] Metaphysical realism stands starkly opposite much of contemporary culture, which either says reality is whatever you want it to be (a form of postmodern gobbledygook) or

[13] James P. Moreland and William L. Craig, *Philosophical Foundations for a Christian Worldview*, 2nd ed. (Downers Grove, IL: IVP, 2017), 159.

[14] Clive S. Lewis, *Miracles: A Preliminary Study* (New York, NY: Harper, 2001), 145.

[15] Gary W. Moon, *Becoming Dallas Willard: The Formation of a Philosopher, Teacher, and Christ Follower* (Downers Grove, IL: IVP, 2018), 193.

[16] James P. Moreland, "Reflections on a Day With My Professor and Friend," in *Eternal Living: Reflections on Dallas Willard's Teaching on Faith and Formation*, ed. Gary Moon (Downers Grove, IL: IVP, 2014), 125.

reality is only what you can see (an updated form of rationalism that has jettisoned spirituality and now goes by the moniker of materialism). It is important for Christians to understand that our foundation for thinking about everything, including leadership, is fundamentally different than these two prevailing beliefs.

I mentioned that epistemology was also the other philosophical category of prime significance that often gets neglected with contemporary discussions of leadership, so let me now briefly explain what this field of philosophy is about. As Moreland again explains, "Epistemology is the branch of philosophy that tries to make sense out of knowledge, rationality, and justified or unjustified beliefs."[17] In other words, epistemology has to do with what "counts" as knowledge, or how someone knows what they know. While this is a vastly complicated field, I bring it up simply to highlight that, again, Christians have such a different understanding than many contemporaries regarding epistemology. For us, Christian Scripture is a fundamental part of our epistemology. If Genesis 1:1 and Colossians 1:17 serve as thesis statements about Christian metaphysics, Psalm 19 and Romans 1 exposit a basic Christian epistemology. We do not believe, as many contemporaries do, in naked experience as the grounds for what counts as knowledge, nor do we limit knowledge to what can be verified through the scientific method, but rather we say that our epistemological framework includes the Trinitarian God's revelation to us through Christian Scripture.

Bringing the two philosophical subjects together, Christian leaders need to understand that everything we say about leadership begins and ends with the Trinitarian God, which is our metaphysical starting point, and that we base our further understanding of all things, including leadership, in the Trinitarian God's revelation to us through Christian Scripture, which is our epistemological starting point. We do *not* begin with anthropology, because to do so is to start from a human-centric perspective that neglects God and instead reverses the great Creator-creature distinction that is at the heart of Genesis 1–2. Carl True-

[17] Moreland and Craig, *Philosophical Foundations*, 61.

man's recent book *The Rise and Triumph of the Modern Self* serves as an exposition of the devastating impact both on an individual and cultural level, with such a human-centric philosophy.[18] But what might it mean to start with the Trinity in actual practice, you might ask, and what might it reveal more specifically about leadership?

The Trinitarian God as Our Best "Case Study" of Leadership

To answer this question, we need to shift gears a bit and move from philosophy to theology. While none other than J. I. Packer warns that Trinitarian study "confronts us with perhaps the most difficult thought that the human mind has ever been asked to handle,"[19] this does not mean that Christians should shy away from the topic. Instead, I have always appreciated what noted Scottish theologian T. F. Torrance said about the Trinity:

> The truth of the Holy Trinity is more to be adored than expressed. The Holy Scriptures do not give us dogmatic propositions about the Trinity, but they do present us with definite witness to the oneness and differentiation between the Father, the Son and the Holy Spirit, under the constraint of which the early Church allowed the pattern and order of God's Triune Life to impose themselves upon its mind.[20]

So instead of trying to explain the contours of trinitarian theology, which theological summarizers like Packer and others do much more brilliantly, I want to see what this wonderful doctrine might have to say to scholars and practitioners of leadership. I affirm the basic outline of the Trinity as set forth in the Nicene Creed, and have come to find great joy in what happens when faith seeks understanding, rather than the other way round.[21] Gregory of Nazianzus was right: "Faith, in fact,

---

[18] Carl Trueman, *The Rise and Triumph of the Modern Self: Cultural Amnesia, Expressive Individualism, and the Road to Sexual Revolution* (Wheaton, IL: Crossway, 2020).

[19] James I. Packer, *Concise Theology: A Guide to Historic Christian Beliefs* (Wheaton, IL: Tyndale House, 1993), 40.

[20] Thomas F. Torrance, *The Christian Doctrine of God, One Being Three Persons* (Edinburgh, Scotland: T&T Clark, 1996), ix.

[21] I'm alluding of course to Anselm of Canterbury's famous phrase in the opening of *Proslogian*.

is what gives fullness to our reasoning," and is not a crutch or a cop-out for the toughest questions and issues.[22] With that in mind, I would like to consider three aspects of the Trinity that have a profound impact on leadership studies: the relationality of the Trinity; the self-existence of the Trinity; and the self-giving of the Trinity.

The relationality of the Trinity is best expressed in the story of the baptism of Jesus in Matthew 3:16–17, where Matthew records: "And when Jesus was baptized, immediately he went up from the water, and behold, the heavens were opened to him, and he saw the Spirit of God descending like a dove and coming to rest on him; and behold, a voice from heaven said, 'This is my beloved Son, with whom I am well pleased.'"[23] As many Christian scholars have noted, including Augustine, love is at the center of the Trinity. In his treatise on the subject, Augustine even described the interaction of the members of the Trinity as that of lover, beloved, and love.[24] Millard Erickson beautifully describes the love the Father, Son, and Holy Spirit have for each other as the type of self-giving, agape love that is so unique in the New Testament: "[The Trinity is]…bound together so closely by the centripetal power of love that they are inseparable. The life of each flows through each of the others, so that each can be said to be the basis of the life of each of the others. None could exist independently of the others."[25] What we discover in the relationship of God the Father, the Son, and the Holy Spirit to each other, according to Augustine, is akin to friendship, and this inter-dependent relationality that is at the heart of the Trinity can help reorient scholars of leadership to the primacy of people and relationships in leadership.[26]

Another aspect of Trinitarian theology that illuminates leadership studies is the aspect of the self-existence of the Trinity. This idea is ex-

---

[22] Gregory of Nazianzus, *On God and Christ: The Five Theological Orations and Two Letters to Cledonius,* trans. Lionel R. Whickham (Crestwood, NY: St. Vladimir's Seminary Press, 2002), 89.

[23] Matt. 3:16–17 (ESV).

[24] Augustine, *City of God* 15.6.10.

[25] Millard J. Erickson, *Making Sense of the Trinity, 3 Crucial Questions* (Grand Rapids, MI: Baker, 2000), 67.

[26] The image of friendship in the Trinity is used throughout the work, but especially in Augustine, *The Trinity*, 6.5.

pressed throughout the Bible, and especially in the prayer book of the Bible, the Psalter. Psalm 90:2 says that "from everlasting to everlasting you are God."[27] Theologically, this idea of God's self-existence and self-sufficiency is known as His aseity, and J. I. Packer explains how neglecting or misunderstanding this challenging aspect of God's nature can impact a Christian:

> In theology, endless mistakes result from supposing that the conditions, bounds, and limits of our own finite existence apply to God. The doctrine of his aseity stands as a bulwark against such mistakes. In our life of faith, we easily impoverish ourselves by embracing an idea of God that is too limited and small, and again the doctrine of God's aseity stands as a bulwark to stop this happening. It is vital for spiritual health to believe that God is great (cf. Ps. 95:1–7), and grasping the truth of his aseity is the first step on the road to doing this.[28]

For scholars of leadership, once we grasp that God is at the very foundation and center of the field itself, and is the paragon and exemplar of leadership, we can then begin to move into the endless ways God's own nature and character provide encouragement and support for our human practice of leadership. With the self-existent, self-sufficient Trinity at the center of our understanding of leadership, we can begin to connect the dots between this doctrine and how it encourages us to be generous leaders. As Dallas Willard explains in *The Divine Conspiracy*, the Trinity is "A Being that exists totally from its own resources…nothing other than God has this character of totally self-sufficient being."[29] The wonder, though, is that this self-sufficient Being shows generosity to His creation, and not just in fits and starts, but in lavish abundance. J. B. Smith says that "God is generous because he lives in a condition of abundance—his provisions can never be exhausted—and God is

---

[27] Ps. 90:2 (ESV).

[28] Packer, *Concise Theology*, 27.

[29] Dallas Willard, *The Divine Conspiracy: Rediscovering Our Hidden Life in God* (New York, NY: Harper, 1998), 81.

moved with compassion because he sees our need."[30] When Christians, and then more specifically when Christian scholars and practitioners of leadership recognize and experience the Trinity's abundant provision, the effects flow out of our lives like streams of life-giving water. As Willard and Black describe, "Living under the care of the Shepherd provides a state of rest, or *shalom*, which involves plenteousness and brings restoration at the deep wellspring of our lives…It is the nature of the Good Shepherd to be good and to lead his sheep onto good paths."[31] The doctrine of the Trinity provides a marked contrast to worldviews of leadership that only see things in terms of scarcity, offering instead a model for truly generous leadership based upon the unlimited resources of God the Trinity.

The third aspect of Trinitarian theology that I want to explore for its impact on leadership is the self-giving nature of the Trinity. The Apostle Paul penned one of the most eloquent descriptions of the amazing self-giving that is present within the Trinity in Philippians 2, but John's first chapter is the New Testament's starting place for the doctrine. There, John says that "The Word became flesh and dwelt among us."[32] As J. I. Packer explains, here is where Trinitarian theology takes on a new dimension:

> Trinity and Incarnation belong together. The doctrine of the Trinity declares that the man Jesus is truly divine; that of the Incarnation declares that the divine Jesus is truly human. Together they proclaim the full reality of the Savior whom the New Testament sets forth, the Son who came from the Father's side at the Father's will to become the sinner's substitute on the cross.[33]

We should be in wonder and awe that the self-existent, self-sufficient Trinity is full of generosity, such that the Son has come to rescue the

[30] James B. Smith, *The Good and Beautiful God: Falling in Love With The God Jesus Knows* (Downers Grove, IL: IVP, 2009), 84.

[31] Dallas Willard and Gary Black, Jr., *The Divine Conspiracy Continued: Fulfilling God's Kingdom on Earth* (New York, NY: Harper, 2015), 16.

[32] John 1:14 (ESV).

[33] Packer, *Concise Theology*, 104.

fallen creation. Augustine's palpable astonishment is evident when he asks: "Could God have done anything kinder or more generous than for the real, eternal, unchanging wisdom of God itself, to which we must cling, to condescend to take on human form?"[34] Is it not incredible that "God does not primarily communicate 'truths' about himself, but rather bestows *himself* as absolute truth and love,"[35] as Hans Urs Von Balthasar reminds us? And this self-giving attribute of the Trinity, most evident to us in the life, death, and resurrection of Jesus the Son, is purposed to bring restoration and redemption. C. S. Lewis elucidates this point quite poignantly in his book *Miracles*:

> In the Christian story God descends to reascend. He comes down; down from the heights of absolute being into time and space, down into humanity; ...down to the very roots and seabed of the Nature He has created. But He goes down to come up again and bring the whole ruined world up with Him.[36]

The self-giving nature of the Trinity is one with numerous applications, but for scholars and practitioners of leadership it should be our nonstop flight to Christian servant leadership. Within the doctrine of the Trinity is the helpful corrective we need to leadership's inherent problems of pride and superiority. As Millard J. Erickson reminds us,

> I would suggest that, if the relationship of the members of the Trinity to one another is intended to be a model for us to follow in relating to one another, then we will be concerned to function in a relationship of equality, of mutual respect, in which we understand that others are as important to God as we are, and treat them as equals.[37]

[34] Saint Augustine, "The Advantage of Believing," in *On Christian Belief*, ed. Boniface Ramsey, trans. Ray Kearney, vol. I/8, The Works of Saint Augustine: A Translation for the 21st Century (Hyde Park, NY: New City Press, 2005), 143.

[35] Hans U. V. Balthasar, *The Glory of the Lord*, vol. 1, *Seeing the Form* (San Francisco, CA: Ignatius Press, 2009), 162.

[36] Lewis, *Miracles*, 179.

[37] Erickson, *Making Sense of the Trinity*, 90.

There is simply no room in the Christian worldview of leadership for pride and smug superiority.

Now, as is most obviously the case, I have not even scratched the surface of the doctrine of the Trinity. I do hope, however, that this brief exploration has been helpful in illuminating connections between theology and leadership. My purpose has been to stimulate thought between these two fields that often do not overlap, because of my convictions regarding the integration of faith and learning. I join with my former colleague David Naugle in affirming that integrating faith and learning "refers to the scholarly activity in which the fundamental doctrines of the Christian faith—God, creation, humanity, sin, and redemption—serve as the theological and philosophical starting points by which the various disciplines are studied, appreciated, critiqued, and developed."[38] This means that every field of study needs to have theology not sprinkled on top of already existing approaches, but used as the starting points to embark upon the whole enterprise. I hope in this next section to briefly sketch a few ways I have tried to integrate faith and learning more deeply into the field of leadership studies.

Application of Trinitarian Theology to the Study and Teaching of Leadership

In the preceding pages I have sought to clarify my central thesis, which is that our perspective on leadership was always meant to be intimately, deeply, and fundamentally connected to the supreme reality of the Trinitarian God. Trinitarian theology should undergird the study and practice of leadership. I have outlined the philosophical foundation this provides to leadership studies, focusing on metaphysics and epistemology, but sought more so to emphasize the theological implications of the Trinity related to three key aspects of nature of the Trinity: relationality, self-existence, and self-giving.

Applying these philosophical and theological foundational ideas to the classroom, though, is the real intent and purpose of a volume

[38] Naugle, "Commentary," 8.

such as this. My previous section was seeking to demonstrate Arthur Holmes's concept of the Foundational Approach to integrating faith and learning, which is where he argues each discipline needs to seriously consider the history of their field, alongside the theological and philosophical starting points that should undergird their study.[39] Now I want to explain how I have tried to teach differently based on my view of the integration of faith and learning. I will explore how each member of the Trinity has impacted my worldview of teaching leadership: first, in recognizing God the Father as the Creator, Sustainer, and Founder of the field of leadership; second, in exalting Jesus as the aim and model of leadership; third, in seeing the Holy Spirit as the teacher in our classrooms.

In DBU's Master of Arts in Leadership, every student takes a core of required courses, including a class called "Christian Worldview of Leadership." We have similar courses for doctoral students and other undergraduate students, but this particular course explores the basic contours of the Christian worldview, focusing in on the unique ways Christians approach leadership. It helps students engage with the biblical metanarrative of creation, fall, and redemption, but also with the basic philosophical questions such as *Who am I? Where am I? What is the problem What is the solution?*[40] Formally teaching through the contours of a Christian worldview requires us to dip into biblical studies, theology, philosophy, and history, among other disciplines, and is often very challenging for students without backgrounds in these subjects. However, the goal is not mastery of the contents of the information about Christian worldview, but is for students to be transformed and renewed in their minds to be able to see leadership from a distinctly biblical and Christian perspective. What we are trying to do by introducing students to a Christian worldview of leadership is to join in the process of helping them discover God's plans for their lives.

---

[39] Holmes, *The Idea of a Christian College*, 52.

[40] I am indebted here to the works of Walsh and Middleton, as well as the work of Ander, Clark, and Naugle.

The field of leadership is just like any other field of study, in that it has basic presuppositions and foundational claims that students need to be able to identify and analyze from a distinctly Christian perspective. We cannot, for instance, just hand students James M. Burns' seminal work on leadership, tell them to read it and understand it, but then not also engage with it from a Christian worldview. As Holmes describes, students need to be able to sift and analyze rather than just take on whatever thought is most accepted in their field: "The Christian revelation claim puts limitations on the scope of scientific knowledge. Its understanding of the human person runs counter to much in Marxist and other forms of naturalistic thinking. One must be alert to such tensions—as well as to commonalities—if one is to think with integrity as a Christian."[41] Our worldview classes attempt to provide students with the tools necessary to think critically about the field of leadership from a Christian perspective. Dallas Willard has argued that "the foundational part of a worldview is always what it considers to be real,"[42] and the biblical answer is that God and His kingdom are what is most real. Boldly teaching that truth helps students see that Christian thinking on leadership does not begin with power, or influence, or any other aspect of a human-centered approach. Rather, leadership begins with God because He is its Creator and Sustainer.

Exalting Jesus as the aim and model of leadership comes directly from the DBU Mission Statement, where our goal is to produce servant leaders, but gets even more focused in the School of Leadership to describe the goal of producing Christian servant leaders:

> The mission of the Gary Cook School of Leadership is to support the University mission by integrating a Biblical foundation of Christian faith and values with academic studies in order to produce effective Christian servant leaders, scholars, and global thinkers who will lead and

[41] Holmes, *The Idea of a Christian College,* 55.

[42] Dallas Willard, *Knowing Christ Today: Why We Can Trust Spiritual Knowledge* (New York, NY: Harper, 2009), 45.

> serve with distinction in their chosen vocations for the glory of God.[43]

To effectively do this requires more than a class on Christian worldview, but requires the curricular process to also focus on developing a Christian imagination that can critically think through contemporary leadership dilemmas with a Christ-centered perspective. This emphasis coheres with Holmes's Ethical Approach to integration, where students need to "explore the intrinsic relationship between the facts and the values of justice and love, a relationship that goes beyond the question of consequences."[44] This means that beyond the hypothetical nature of many ethics conversations, we as educators need to help students wrestle with ethical issues in actual practice so ethics is shaped more by the wisdom of Scripture than by what Charles Taylor has termed the prevailing "social imaginaries" to which students often unconsciously subscribe.[45] Holmes makes the point that "questions of justice and mercy haunt us continually, calling for active integration of factual understanding with moral values rooted in the Christian faith,"[46] which means that students of leadership need help to approach the specific questions of justice and mercy that haunt the field of leadership with a foundation that Jesus is the aim and model of leadership and can provide wisdom that no other source can provide in thinking through ethical challenges. Pedagogically, the best ways we have found to stimulate this kind of critical thought is to utilize case-study exercises in class and with writing assignments, often asking the students to reflect on their own leadership contexts so theory does not remain distant from practice. This often leads to robust classroom discussions, as students have had time to think through thorny scenarios on their own before class, rather than being cold prompted by an ethical question in class and asked to formulate a response with limited thought. The overarching goal is for students to

---

[43] "Mission Statement," School of Leadership, Dallas Baptist University, accessed June 14, 2022, https://catalog.dbu.edu/undergrad/leadership/general-info.

[44] Holmes, *The Idea of a Christian College*, 51.

[45] Charles Taylor, *A Secular Age* (Cambridge, MA: Harvard University Press, 2018), 171–76.

[46] Holmes, *The Idea of a Christian College*, 50.

see that Jesus offers a different way to think through such issues, that in fact "there is a body of uniquely Christian knowledge, one that is available to all who would appropriately seek it and receive it."[47]

Once we recognize God at the center of all things, the "architect and builder" as the book of Hebrews says,[48] the starting place for all our thoughts on leadership, and then exalt Jesus as our aim and model of leadership, we are then naturally able to affirm Jesus' teaching that the Holy Spirit will "guide you into all the truth."[49] As Robert Fryling, author of *The Leadership Ellipse* has argued, the promptings and guidance of the Holy Spirit "is one of the greatest leadership resources we have."[50] The way I have sought to apply this to my teaching has been to recognize and affirm the Holy Spirit's leadership while we are in class together as well as while we are doing our work for class assignments throughout the week. This is by no means an easy thing to work out and practice, but it also does not require complex pedagogical methods to simply try. In my own thinking, I see this drawing on Holmes's Attitudinal Approach to integrating faith and learning, where he says, "The most important single factor in the teacher is the attitude toward learning. By virtue of what a teacher is, his students can stand on his shoulders and peer further in their day than he did in his. From the teacher the alluring contours of a Christian mind begin to emerge."[51] What this means is that when I initiate the students into recognizing the leadership of the Holy Spirit in our class discussions and assignments, the students are then able to respond and be open to the Spirit's promptings. They might not know exactly what this means, but they will most definitely pick up on how they see me practicing it, either for the better or for the worse. This is where the vulnerability of teaching becomes challenging because we set lofty ideals and goals that we so often fail at miserably. I know I do. However, we can continue to seek to model what it might

[47] Willard, *Knowing Christ Today*, 7.

[48] Heb. 11:10 (NIV).

[49] John 16:13 (ESV).

[50] Robert Fryling, *The Leadership Ellipse: Shaping How We Lead by Who We Are* (Downers Grove, IL: IVP, 2009), 47.

[51] Holmes, *The Idea of a Christian College*, 50.

look like to allow the Holy Spirit to be our teacher through the way we listen to each other, the way we think before blurting out our emotionally-charged responses, and the way we try to come to an understanding of truth, rather than simply seeking to get a nugget of leadership wisdom here and there, or simply get through the particular class on the way to something else. I am focusing here on the importance of being present, whether in the classroom or doing homework (and for that matter, in everything we do!), because I have been shaped by Eugene Peterson's teaching on the role of the Holy Spirit in helping us be present to God's work in and around us. In *Practice Resurrection*, Peterson says the "Trinity is the church's way of learning to think and respond relationally to God as he reveals himself to us as Father, Son, and Holy Spirit."[52] The personal nature of the Trinity is clearly evident in the work of the Holy Spirit, where Peterson continues by saying, "Holy Spirit is God present with us, making us personal participants in all his work, empowering us to be present in all his work."[53] I love that last phrase, "empowering us to be present in all his work," because it gives me vocabulary for my role as a teacher. I can seek to create spaces in my classroom (and outside, through the assignments) where students can learn to be more attentive to the leadership of the Holy Spirit by simply learning to be present, open, and available. I believe this is vitally important because it can hopefully help students become practiced in the ways of the Holy Spirit's leadership in their life, responsive to how it allows them as leaders to be followers first. As Peterson reminds, "The Holy Spirit is God's empowering presence, and what he empowers in us is a life of blessing and salvation, a life of resurrection. It is most definitely not a life of self-will, a life of self-righteousness, a life of using God to get what we want."[54] As I have said already, the field of leadership is rife with pride, superiority, and arrogance, and for Christian leaders to be different from the world

---

[52] Eugene H. Peterson, *Practice Resurrection: A Conversation on Growing Up in Christ* (Grand Rapids: MI, Eerdmans, 2013), 198.

[53] Ibid., 199.

[54] Ibid., 202.

requires us to learn at the feet of Jesus, by the power of the Holy Spirit, for the glory of God.

Conclusion: Reflections on the Challenges of Teaching Leadership

As I mentioned at the beginning of this chapter, there are unique challenges to teaching leadership that have caused me to reflect more deeply on my Christian faith and its relationship to the field of leadership. The bulk of the rest of the chapter has been my attempt to explain how I have increasingly grown to see the integration of Christian faith with leadership, primarily through the lens of Trinitarian theology. I want to conclude, however, with a few personal words of how I have experienced joy in teaching this wonderful subject, but to do so I want to revisit the three challenges I highlighted: that the field of leadership is largely human-centered rather than God-centered, that much curricula is aimed at mastery rather than life-long learning, and that skills are prioritized more often than character development.

One of the greatest joys I have experienced in teaching leadership has been in seeing students clarify first principles in their own lives. Personally, Augustine's idea of ordered loves, expounded in a variety of his writings but most vividly for me in *On Christian Teaching*, helped me understand how our affections impact the way we direct our steps, either positively toward God, or negatively away from Him and more to our own selfish desires. He says "living a just and holy life requires one to be capable of an objective and impartial evaluation of things; to love things, that is to say, in the right order, so that you do not love what is not to be loved, or fail to love what is to be loved, or have a greater love for what should be loved less."[55] The core of this teaching is what Proverbs 4:23 exhorts, that you should "keep your heart with all vigilance, for from it flow the springs of life."[56] As I have come to see our Trini-

[55] Saint Augustine, *Teaching Christianity (De Doctrina Christiana)*, ed. John E. Rotelle, trans. Edmund Hill, vol. I/11, The Works of Saint Augustine: A Translation for the 21st Century (Hyde Park, NY: New City Press, 1996), 122.

[56] Prov. 4:23 (ESV).

tarian God as the foundation and source of the field of leadership, and have been able to share this truth with my students, I have experienced the joy that comes from helping students clarify first principles.

The Lord has also been so good to allow me to experience the joy of helping students understand the rich resources available to them to grow in wisdom and knowledge as a leader. I have come to see each class I teach as an opportunity to share not only a body of knowledge about the subject of leadership, but also as an opportunity to open students' eyes to the wide panorama of God's Kingdom. C. S. Lewis argued in *The Abolition of Man* that "The task of the modern educator is not to cut down jungles but to irrigate deserts."[57] Joel Heck, a Lewis scholar, explains that it is not enough to simply instruct against false teachers. Instead, educators must encourage stimulating and deeper level learning both in and out of the classroom.[58] What I have come to understand along these lines is that there is more joy to be found in treating students not as receptacles needing to be filled with facts, but as men and women that need to be cultivated and encouraged in their overall process of learning and growth. There are, indeed, rich resources for us all to draw from in our journey of growing in wisdom and knowledge as leaders, and our common source is Christ Jesus Himself, in whom, as Paul said, "are hidden all the treasures of wisdom and knowledge."[59]

Finally, while the field of leadership itself may be one that undervalues character development, I have come to experience the joy of helping students see it as the central task of growing as a Christian leader. Dallas Willard's teaching helped me understand that giftings, while important, will only take you so far in leadership, because giftings are secondary to character. Usually, the field of leadership more or less looks at it as the other way around, but as Willard goes on to explain, the focus of growth in Christ comes out in the fruit of our very lives:

---

[57] Clive S. Lewis, *The Abolition of Man or Reflections on Education With Special Reference to the Teaching of English in the Upper Forms of Schools* (New York, NY: Harper, 2001), 13–14.

[58] Joel Heck, *Irrigating Deserts: C. S. Lewis on Education* (St. Louis, MO: Concordia Academic Press, 2006), 12.

[59] Col. 2:3 (ESV).

> Life in the kingdom is not just a matter of *not* doing what is wrong. The apprentices of Jesus are primarily occupied with the positive good that can be done during their days "under the sun" and the positive strengths and virtues that they develop in themselves as they grow toward the kingdom. What they, and God, get out of their lifetime is chiefly the person they become. And that is why their real life is so important. The cultivation of oneself, one's family, one's workplace and community—especially the community of believers—thus becomes the center of focus for the apprentice's joint life with his or her teacher. It is with this entire context in view that we most richly and accurately speak of "learning from him how to lead my life as he would lead my life if he were I."[60]

In sharing this wisdom with students, I have seen the burden of naked self-improvement lose its grip and be replaced with the better yoke of discipleship to Jesus. The paradoxical truth that Jesus knew, of course, is that aiming at character development will naturally lead one to become quite skillful, but it will add the further blessing of combining wisdom with the skill.

My journey of teaching leadership has been very frustrating at times, but I think this is because good leadership plays such a vital role in the health of God's people and has such an impact on God's overall mission. The prophetic witness of Jeremiah and Ezekiel describe God's frustration with His under-shepherds in vivid detail, underscoring the detrimental effects of bad leaders but also highlighting the blessing of godly leadership. Along the way, though, my frustration has also been turned into unexpected joys. I hope that what I have articulated over the course of this chapter has helped you understand not only my journey of seeing the integration of Christian faith with the subject of leadership but has also encouraged you in your life to see leadership as intimately, deeply, and fundamentally connected to the supreme reality of our Trinitarian God.

---

[60] Willard, *The Divine Conspiracy,* 284–85.

Chapter 6

Integrating Faith in the Pre-Medical and Biological Sciences

By Jonathan M. Cooper[1], Drew Ivey[2], and Curtis Lee[3]

Introduction

Any discussion of the integration of faith and learning will inevitably lead to the question of how the Christian faith can be integrated with the study of the natural sciences. Ironically, as Holmes mentions in his book the integration of faith and science is simultaneously one of the most frequently examined topics in the field of faith and learning integration while also one of the most challenging to display. However, we believe that the harmony between the Christian faith and the study of natural sciences has clear and compelling biblical foundations and can be displayed concretely in different models of faith and learning integration.

As a Christian institution of higher learning, we should realize that the integration of faith and learning is important in the educational maturity of the student. In the field of science this concept is certainly worthy of academic discussion. There is the point of view that says

[1] Jonathan Cooper serves as Assistant Professor of Biology and Chair of the Biology department at Dallas Baptist University.

[2] Drew Ivey serves as Assistant Professor of Biology/Science Safety and Lab Manager at Dallas Baptist University.

[3] Curtis Lee serves as Professor of Biology at Dallas Baptist University.

for science to be valid it must be free of religious influence. In other words, bringing in a spiritual aspect would result in a skewed or biased approach to finding truth, and the ability to remain objective would be lost. From the other side there could be individuals that desire to live a life of spiritual commitment and discipline that might tend to impose restrictions on scientific inquiry because of the inability to reconcile scientific discovery to Scripture. Each of these points of view are starting from a wrong perspective. They both fail to take in account the complete sovereignty of God. The physical and the spiritual world are not completely unconnected, but should instead be viewed as inseparable and understanding the world around us must be undertaken with a unified, wholistic approach, and thus the search for the whole truth requires the integration of faith and learning.

All of creation affirms God's sovereignty. Scriptural truths[4] proclaiming this fact are beautifully captured in the following words of the hymn "This Is My Father's World,"

> This is my Father's world,
> And to my listening ears
> All nature sings, and round me rings
> The music of the spheres.
> This is my Father's world:
> I rest me in the thought
> Of rocks and trees, of skies and seas—
> His hand the wonders wrought.[5]

The Christian faith has at its core love for and worship of the Triune God, who has revealed Himself in the Scriptures (Hebrews 1:1–3) and in the natural world (Romans 1:20). Science has at its core the study and knowledge of the very same natural world in which this God has revealed Himself. Therefore, an essential goal of a Christian university

[4] Ps. 24 :1–2; 1 Cor. 15:25.

[5] Maltbie D. Babcock, "This Is My Father's World," Hymnary.org, accessed August 15, 2022, https://hymnary.org/text/this_is_my_fathers_world_and_to_my.

education should be the illustration of how Christian faith can be integrated with the study of the natural sciences.

Furthermore, to those who would object to the very notion that faith and learning in the natural sciences is possible, one argument in its favor is the number of scientists who are leaders in their fields, while also being outspoken and committed Christians. Examples of these include Francis Collins, M.D., Ph.D., former director of the NIH and of the Human Genome project; John Lennox, Ph.D. Professor Emeritus of Mathematics at the University of Oxford; James Tour, Ph.D., Professor of Chemistry at Rice University, and others. Another argument in favor of the possibility of faith and science integration is the history of science, in which many great scientific achievements were made by individual scientists and inventors who show the compatibility of their Christian faith with their pursuit of scientific exploration (Kepler, Newton, Mendel, Morse, Carver, etc.). Furthermore, in the contemporary context in the United States, many undergraduate universities with an expressly Christian commitment (even across a wide theological spectrum) all contain and promote programs in science and medicine (Baylor, Notre Dame, Biola, Cedarville, Liberty, DBU). These examples do not deny that many people can and do study science from worldviews other than that of the Christian, but they rather point out the fact that the pursuit of science is not *inherently* incompatible with an explicit commitment to the Christian faith. The key issues then really do not stem from the question of *whether* one can integrate faith and science, but rather from the questions of *why* and *how* is this done? In what practical ways can this be accomplished? What steps need to be taken to accomplish a successful outcome in student understanding when it comes to integrating faith and science in their lives? It is not an option to have a program where Science and Faith are kept separate, but instead a method of developing a program that incorporates both ideas should be developed and refined.

The Christian faith *can* be integrated with natural science, because it presents a worldview that accurately describes the world we live in, it accurately describes reality and provides the best framework for two of the most important aspects of the scientific enterprise: why and how you *study* science, and why and how you *apply* science. The Christian worldview speaks to both of these issues. A Christian worldview informs why and how one studies science, as it impacts things like the motivations for scientists to study what they study. It provides guiding principles of ethics and truthfulness, which are essential for the proper conducting and reporting of scientific experiments, as well as for their application.

Theological Underpinnings for the Integration of Faith Into the Sciences

What then are the specific biblical or theological underpinnings for these claims? It is amazing the number of references in the Bible that address the natural environment. All of creation shouts for joy.[6] One framework for viewing how the integration of faith and learning relates to the study and practice of the natural sciences would be to view how this endeavor fulfills the First and Second Great Commandments:[7] (1) love the Lord your God with all your heart, soul, mind, and strength, and (2) love your neighbor as yourself. There should be a two-fold goal, emphasizing the true nature of God and understanding that mankind is made in His image.

At the core of everything, we should think about the integration of Christian faith and science as a love for God that manifests itself in revealing how science reflects and magnifies the character and nature of God. To begin at the Beginning, we study science through an understanding that the God of the Bible is the Creator of the world.[8] He spoke, and it came to be. Not only is He the Creator who began everything at some point in the past, but He is also the ever-present Sustainer of the universe, and every living thing in it.[9] More specifically, as Christians, we do not merely confess that God the Father is the

[6] Psalm 66.

[7] Mark 12:30–31.

[8] Gen. 1:1; Ps. 33:6–9.

[9] Ps. 89:11 (All creation belongs to God); Ps. 145:15–16 (God gives food and satisfies the desire of every living thing); Jer. 5:22 (God is the one who sets the boundary for the sea); Acts 17:25 (God gives to humanity life and breath and everything).

Creator and Sustainer of the natural world, but so is God the Son, our Lord Jesus Christ.[10] In the creation God has made, His attributes are on display.[11] The very heavens themselves declare the glory of God.[12] God being the Creator of the world impacts how we study and apply science, because we know this is our Father's world, and as we make scientific discoveries we are, as Johannes Kepler is quoted as saying, "Thinking God's thoughts after Him." Lastly, the Christian worldview understanding of the character and nature of God provides a logic for studying the natural world in such a way that one would expect to see a world of simultaneous order and decay. There is order because God is a God of order,[13] and decay because we live in a fallen world in which even the creation itself is affected by human sinfulness.[14]

Science must be studied and applied according to the highest standard of truthfulness. If not, then other scientists and the general public may lose confidence in the reliability of the scientific process, and styme further scientific discovery. The Christian worldview, however, provides the motivation for truthfulness because truthfulness and truth-telling are intrinsic to the nature and character of God. We must tell the truth because God is a God of truth.[15] God's care for truth extends even into His abhorrence of unjust weights and measurements,[16] which provides motivation for the Christian student of science to study, practice, and report scientific findings with the highest level of precision, accuracy, and integrity possible. Not only this, but these facets of God's care for truth should guide and guard the professor or instructor of the natural sciences, as well, to pursue truthfulness in their teaching, and seek justice, equity, and integrity with their grading.

---

[10] Hebrews 1 (He upholds all things by the word of His power); Colossians 1 (In Christ all things hold together); John 1 (Apart from Him nothing was made that has been made).

[11] Rom. 1:20.

[12] Ps. 19:1.

[13] Ps. 8:3 (God set the moon and stars in place); Prov. 3:19 (God founded the earth by wisdom).

[14] Gen. 3:17 (The ground is cursed); Rom. 8:20–22 (Creation was subjected to futility and it groans).

[15] Ps. 51:6 (God delights in truth in the inward being); Prov. 6:16–19 (God hates lies); Titus 1:2 (God never lies); Heb. 6:18 (It is impossible for God to lie); John 14:6 (Jesus is the truth); John 17:17 (God's Word is truth).

[16] Prov. 20:10.

In seeking to fulfill the second great command to love one's neighbor as oneself, a Christian worldview also impacts the "why" and "how" when applying scientific knowledge. While the natural sciences may tell a great deal about what can be done, they are incapable of telling what should be done and why. As Albert Einstein is quoted as saying, "You are right in speaking of the moral foundations of science, but you cannot turn around and speak of the scientific foundations of morality.[17] A Christian worldview is able to provide ethical foundations for the application of science, providing a guiding framework for navigating complex bioethical issues. This begins by the biblical truth that every human being is uniquely made in God's image.[18] Accordingly, each human being is to be treated with a level of dignity and respect not awarded to any other creature. Furthermore, a Christian worldview gives value to each human being even before birth.[19] This deeply affects ethical issues related to the application of scientific discovery to the full span of human life from womb to tomb. This also provides guidance for how scientific experiments can be done on human beings, since it makes a great difference if human beings are made in God's image as opposed to being considered more as highly sophisticated animal test subjects. It is also a motivation of love of neighbor, which should motivate the student and practitioner of science to pursue truthfulness and accuracy in conducting and reporting scientific experiments, as one of the first examples given after the first command to love one's neighbor as oneself is God's command to His people that they do "no wrong in judgment, in measures of length or weight or quantity."[20] Furthermore, decisions about how to apply science should be made out of a humble heart of service for love of neighbor and following the example of Christ.[21] It is this heart attitude which will guard the student and the scientist from

[17] "Science and God," *The Forum* 1930-06: Vol 83 Iss 6, June 1930, 374–75, accessed March 9, 2024, https://archive.org/details/sim_forum-and-century_1930-06_83_6/page/374/mode/2up.

[18] Gen. 1; Ps. 139.

[19] Ps. 139; Jer. 1; Luke 1.

[20] Lev. 19:35–36 (ESV).

[21] Mark 10:45 (The Son of Man came not to be served but to serve); Mark 12:31 (You shall love your neighbor as yourself); Phil. 2:1–4 (Consider others as more important than yourself).

pursuing the natural sciences from a desire for self-glory rather than for God's glory.

Lastly, as it pertains to the natural sciences related to the advancement of medicine and the care of human health, the Christian worldview provides a motivation to pursue medicine in the first place. This can be found in the Gospel's account of Christ's heart of compassion for the spiritual and physical needs of others, as His power and authority over creation were shown in His miraculous healings.[22] And while the Christian's pursuit of learning about the human body and then applying that knowledge to treat disease is not an exact parallel, it does echo that compassion. It is not for no reason that Christians have been a leading force behind the development of hospitals throughout history and even seen today in major Methodist, Presbyterian, and Baptist healthcare networks.

Practically Integrating Faith Into the Sciences at DBU

Attitudinal Approach

With these theological underpinnings in mind, how can the Christian faith be practically integrated? How do the faculty perceive and then project this idea of integration of faith and learning? It is important to remember that a culture of anti-intellectualism cannot be allowed to infiltrate the environment of learning. Professors need to model a love for God and love for the discipline that leads to a true state of intellectualism. One level at which faith and learning are integrated in the classroom is the level of attitude, that is the attitude with which Christians should think about learning, and in this case, in the context of studying and learning about the natural science. This is achieved firstly as professors model a love for God and worship of His majesty as seen in the created world. We have been captivated by the wonder of the natural world, and we seek to share that with others. This can come through the way we discuss topics. For example, rather than merely describing

[22] Matt. 14:14.

a natural phenomenon, a professor can exclaim, "Isn't that amazing? What an amazing gift to us by God!"

The attitudinal application of the Christian worldview is also seen in the ways in which scientific integrity is emphasized in an "Introduction to Scientific Literature" course. In this class, we discuss the importance of integrity and truthfulness in the collection and reporting of scientific data. For just as in Proverbs 11:1 ("A false balance is an abomination to the LORD, but a just weight is His delight" [NASB]), so also does the Christian in science need to strive for the highest level of accuracy in scientific data collection and reporting. This affects how we do laboratory exercises and how we report our experiments in lab notebooks. Furthermore, we exhort students to pursue academic integrity (avoiding cheating, plagiarism, and sloppy research) because of God's care for truth. For the Christian student of science, and any discipline, we pursue academic integrity because God is a God of truth, and because lack of integrity is a lack of love to our neighbors.

We additionally encourage students to integrate their Christian faith into their attitude toward science via our annual Dr. Herb Robbins Undergraduate Research Symposium. We regularly encourage students to develop their own passion to pursue scientific/medical research through research internships. We then give students an opportunity to present their research at the Dr. Herb Robbins Symposium. We select a keynote speaker for the symposium who is an alumnus of our college who can discuss his/her research, but who can also describe in part how his/her Christian worldview has impacted his/her career. This further models the attitudinal framework for faith and learning integration in the natural sciences.

Ethical Approach

Along with this, the students should understand that now that they know the wholeness of faith, their lives should reflect that idea. Students need to remember the Damoclean idea of "With great knowledge comes great responsibility." Therefore, a second level at which Christian faith and learning of the natural sciences can be integrated is at the level of ethics. Ethical values need to be introduced to the students.

Namely, what should Christian's value with respect to the study and application of science? At our university we do this through a variety of ways. Firstly, we offer a designated course on Bioethics in which case studies of ethical scenarios are examined from a Christian perspective in areas such as end of life, ethical conduct of human research, research integrity, and ethical reporting of findings in biotech industry.

In this course, students can be led to examine the Christian worldview implications on ethical issues in science though the asking of thought-provoking questions. Here are some examples. What does the Bible say about genetic manipulation, or stem cells, or abortions? Our worldview connects us to this. Scripture may not speak to all the specifics of these things, but can the morality of God and the morality given to us in the Bible dictate our response to such medical situations? Foundationally the first role of a Christian is to be a servant and disciple. The second role is that of father, mother, husband, wife, and then one's profession can come into your decisions. Can one perform abortions as a physician and still be a follower of Christ? Does "my body my choice" apply when all of you is created in His image, and for His purpose? Does that apply when your decisions are for His kingdom not yours? Should we use genetic manipulation to remove all genetic diseases, or to create a child with certain traits we want versus what God wants? Or is that ability part of the plan since God gave man the ability to think and grow? Lastly, if God was a physician would He spend His time prolonging life or delaying death? Our worldview as a Christian is founded in His words and truths; we want our students to be equipped to be strong enough to rest on that truth rather than simply what the world or western culture values.

We also approach how a Christian worldview impacts key ethical dilemmas in science through lectures and panel discussions facilitated in the venue of DBU's Friday Symposium lecture series. These discussions are opportunities to engage in ideas that are or soon will be in front of students in their fields. Recent topics have included discussions on end-of-life issues, care of the environment, the credibility and reliability of scientific information, the Christian response to the COVID-19 pandemic, and the ethics of gene editing. In these discussions of important ethical questions, we are able to integrate Christian faith and learning by seeking to apply biblical truth to how we think about these issues, and to how we propose to address them as Christians.

We also discuss the impact of research ethics misconduct/lack of reproducibility in our "Intro to Scientific Literature" course. Likewise, in one of our biology/pre-health major-specific sections of Foundations for Excellence (a mandatory course for all Freshmen), we also discuss the importance of ethical character in the relationship between healthcare provider and the patient. We then also point out this type of character is not only something that should be developed in the future but is also something the students can be working on now. We would like for them see that their character and their consideration of ethical issues now will have a tremendous impact on their future character as a scientist or healthcare professional.

Foundational Approach

A third level at which Christian faith and learning can be integrated in the study of the natural sciences is at the Foundational level. That is, it is important for Christian students of science to see the impact of history, philosophy, and theology upon the foundation of the scientific enterprise. There must be development of foundational concepts that we are able to build upon. Isaac Newton got it right when he said he stood on the shoulders of giants. The accomplishments of great thinkers who have come before enable the advancement of great thinkers today. Students need to learn about the history of scientific thought.

Some of the foundational theological underpinnings of the study of science from a Christian worldview are stated above, and some of these are discussed in class settings. But in one specific example, as part of teaching Biochemistry, students are assigned to read *Christianity: Coherence or Conflict* by chemist Dr. Fritz Schaefer, and in this book, students are confronted by a brief history of the impact of scientists within the historical development of western science, as students can see that many influential scientists or inventors have brought their faith with them to their studies, not seeking to separate their faith from their science.

One topic in which historical, theological, and philosophical foundations of the Christian worldview are important for natural science students at a Christian university to understand is the topic of evolution. Evolution is such a vast and multidimensional concept, and I find most American Christians fail to grasp the complexities of the topic. In one of our freshman biology classes, a key part of the curriculum is a discussion of the evolutionary paradigm, particularly in the ways in which it touches on the biological sciences. One professor creatively begins a discussion of this topic by relating an incident that happened on our campus a few years ago. We were training students for a mission trip to Bangladesh to help a community that had a poisoned water supply. We were going to show the community how you could grow fruits and vegetables via hydroponics. We bought 52 goldfish (their biological waste is utilized by the plants and is a natural fertilizer). Since we do not keep live animals as pets, the fish were to be properly discarded. However, one technician, desiring to spare the fish from this fate, decided to hide the fish in a dark storage room instead. These 52 fish had no filters, no heat supply, no vegetation, and no steady food supply (they were fed when a worker remembered, but at times they would go weeks without food). After 3 months, the fish were found and amazingly 3 had survived. They had no sunlight, minimal food, and with water that was both acidic and cooler than what goldfish typically need to survive. One of these fish, affectionately named Frederick lived for nearly 18 months. The professor then leads a healthy discussion about this case study of goldfish adaptation and how it relates to the discussion of evolution within the scientific community of modern times. In the context of this light-hearted thought experiment, students are then challenged to consider God's role in the adaptation of certain creatures in various environments. The professor guides the discussion to help show that this type of scenario does not preclude the work of God as Creator of all things, irrespective of the extent of species adaptation.

Building upon this discussion of the goldfish scenario, in another freshman biology class students are encouraged to consider the different perspectives on the issue of biological evolution that are advocated by different organizations staffed by many Christians, who seek to relate the scientific consensus to the biblical account of creation and God's work in nature. Organizations that seek to relate the biblical data about creation with scientific discovery and theory include BioLogos, a leading proponent of evolutionary creationism; Reasons to Believe, proponents of "old earth" creationism; the Discovery Institute, proponents of intelligent design (a not explicitly Christian view of the natural world); and Answers in Genesis or the Institute for Creation Research, who are proponents of "young earth" creationism. Students are encouraged to examine how these organizations attempt to reconcile modern scientific consensus with the Scriptures, and then challenged to be convinced in their own mind which of these models offers the best relationship of the two.

An additional way in which students are exposed to foundational aspects of the integration of faith and science takes place in our Anatomy and Physiology class. In this class students engage in the history of science through writing assignments that examine key events in the development of the sciences studying the human body. Not only is the theological and historical foundation of science discussed from a Christian worldview, but so also are some of the philosophical frameworks. This is done in part in bioethics, but it is also done in our non-majors' biology class, "Principles of Biology." In this course we discuss the "Nature of Science" and how science is a tool to learn something about the natural world, but it is not the only tool; there are other created things beside the purely natural, and other ways to learn true information, such as theology and philosophy. As Christians, we thereby simultaneously reject materialistic naturalism (all existence is merely comprised of material) and scientism (that only science can produce reliable knowledge about reality). As Christians we can use the tools of philosophy and theology to appreciate the gift and power of science and the scientific method to provide ways to worship God and love and serve our neighbor.

Worldview Approach

Finally, the last and most compressive way in which Christian faith and learning about the natural sciences can be integrated is at the level of worldview integration proper. One of the most influential thoughts in the church today is the concept of worldview. Dr. David Naugle defined it this way: "a view of the world and the resulting way of life within it."[23] The study of science and faith allows for a comprehensive understanding of creation. This means that being a Christian affects the way one views everything. This will include the study of science as has been primarily discussed above. But it also includes the application of science, the way one views one's career as a scientist, the way one uses one's knowledge and love for science for the good of others, the types of service projects one chooses, or the types of careers one pursues.

In our classes, we introduce worldviews with a very simplistic definition. A worldview is a collection of beliefs centered around the most valuable issues in a person's life. An individual's views about those valuable issues are the building blocks of a person's values, and those values are the windows of understanding in which we interpret the world in which we live. Given that everyone can have a worldview, how might those that consider themselves as disciples and followers of a mighty Creator create a worldview?

A professor should guide students to grow their worldview, push boundaries of what is known and let a student discover the values that will shape their life. Moreso, a professor at a Christian university should encourage the development of their students' Christian worldview with three main ideas: 1) God has revealed absolute truth in His Word, 2) Those truths should be at the center of a Christian's walk and purpose,

[23] David Naugle, "Worldview and a Christian Worldview," unpublished manuscript (Dallas Baptist University, 2003), accessed November 27, 2023, https://www.dbu.edu/naugle/academic-papers/_pdfs/11/worldview-and-a-christian-worldview.pdf.

and 3) Christians are to take His truths earnestly, allowing it to teach, correct, and form our worldviews.

As to the first, we make it clear we are servants of God, students of His inspired Word, and disciples of His. Beyond that my particular professional role is as a molecular biologist/immunologist. One thing I have learned, and that I pass on to my students, is the wisdom in knowing just because science knows how something works, does not correlate to knowing how it was made. For example, we know how physics makes the universe work, but its origin is quite disputed. My relationship with God began my senior year of college so I have that understanding of the substance of both views. Much of these discussions are based on that fact and the fact I live in the world, but I am not of it. As I teach, I pull material from Ronald H. Nash's book *Worldviews in Conflict: Choosing Christianity in a World of Ideas*.[24] The material from this book helps us in our class as we deal with issues of God, reality/truth, knowledge/wisdom, right/wrong, and the very idea of humanity. This presents important topics for discussion, especially if a non-Christian is in my class. We discuss the existence of God, how he brought an ordered system out of chaos, the interplay of faith and reason for a scientist, and how we as Christians view right and wrong within the context of moral laws seen in God's character and the Bible.

In order to get to the point where we are able to tackle this big worldview issue, we first start small. It is important to remember that for a student to be able to integrate faith and learning they must gain practical skills along with the academic knowledge of the classroom. The faculty play an important role in this process and work alongside the students in order to accomplish this outcome. This process begins the first time that the student is admitted to the program. The registration process is actually the start of building community. Students are introduced to the faculty that will be helping them register for their first classes at the institution. The professors who really care about the students demonstrate faith and learning. Students see the first steps of

[24] Ronald Nash, *Worldviews in Conflict: Choosing Christianity in a World of Ideas* (Grand Rapids, MI: Zondervan, 1992).

a unique approach to education. The faculty at this first introduction start the mentor relationship, which will continue until graduation and even beyond.

The biology department has the opportunity to enroll the students in one of their first required classes, FOUN 1101 (hereinafter "Foundations"). The goal of the Foundations class is two-fold: 1) to help prepare them for success in college; and 2) to begin to develop their sense of community, identity, and worldview. As to the first goal, the first year of college is a significant time in a student's life. Changes are happening daily. For many students it is the first time they will be away from home and in a new environment. It is the first time that students will be required to be responsible for their own actions. And for some, it will be a time when they need to determine the role of faith in their lives. For this reason, in this Foundations class, students will learn such things as how to be successful in college, how to plan for future careers post-graduation, and what is a worldview. Each one of the classes is taught by a faculty member who will help them understand the pathway to develop into successful students. In this class, I have students engage in multiple exercises and discussions that help them as they develop their worldview. I ask a lot of questions for the students to think on after we discuss big topics such as God, reality, truth, etc. I also have them write a paper on what shapes their Christian worldview more, culture or the Bible? After the paper is turned in, I always ask the students that said the Bible shapes their worldview more how many hours a week they watch TV, how many hours they listen to secular music, how many hours they read secular books, and then how much time they actually spend reading their Bible. After asking these probing questions, I then have them rewrite the paper. Asking such questions, and having the students think on them, I see it helps guide them to establish their own worldview versus me just making theirs look like mine.

Secondly, the Foundations class will help the students to develop a sense of community. Since all of the students enrolled in the course have the same interest, they develop together and share a family experience that will follow them throughout the academic experience. This allows them to develop deep friendships with other students who share similar learning experiences.

As you can see, the integration of faith and learning comes about by interaction between people. The Department of Biology has several unique events that build these relationships. Every year the College of Natural Sciences and Mathematics celebrates the start of a New Year. At the start of the fall semester students will be welcomed to the academic year by a social event. During this event, all of the students and faculty come together to fellowship and get to know one another. Significant relationships are started at this event. Faculty meet new students and begin sharing with them. Upperclassmen meet new freshman and transfer students and encourage them. One of the goals of coming together is to develop mentoring opportunities for both faculty and upperclassmen as they interact with the new students and continue to develop community.

Another unique experience for biology majors is the opportunity for the students to do scientific research. The biology department is too small to support a strong research program for undergraduates, so our students are encouraged and supported to do research at other institutions. Every year the department will give a seminar on how to apply and where to apply for these research opportunities. Many of our students have been successful in doing these projects.

Likewise, in other courses taught in our department, we are able to discuss the impact of the Christian worldview on the whole person of the student and how a Christian worldview influences one's view of higher education, one's character, one's use of time, one's pursuit of academic integrity and excellence, one's reasons for going into science, research ethics, bioethics, pursuing all of education as a Christian, etc.

The department has another class that is required by all of our students. It is the capstone class BIOL 4101 "Senior Seminar." In this class, the department provides the students with a curriculum that continues to reinforce practical faith and learning. The students learn how to transition to a post-baccalaureate program. Ideas such as professionalism, empathy, networking, and service are emphasized as the students prepare for the next transition in their lives. We discuss topics such as how science has impacted our worldview, how God's creation has impacted His Kingdom, and how to develop a Christian worldview of being a science/healthcare professional.

In addition to these in-class experiences, students are encouraged to practically apply their Christian worldview through service-learning projects where we emphasize ways in which our Christian worldview as scientists/healthcare professionals motivates us to use our time and energies to serve others in areas related to our courses of study. These include extracurricular summer research projects, outreach interests from our Global Health Organization, local area service projects sponsored by the Tri-Beta National Biology Honors Society, individual medical mission trips experiences and school sponsored international study and service trips to Bangladesh and to Jamaica. All in all, we seek to develop students as wholistic individuals who serve God through not only their endeavors in the classroom, but outside the classroom as well.

Conclusion

We will conclude this chapter with the testimonies of two of our recent graduates, who beautifully summarize the experience of integrating faith and learning in the Biology department:

> Faith Sawyer – DBU Class of 2020, PhD Candidate at Baylor College of Medicine in Houston, Texas
>
> In a society that seeks to justify immorality by insisting that truth is relative to one's opinions and beliefs, the incorporation of faith into learning requires a counter-cultural approach to one's education. The Bible is immensely relevant to every topic of education—including history, politics, science, and ethics...To integrate faith into learning, one must approach one's education with an open mind and an open heart, every idea prayerfully filtered through the lens of Christianity and tested according to the truths of God's Word.

My DBU professors approached education from an attitude of humility and kindness. Instead of seeking to indoctrinate students with a predetermined conclusion, they encouraged us to think critically about topics in the pursuit of truth by facilitating Socratic discussion and listening to alternative perspectives, which emboldened me to come out of my shell and contribute to class discussions. Most importantly, my countless meaningful interactions with my professors allowed me to observe the lasting impact of a professor on shaping a student's worldview and leading them to Biblical truths. My DBU professors so profoundly impacted me that I decided to teach at the college level at the conclusion of my doctoral education in hopes of also making a meaningful difference in the lives of students by guiding them to a Christian worldview.

As a biomedical scientist, my life revolves around the constant desire to learn more about God's creation to make scientific discoveries that might impact humanity. This process is not easy, as it involves constant failure in my experiments, disproving my many hypotheses, and facing the vast expanse of the unknown, trying to find the common thread that connects one biological phenomenon to another. Since God knows all things and fully understands all of his creation, I integrate faith and learning in my life by seeking to include God in the process of unraveling the mysteries of his designs. I constantly pray for success in my experiments and seek him for direction, and by allowing him to guide me, I can give him all of the credit for my successes.

Leslie Omiere – DBU Class of 2022, MD/MPH Student at UT Health Science Center in San Antonio, Texas

With time, I've recognized more fully that learning, in and of itself, is truly a personification of faith. There is a curiosity in learning that pushes one to dig deeper, to understand the hidden things in the pictures we try to see more clearly. It's a search for truth, and a belief that there is something meaningful and purposeful in the knowledge we acquire. With this view, I cannot untether my faith from my learning, because not only is it the light on my path of discovery but it is the very thing that bends my heart towards the desire for knowledge.

My professors were the very vessels that the Lord so kindly used to help me appreciate and value the purpose of knowledge. Without faith, it's quite easy to become jaded by the amount of information that is out there in the world. Fortunately, faith brings life and meaning to the seemingly dull or monotonous facts found within textbooks or research databases. My professors exemplify this so well in their passion and drive. They have brought a sense of revival to our education, and it's a beautiful illustration of what happens when faith and learning are integrated.

St. Bernard of Clairvaux beautifully expresses that love is the act of seeking knowledge in order to serve. This encapsulates the integration of faith and learning from a point of view that keeps the bigger picture in sight. Every effortful grasp for knowledge that I commit to is the embodiment of faith lived out because my pursuit of knowledge has become my labor of love.

Chapter 7

Integrating Faith in Mathematics

By Stewart M. Tung[1]

Introduction

In this chapter, I will address how to integrate faith and learning in mathematics and how that process prepares Dallas Baptist University students to integrate their faith into life and future callings. To do so, the integration of faith and mathematics will be motivated by two questions often asked by Christian students struggling in a math class. Following this, various articles or books regarding the integration of faith and mathematics will be briefly and informally sampled and discussed. Next, I will share how to integrate faith and learning categorized according to Arthur Holmes's paradigm of Foundational, Ethical, Worldview, and Attitudinal Approaches to the integration of faith and learning. Practical ways the integration of faith and mathematics is accomplished without regard to a particular course's curriculum will then be shared. After this, examples of curricular integration of faith and learning related to specific math course topics will be presented. Finally, samples of student responses to devotional reflection questions will be provided that show how what has been done prepares DBU students to integrate faith into life and future callings.

---

[1] Stewart Tung is Professor of Mathematics in the College of Natural Sciences and Mathematics at DBU.

Theological Foundations for Integrating Faith in Mathematics

Two questions frequently posed by desperate Christian students who are struggling in a math class are examined as a motivation for the integration of faith and mathematics. The first question is, "Can God help me learn math?" The answer is obviously yes, but not in the way that it is popularly assumed that God would help, with a bolt of miraculous insight out of the blue and with no pedagogical context or spiritual growth. The second question is, "Could increasing my mathematical understanding enhance my love for Jesus?" The answer to this question is less obvious and is by no means an easy goal to achieve in practice, yet clearly addresses the importance of the integration of faith and mathematics.

Regarding what others have previously attempted regarding the integration of faith and math, Johannes Kepler (1571–1630) famously wrote, "The chief aim of all investigations of the external world should be to discover the rational order and harmony which has been imposed on it by God and which He revealed to us in the language of mathematics."[2] Here, Kepler, from the perspective of a Christian worldview, is calling for an understanding and use of mathematics as a means to describe and discover order and harmony revealed by God as its divine engineer. From this starting point, mathematics is a tool for greater worship of our Creator and insight into His character.

Much more recently, Russell Howell and James Bradley, mathematics professor and professor emeritus at Westmont College (Santa Barbara, California) and Calvin College (Grand Rapids, Michigan) respectively, published a book in 2011 titled, *Mathematics Through the Eyes of Faith.*[3] In it, the authors address the integration of faith and mathematics with questions that challenge whether or not mathematical concepts point to a greater reality beyond themselves and whether chance and

[2] Johannes Kepler, "Thesis XX," in *De fundamentis astrologiae certioribus*, accessed November 27, 2023, https://apologetics315.com/2013/08/johannes-kepler-on-god-and-science/.

[3] Russell Howell and James Bradley, *Mathematics Through the Eyes of Faith*, Through the Eyes of Faith Series (New York, NY: Harper, 2011).

God's sovereignty are mutually exclusive. Their discussions on truth and the exercise of mathematical proof would be a useful supplemental reading exercise for the author's students in upper-level mathematics courses that required proving theorems and homework problems. Here the idea of proof to discern truth would be the integrating connection between math and faith, as students seek truth in all its forms as part of God's truth and as they train themselves as truth-seekers to discern any kind of truth from error, whether mathematical or Christian.

Jason Wilson, professor of mathematics at Biola University, discusses the integration of faith and mathematics in a 2015 article entitled, "Integration of Faith and Mathematics from the Perspectives of Truth, Beauty, and Goodness."[4] He utilized Alister McGrath's scheme of "truth, beauty, and goodness, viewed as different perspectives of the same mathematical phenomena."[5] Wilson also applied John Coe's faith-learning integration scheme of "conceptual [content through the lens of a Christian worldview], methodological [possessing a humble and teachable attitude toward content], and teleological [what God calls me to do with content] components."[6] His goal was to "combine the two complementary approaches to enrich the project of mathematics-faith integration and help apply it not only to the head but also to the heart."[7] "The perspectives and dimensions [he] described" were intended "to provide mathematics educators with ways to go beyond the usual secularized mathematical content and connect it with the Creator and the students' relationship with Him."[8] What Wilson does in general with his provided examples, I have, in this chapter, attempted to apply to specific math topics, pursuing specific content through the lens of a Christian worldview (conceptual dimension of faith integration), exemplifying and encouraging a humble and teachable attitude toward math subjects (methodological dimension of faith integration),

---

[4] Jason Wilson, "Integration of Faith and Mathematics from the Perspectives of Truth, Beauty, and Goodness," *Perspectives on Science and Christian Faith* 67, no. 2 (June 2015): 100.

[5] Ibid.

[6] Ibid.

[7] Ibid.

[8] Ibid.

and through avenues such as reflection questions and helping students carefully consider what God is calling them to do with a particular math assignment (teleological dimension of faith integration).

As a final example, Josh Wilkerson provides many helpful tools for the integration of faith and mathematics. One interesting practical guide to the integration of faith and mathematics is his article, "A Math Catechism (UPDATED)."[9] In his catechism, he suggests as part of a kind of mathematical catechism a series of insightful questions and their suggested answers based on previous writings or upon his own philosophy of integration such as, "How then is the Christian to understand mathematics?"[10] and, "How does a Christian understanding of God, creation, and humanity lend insight into grasping the effectiveness of mathematics?"[11] In contemplating the questions to such answers regularly as part of a catechism, the integration of faith and math is promoted and revisited especially during the introduction to math lessons.

Having briefly surveyed what others have previously done in integrating their faith and the subject of mathematics, the integration of faith and math at DBU is explained with a well-known saying, "Give a man a fish and you feed him for a day but teach a man to fish and you feed him for a lifetime." When I integrate faith and learning in mathematics, I desire not only to draw one-time connections between a Christian worldview and mathematical content, but also to train students to use a mathematical approach to clarify or explain spiritual truth and apply their faith in practical ways in order to succeed or serve in their mathematical careers. Students are encouraged to make use of the interplay of mathematics and a Christian worldview from the very purposes of each subject. On the one hand, mathematics was developed as a methodology for accurately modeling and describing truth to be understood or applied. For this very reason, mathematics can be used to effectively describe particularly abstract or supernatural

[9] Josh Wilkerson, "A Math Catechism (UPDATED)," *God and Math: Thinking Christianly About Math Education*, September 10, 2021, https://godandmath.com/2021/09/10/a-math-catechism-updated/.

[10] Ibid.

[11] Ibid.

Christian worldview concepts such as an infinite God or unfailing love. Therefore, if students are trained to use math to understand or predict how an abstract or infinite world works, they will also be able to use mathematical thinking to understand or predict how an infinite God interacts with a natural world ruling from an abstract spiritual world governed by spiritual laws.

On the other hand, the very purpose of a Christian worldview is to seek out the God of truth and contemplate all truth, especially mathematical truth, since it describes in detail the language of the natural world's beauty and tragedy and the human communities who inhabit it with their aspirations, problems, and suffering. For this reason, a Christian approach to the learning of mathematics never shuns such ideas simply because no connection between theology and math is obvious, but holistically understands that God could be revealed and glorified by a more precise understanding of His creation or of the nature of truth itself. This approach could be categorized as a kind of foundational integration of faith and learning, applying a cross-disciplinary approach to apply personal faith as a reason to learn mathematical content or use math to clarify spiritual truth or design solutions to alleviate human suffering or steward creation, about which God cares deeply.

I also seek to help students consider the idea of mathematical truth as a part of the totality of truth from the perspective of a Christian worldview. In this context, mathematical truth applies to a fallen world with unsolved problems, the provision of redemptive solutions, and the calling of God toward hard work, integrity, excellence, and suffering, even suffering caused by difficult mathematical content or human fallibility or both. This approach could be categorized as a kind of ethical integration of faith and learning, addressing the learning and applying of mathematics to solve academic and real-world problems related to values and morals in a fallen world.

Sometimes Christian liberal arts students need motivation to learn difficult and often dry abstract mathematical ideas. For those who seek to love and obey the God of the Bible, but struggle with finding purpose in learning so-called secular mathematical ideas, there is unspeakable joy in discovering God or His truth in a deeper way by making an appropriate connection to the surprising illumination of a mathematical concept. Here is where a Christian worldview reaches beyond just the need to know for some utilitarian purpose and calls the Christian to be an informed truth-seeker investigating a deeper understanding of the God of truth. This approach could be categorized as a kind of worldview integration of faith and learning, believing that all truth, and especially mathematical truth, belongs to God, whether labeled as sacred or secular, and is worth exploring, discussing, reflecting upon, confessing, redeeming, and applying.

A worldview integration of faith and learning naturally leads to a valuable principle of humility in Christian education. Just because a Christian student cannot see at this moment why he or she needs to know a particular math topic does not mean it will never be known what these truths, stacked one upon another, might build toward. For the result, either a necessary knowledge base or a strengthened mental capacity could empower such a devout truth-seeker to genuinely love God not with a mathematical fraction of one's mind, but with all of it in totality as the Lord commands. When I approach my students as a shepherd of the integration of faith and mathematical truths, it could be categorized as an attitudinal integration of faith and learning, endorsing a positive mindset toward a liberal arts education even if it involves writing papers and reading books that math students usually want to avoid.

In conclusion, to answer the motivating questions for this chapter, God helps the struggling student learn math through answers to prayer in the context of a caring Christian community of learners whose goal is holistic edifying education. This includes a call to a humble attitude toward truth-seeking, with a renewed motivation to learn surprisingly faith-relevant mathematics toward the ultimate purpose to know, love, and serve Him better. Likewise, it also includes spiritual growth as the seeker improves study habits, learns from mistakes, and resolves to seek excellence and build character for His glory. Symbiotically, a faith-integrated understanding of mathematics generates awe and wonder at God's creation and power, equips the math learner to serve others with useful mathematical modeling and applications, and reveals that the math-learning process helps you learn better and think clearer to love and worship God in fresher and fuller ways.

Practical Applications

Having discussed my general approach to the integration of faith and learning in mathematics, I now provide specific examples of such integration at DBU. Integration is first presented in ways that are not specific to a particular math course. For example, one could use this approach in any math class that is taught. In the following section, faith and math integration topics are addressed for specific math courses such as College Algebra or Calculus and Analytic Geometry.

Instead of simply lecturing on integration principles, faith and math connections are achieved by asking reflection questions, either as small group discussions in a face-to-face class or by way of online discussion board questions that are required as part of attendance. Student feedback comments are then guided toward the desired discoveries by instructor responses or intentional classroom discussion. Here follow some examples.

- A question for reflection based on Matthew 11:28–30: "Can God help you learn mathematics? How does He accomplish this?"
- A series of questions for reflection: "Is it possible to love God and hate math at the same time? If I replace the word "math" in the previous question with the word "truth" does that change your answer? Why? What is math?" (Spoiler alert: we really do not hate math, we hate the failure, frustration, arrogance, and ignorance of mathematically challenged creatures languishing in a fallen creation. In conclusion, most people will grudgingly admit the value and the challenge of learning the precise, logical, and beautiful mathematical language in which the universe was written.)
- A question for reflection based on 1 Corinthians 10:31 and Psalm 150:1–6: "Is it possible to worship God in your math class? What

would it look like? Could understanding the essence of math enhance your worship of God? What is math?" (Spoiler alert: the laws of physics the heavens obey, the description of acts of God's power, trumpet sounds, harp and lyre sounds, strings, flutes, the clash of cymbals and echoes of sound are all mathematically described, explained, and controlled. Therefore, appreciating math and using it to describe and control sounds enhances musical worship and adoration of God, as well as demonstrating loving God with your mind. Do you like or love that sound? That is the sound that math makes or controls.)

- A question for reflection applying Luke 2:43–52: "What humble approach would Jesus take in solving this difficult math problem?"
- A question for reflection applying Luke 6:46–49: "Why does Jesus think it is important to do your math homework?"
- A question for reflection considering Ecclesiastes 1:17-18 compared to 1 Corinthians 13:2 and the disillusionment of acquiring wisdom and knowledge without the utilization in service to others out of love.
- A personal prayer request reflection: "What kinds of mathematical and non-mathematical things would you like to pray for at this time? Is there a connection between the two? Why or why not?"
- An opening prayer for a particular mathematical lecture topic: "Dear God of wisdom and truth, open our minds to be equipped with the truths and skills necessary for the calling to which You have called us and help us learn to love You with our minds as well as our hearts throughout this upcoming mathematics topic."

Next, I will address integration topics that belong to a standard curriculum in courses taught at DBU such as College Algebra or Calculus and Analytic Geometry. The following are topics addressed in the course, *Mathematics for the Liberal Arts*:

- Set Theory: Let W=the set of all things you are worrying about right now. Let P=the set of things that you are praying about right now. Let T=the set of things you are giving thanks for right now. A question for reflection: "Are the sets equal, are they disjointed, and what are the intersections of the sets as related to Philippians 4:6–7?"
- Logic: Conduct a logical analysis of John 14:15 and the "if then" logic statement. (Spoiler alert: loving God is not about warm and fuzzy feelings; it is about obedience especially when you don't feel like it.)
- A question for reflection on Personal Finance, Compound Interest, and Proverbs 13:11: "What can we learn about the power of compounding interest and the wisdom of deferred gratification?"
- Metric Conversion: A question for reflection: "Which of you by worrying can add one cubit [equivalent to 45.7 cm] to his stature?"[12]
- A question for reflection on Geometry applied to Ephesians 3:16–21: "What is the relationship of volume formulas to grasping the metaphorical dimensions of understanding the love of Christ?"

The following are topics addressed in the course, *College Algebra*:

- A question for reflection on 2 Corinthians 5:21: "Can Algebra save your soul?" (in relation to the substitution principle in the definition of a solution to an equation).
- A question for reflection on the radius formula for an equation of a circle, distance from the center, relational distance from Jesus Christ, and the connection to Jesus and abiding in Him from John 15:4–7.
- A question for reflection on Galatians 2:20 and living the life of best fit compared to finding the equation of the line of best fit.

[12] Matt. 6:27 (NKJV).

- A reflection on the concept of a vertex of a parabola being the highest or lowest point of the graph and Jesus' words in John 13:12–17 in conjunction with the discussion question, "Is Jesus the metaphorical vertex of your parabola?"
- A reflection on Matthew 6:19–21 and comparisons to what determines the far left and far right behavior of a polynomial and what determines your eternal destiny.
- A reflection on 2 Timothy 2:2 and the relationship of the power of exponential growth to the supernatural power of spiritual multiplication through one-on-one discipleship under the crucial assumption that everyone participates.

The following are topics addressed in the course, *Finite Mathematics for Business Analysis*:

- A reflection on Hebrews 5:12–14 applied to drawing connections between mastering matrix algebra, which can be characterized as multidimensional numbers operating with multidimensional arithmetic rules, and the parallels to spiritual maturity and eating solid food.
- A question for reflection on Matthew 11:28–30: "How is Linear Programming like spiritual growth and how is it different?"
- A question for Discussion: "How should people who believe in an omniscient and omnipotent God deal with uncertainty in probability and statistics?"
- The following are topics addressed in the course, *Calculus for Business Analysis*:
- Relating average rate of change and journaling between two entries and living every moment under the influence of the Holy Spirit and the instantaneous rate of spiritual change according to Ephesians 5:15–18.
- A reflection on spiritual and mathematical maturity and the concept of learning the definition of the derivative versus just memorizing the differentiation rules compared to eating meat or just drinking milk in Hebrews 5:11–14.

- A reflection on the Texas Chain Rule Massacre, a humorous look at Proverbs 14:12 and the mistakes calculus students make when incorrectly applying the chain rule for function composition derivatives on the specific function .
- A reflection on the relevance to God's power and presence in good times and bad in the story of 1 Kings 20:23–30 where good times and bad times are described metaphorically like hills and valleys as it relates to local extrema and how to find them using calculus concepts.
- A reflection on the comparison between how to optimize one's efforts both mathematically and spiritually using Colossians 3:22-33 (which calls us to do our best for the Lord) as a guide.

The following are topics addressed in the course, *Calculus and Analytic Geometry I:*

- A reflection on the analogous concepts of limits and divergence and God's limitless commands and perfection found in Psalm 119:96.
- A reflection on the similarities and differences between the concepts of mathematical continuity and continuity in prayer found in 1 Thessalonians 5:17.
- A humorous reflection discussion on the question: "Who sinned and what is the solution?" applied to the incorrect application of the derivative of the sine function $f(x)=sin\ x$ as $f'(x)=sin$ as found in John 9:1–5.
- A reflection on the principle of self-examination before relational confrontation found in Matthew 7:3–5 and the crucial step of a similar simplification "taking the log *(arithm)* out of your own eye" before applying the logarithmic implicit differentiation method to find the derivative of the equation .
- A discussion reflection question: "How is the approximation of a solution using Newton's Method similar and different to drawing closer and closer to Christ with Jesus' Method in Matthew 11:28–30?"

- A reflection on the similarities and differences between the examples of integration of faith and learning by Solomon and Jesus in Proverbs 1:5–7 and Matthew 6:25–26 and the integration of a function that makes use of the Power Rule for Integration in Calculus on a formula that spells out the word, "faith."
- A reflection on the similarities and differences between doing the work of God as described in John 9:1–11 and finding work done over distance using an integral formula in calculus.

The following are topics addressed in the course, *Calculus and Analytic Geometry II*:

- Based on the example of a young Jesus in Luke 2:46–52, reflect on the phrase, "What Would Jesus Do?" to solve an integration method problem such as Integration by Parts, Trigonometric Integrals, Inverse Trigonometric Substitution, or power series convergence problem (or any math problem).
- A reflection on a comparison of the method of Partial Fraction Decomposition and "what stinks about it" and the value of the statement that a partial fraction of Lazarus decomposed in the story found in John 11:21–44 regarding Jesus as "the Resurrection and the Life."
- A reflection comparing the process of following the examples of Christians who have lived exemplary lives with following the examples of previous solved antiderivatives from a table of integral formulas based on Hebrews 13:7.

The following are topics addressed in the course, *Calculus and Analytic Geometry III*:

- A reflection on the process of drawing and doing calculus on three-dimensional objects on a two-dimensional piece of paper and relating that to making a two-dimensional Bible page doctrine become a three-dimensional reality lived out as it relates to James 1:22–27.

- A reflection on Psalm 19:1–14 and the difficult and challenging vector calculus that describes the motion of heavenly bodies in Kepler's Laws and avoiding mathematical mistakes caused by laziness, arrogance, or stubbornness that refuses to acknowledge errors.
- A question for reflection on Proverbs 4:23 and the concept of the domain of a function, that is, what numbers or vectors are allowed to be plugged into a real-valued function of several variables and what numbers or vectors are not applied to filtering our hearts and minds so garbage in does not become garbage out.

The following are topics addressed in the course, *Elementary Foundations of Mathematics* (An Introduction to Mathematical Logic):

- Utilizing a Scripture logic project: "Analyze the logical statements and the truth table constructed from 2 Chronicles 7:14 as well as a favorite Scripture verse and perform a logical analysis of a truth table of those verses. What are the spiritual and practical applications of applying logic to these verses?" As part of the project, a truth table analysis of each students' favorite verse or verses is then presented as class devotionals and spiritual applications based on logic analysis.

The following are topics addressed in the course, *Introduction to Probability and Statistics*:

- Probability and Counting: A reflection on Psalm 90:10–12 and Luke 14:28–32 and the accurate accounting and counting necessary for wise and accurate decision making and calculation of probabilities.
- Biblical Probability Distributions: Luke 15:11–32 and the Story of the Prodigal Son. A reflection question: "A prodigal son leaves his father to spend his share of the inheritance. On any given day, the prodigal has a 1/10 chance of returning to the father. Let X=the number of days that the father waits until his prodi-

gal son returns. Which discrete random variable distribution best represents this situation? What is the expected number of days the father will have to wait to see his prodigal son return?" Application Discussion: "How can one increase the probability that the prodigal returns? How can one reduce the number of days that your Heavenly Father has to wait for the prodigal? How does this apply to you?"

- Biblical Probability Distributions: Mark 2:1-12 and the story of the Four Friends of the Paralytic. A reflection question: "Suppose a paralytic needs four friends to carry him to Jesus to be healed and suppose that on average, the possibility of successful friend request is 1/5. Let X=the number of friend requests needed to reach 4 friends. Which probability distribution best describes this situation? What is the expected number of friend requests needed to get 4 friends?" Application discussion: "How willing are you to answer a friend request? What could be done to help yourself be more willing to answer a friend request?"
- Biblical Probability Distributions: Luke 17:11–19 and the story of the Ten Lepers Healed by Jesus. A reflection discussion: "Suppose Jesus healed ten lepers and suppose there is a 50% chance that a given leper will return to Jesus to give thanks. Let X=the number of lepers who return to give thanks. Which probability distribution best describes this situation? What is the number of lepers that is expected to return and give thanks?" Application discussion: "You have been healed or saved by Jesus, what is the probability that you would return to give thanks?"

The following are topics addressed in the course, *Linear Algebra*:

- A discussion reflection based on Psalm 127:4–5: "Your life is like a vector with direction and magnitude (length of a directed line segment). Are you pointed in the right direction and how much impact are you having on others?"
- A reflection relating the ten commandments to the ten vector space axioms and looking for similarities and differences for the

purpose of helping students memorize both the ten axioms and the Ten Commandments (see Exodus 20:1–17).

The following are topics addressed in the course, *Abstract Algebra I*:

- A discussion question on Lamentations 3:22–23: "How is God's infinite love and forgiveness like the Principle of Mathematical Induction?"
- A discussion question on James 2:8–10: "How is satisfying the group axioms to become a group like satisfying the requirements of the law to be perfect in God's eyes?"

The following are topics addressed in the course, *Theory of Calculus: Real Analysis I*:

- A reflection on John 13:12–17 and the concept of the greatest lower bound of a set (lower than everything in the set and yet the greatest of all lower bounds) and the parallel to Jesus being the greatest among all servants, but also being willing to serve the least of the lowest.
- A discussion question on the concept of the Interior and Boundary of a set (every open neighborhood of a point intersects both inside and outside of the set) and how it relates to believers who must be in the world and not of the world according to John 17:15–19.

Service Learning

At Dallas Baptist University, we have designated service-learning mathematics courses that have a service-learning project or paper requirement. The integration of faith and learning of mathematics can be most appropriate in a service-learning course where the harvesting of content-specific academic learning is done through analysis of the reflections of students in a designated servant-leadership journal. Questions (three samples are provided below) are reflected upon and the connections are discussed and attempted between mathematical content and skills addressed in a proof class and acts of service to humanity in their assigned service-learning project or research paper:

- "How can the mathematical skills of critical thinking and problem solving be applied to nonmathematical problems such as poverty, war, crime, hunger, clean water, disease, health education, affordable health care, and educational equity?"
- "How would critical thinking skills developed in math classes help me to decipher between truth and spin in the marketplace of ideas? As an informed voter, what difference might that make?"
- "How does better mathematics or better mathematicians make a better world?"

A guide to an integration of mathematics and community service is provided for the student to help make important connections in the integration of faith and learning and to harvest mathematical content learning from community service activities while reflecting on these questions. Three sample connective suggestions are provided below:

- "Spending time on task-learning advanced calculus topics or abstract algebra while tutoring is a means by which you can help people in the community who are struggling with mathematics and master difficult abstract concepts yourself by playing with similar concepts at the specific case level."
- "While it is good to be able to do math yourself, it is best to learn the skill of passing on mathematical reasoning to others so they can master mathematical and critical thinking skills within the context of a Christian Worldview for the rest of their life."
- "One aim of the service project in Analysis this semester is to help us interact with people that are not like us and to increase our sympathetic understanding of their way of thinking and way of life."

Examples From Students

As for examples from students regarding their own integration of faith and mathematics in a possible future calling, included are the following examples. The first comes from a student in an Advanced Calculus class named *Analysis I* as part of a service-learning project tutoring students in statistical topics. She writes about struggling with integrating her faith with her mathematical content, but ultimately discovers that integration can occur through emotional support and encouragement in the process of helping someone learn statistics and not just by making connections with equations or content topics. She writes:

> I really struggled with connecting the (mathematical) material to the Bible but excelled with connecting it to my students' emotions. This is...something I would want to work on as I want to find ways to correlate the (mathematical) content with (my faith). However,...the material did present opportunities to integrate faith, less so because of the (mathematical) material itself and more so because of the impact it was having on the students I tutored. Often...they would become dejected, distraught, or hopeless after struggling with a concept...expecting too much of themselves. Being able to support them mentally, emotionally, and spiritually was a result of the meaningful conversations that were had about the truth of the Bible and how it applies to even things such as our anger at a math problem. Ultimately, I was able to have some amazing conversations and I am incredibly grateful for that.

The second example comes in response to the following integration of faith and mathematics reflection question on personal finance, compound interest, and Proverbs 13:11: "What can we learn about the power of compounding interest and the wisdom of deferred gratification?" A student in a *Finite Math for Business Analysis* class identified practical action steps and combined it with prayer as she wrote:

> I am working on getting a job, so my plan to be a good steward of the financial resources that will be entrusted to

> me is to pray over every check. God blesses us in a way that we can then bless others; there will certainly be times when God wants me to help others with money, so I will pray about what area of my life He wants me to do this.

A final example is an interchange from two students in an *Introduction to Probability and Statistics* class regarding the reflection on a Biblical Probability Distribution: Luke 15:11–32 and the story of the Prodigal Son. The reflection question was:

> A prodigal son leaves his father to spend his share of the inheritance. On any given day, the prodigal has a 1/10 chance of returning to the father. Let X=the number of days that the father waits until his prodigal son returns. Which discrete random variable distribution best represents this situation? What is the expected number of days the father will have to wait to see his prodigal son return? Application Discussion: How can one increase the probability that the prodigal returns? How can one reduce the number of days your Heavenly Father has to wait for the prodigal? How does this apply to you?

The student responded to questions with correct mathematical understanding as well as provided a solid attempt at an integration of faith and math reflection on the application prompt when he wrote:

> Geometric Distribution=10; We can increase the probability that the prodigal son returns by waiting longer. This teaches us that as Christians trying to spread the Gospel, we should be patient with the people we are trying to point toward Christ. In order to reduce the number of days, we have to make the prodigal son more willing to return and have a higher chance to return, which we can do as Christians when we show love to nonbelievers.

An interesting reply to the same prompt from another student yielded the observation of a connection between the mathematical understanding of the problem and the spiritual application of the solution:

> It's interesting seeing math problems within a Christian context like the ones above. I especially liked the Prod-

igal Son's story. We should all strive to be more Christ-like in everything we do. Forgiveness is often hard, however, when we consider what Christ did on Calvary, our petty arguments seem to fall flat.

Conclusion

Having reviewed the current literature on the integration of faith and mathematics learning, provided examples of how this integration takes place at DBU, and hearing from the testimonies of specific students who have experienced a deeper level of faith integration in the study of mathematics, it is my hope and prayer that the reader has gained valuable insight into the integration of faith and learning and has been inspired to discover new and even better connections between faith and the learning of mathematics.

Chapter 8

Integrating Faith in the Study of Music and Art

By Wes Moore,[1] Jennifer Weaver,[2] and Jim Hutchinson[3]

Introduction

Beauty and transcendence are terms often associated with the work of the artist. A certain lushness of color, a symmetry of design, or feeling of overwhelming intensity can transform us from the routine to the sublime. Yet beauty can also be a troublesome concept when one considers the well-used phrase, "beauty is in the eye of the beholder." Is beauty a mere transaction of personal opinion, supremely subjective in its assessment, or is more objective criteria also to be accounted for when participating with great works of art? As Christians, how do we think about the beautiful and the transcendent? How do we bring faith to bear on our understanding of art?

There is a grand, almost operatic picture of divine transcendence in Isaiah 6:1–4. It says:

> In the year that King Uzziah died I saw the Lord sitting upon a throne, high and lifted up; and the train of his robe filled the temple. Above him stood the seraphim. Each had six wings; with two he covered his face, and with two he

---

[1] Wes Moore serves as the Dean of the College of Fine Arts and Professor of Music at Dallas Baptist University.

[2] Jennifer Weaver serves as a Professor of Music at Dallas Baptist University.

[3] Jim Hutchinson serves as the Associate Dean of the College of Fine Arts and Professor of Visual Arts at Dallas Baptist University.

> covered his feet, and with two he flew. And one called to another and said, "Holy, holy, holy is the LORD of hosts; the whole earth is full of his glory!" And the foundations of the thresholds shook at the voice of him who called, and the house was filled with smoke (ESV).

This passage presents us with a powerful and visceral image of transcendence, an otherworldly vision of transformation and yes, beauty. The iconic images of seraphim with full sculptural manifestations derived from ancient Israel, the detailed relief sculptures of the Temple, the mysterious smoke, the train of a bejeweled, royal robe, the vocal chants of "Holy, holy, holy." This is a common way Christians have thought about beauty and transcendence throughout history despite being sometimes divided over theological conflicts concerning the usage of music and the arts.

Another, more subtle way we can think about the intersection of faith and art is through the concept of revelation. This can be a global, corporate revelation as in the idea that the arts reveal the values of a society. Painting, sculpture, music, architecture, drama, broadcast media, and graphic design often serve as a mirror to hold up to culture and reflect both the goodness and depravity of humankind. The artistic products left by that culture can be markers for future civilizations as to the values and mores of the time. The idea of revelation, though, can also be more intimate and personal. A song or hymn can reveal a spiritual truth about the nature of God. A photograph can evoke memories of childhood experiences and either happy or painful times with family or friends. An architectural monument or building can reveal acts of conquest and terror as well as moments of national unity and solidarity. Drama or film can reveal the truth of history in all its rawness and cruelty, or it can also redeem that truth with stories of ultimate reconciliation, hope, and spiritual renewal.

In this chapter, you will hear from two wonderful university colleagues, a painter and a music theorist and singer. They will share from the deep well of many years of experience as scholars, practitioners, and teachers of their craft. The knowledge of their content areas is extensive and the abundance of faith and life experience they bring to their teaching is most profound and valuable to their students and colleagues. In one, you will see a deep exploration of a philosophical/theological approach to the teaching of the visual arts. In the other, a more practical, case-study approach to the teaching of music theory. You will see revealing journeys of the mind, heart, and soul as they seamlessly weave the truth of faith with the truths of their disciplines while taking their students on the journey with them. It is most inspiring.

Finally, as we contemplate our work as scholar/artists who are also Christians, we must address the temptation to shoehorn our own agendas as we integrate our faith with our art. This can be easy to do if we are in a rush to fulfill a pedagogical mandate or teaching deadline. Nothing could be more damaging to our work and influence with students if we were to easily succumb to this path of least resistance. It takes thought, prayer, living with and getting our hands dirty with the messy work of teaching and artmaking to teach holistically and lovingly from a Christian perspective. As we do this work, we are often tempted by the seduction of the shiny new and relevant or beset by the tyranny of the urgent. Both can dilute our best and deepest work by diminishing an integral connection to enduring excellence and the divine. Our course is clear, but the chances for distraction are great as well. Harold Best, in his great work, *Music Through the Eyes of Faith,* says it well, "God remains God, ready to swoop down in the most wonderful way, amidst the flurry and mystery of newness and repetition, to touch souls and hearts, all because faith has been exercised and Christ's ways have been imitated. Meanwhile a thousand tongues will never be enough."[4]

The Visual Arts

Made in the Image of God

By and large, Christian artists believe God has endowed them with the unique ability to create and that by exercising that ability, they magnify His own inimitable creativity. As Christian art educators, this un-

[4] Harold Best, *Music Through the Eyes of Faith* (New York, NY: Harper, 2013).

derlying principle remains constant, and we seek to deliberately weave them into our daily instruction. Art training in the DBU Art Department proceeds from the truth that God Himself is the true Creator, uniquely capable of producing original work. Simply put, He can create matter and living organisms from nothing, beginning at the molecular level. In turn, mankind—His pinnacle creation—can also create original works, but only in the context of existing matter. In this way, mankind's highest artistic achievements are clever imitations at best, using the physical tools and substance provided by the Creator. Nonetheless, humanity is enormously fulfilled by the measure of creativity handed down to them, adorning His creation with proven aesthetic principles. In all of our classes, we acknowledge that creativity, given by God, is a precious gift and pursuing mastery of that gift is a joyous and rewarding search.

Regrettably, the fall of mankind brought about the perversion of creativity. Indeed, the world has been filled with humanity's aesthetic contributions, but sadly, an equal portion has been dedicated to mediocrity and even downright ugliness. To study this further, DBU's art history courses are taught from a biblical perspective, measuring the motivations of historical artists and their movements against the principles of God's Word. What extenuating circumstances caused these artists to produce such work? Were they driven by war, oppression, or poverty? How did they arrive at an attitude of total frustration, ruled by nihilism or humanism? Do their philosophies align with biblical principles?

Though these negative examples are touched on briefly and used as object lessons, more time is given in class to the works of notable artists who have utilized their talents to further beautify God's creation. Keeping our focus on positive and useful form of art, we take our very first case study from the Bible itself, where *Yahweh*-God commissions the artisans of His tabernacle:

> The LORD said to Moses, "See, I have called by name Bezalel the son of Uri, son of Hur, of the tribe of Judah, and I have filled him with the Spirit of God, with ability and in-

> telligence, with knowledge and all craftsmanship, to devise artistic designs, to work in gold, silver, and bronze, in cutting stones for setting, and in carving wood, to work in every craft. And behold, I have appointed with him Oholiab, the son of Ahisamach, of the tribe of Dan. And I have given to all able men ability, that they may make all that I have commanded you.[5]

When God ordered the building of the Tabernacle, He authorized only the best artisans to fulfill His work. Trained in proven techniques by the Egyptians, Bezalel and Oholiab created each piece with excellence and sophistication. Throughout the biblical discourse, all artistic artifacts commissioned by God were crafted with excellence. Yet, in all of God's direction, He allowed the personal styles of each artist to shine through, even allowing for personal interpretation in matters of color and form. This is an exciting prospect for the Christian artist.

Later, when Solomon built his Temple, the same care was taken to portray excellence in everything that was made. Solomon did this out of respect for God and His principles. Still, in all of its symmetry and order, the personal interpretation of every detail was left to the artisans. Likewise, in Gothic times, artisans from all over Europe gathered to build lofty cathedrals. In this way, they integrated their work flawlessly, not concerned with being personally identified. Like the Tabernacle and Solomon's Temple before, the Gothic Cathedral stood as the perfect integration of aesthetic form and order so it would edify the believer,[6] preserve the techniques handed down with excellence,[7] and glorify God.[8]

Our Three-Fold Purpose as Christian Artists

In the DBU Department of Visual Arts, our practical instruction is woven together with three New Testament principles: *Edification, Preservation,* and *Glorification. A three-stranded cord is not easily broken* (Ecclesiastes

---

[5] Exod. 31:1–6 (ESV).

[6] 1 Cor. 10:23–24.

[7] 1 Cor. 14:40.

[8] Eccles. 12:13; 1 Cor. 10:31.

4:12); likewise, these three bring authenticity, integrity, and security to one's own self-expression in any form, whether it be gallery art, portraiture, graphic design, or illustration.

Edification

In Scripture, Christians are exhorted time and again to *edify* those around them, whether in the church[9] or in the marketplace.[10] Simply stated, edification is the act of uplifting or building up, which, for the believer, should be the natural outflowing of his or her daily life.[11] But we cannot be disingenuous. As artists in a fallen world, we sometimes forget to consider the effects our visual manifestations will have on others.

As we teach our students on a daily basis, we try to teach by word and example that for the Christian artist, edification might involve setting aside one's personal interests or desires, whether temporarily or long-term, for the express purpose of building up those they've been entrusted to influence. In visual art, this could simply be the avoidance of dubious subject matter so as not to subvert another's thinking toward questionable issues. In Romans 14:19, the Apostle Paul frames this beautifully when he says, "Therefore let us pursue the things *which make* for peace and the things by which one may edify another" (NKJV). When a painter or sculptor genuinely adopts this principle, it becomes impossible to portray the sordid or ugly.

Edification in visual art also indicates the form or visual language the work of art may take. Certainly, there are forms of expressionism or abstraction that can convey a sense of beauty or repose. Still, on a deeper level, such paintings often express the artist's personal emotion and might appeal to only a few. Bearing this in mind, the motivations behind these forms of visual expression must be carefully examined to avoid feelings of confusion or despair, which do not so easily cohabitate with edification. "For God is not *the author* of confusion but of peace."[12]

---

[9] 1 Cor. 14:4.

[10] Rom. 14:19; 1 Cor. 8:1.

[11] *Mariam-Webster's Dictionary*, s.v. "Edification," accessed November 27, 2023, www.merriam-webster.com/dictionary/edify.

[12] 1 Cor. 14:33 (NKJV).

Hoping to instill this basic tenet in the lives of our students, we encourage them to examine their artwork, both stylistically and thematically, by the light of God's word.

Preservation

Beginning in the foundational year of our visual art programs, DBU students are urged to preserve those principles that uphold orderliness, craftsmanship, and a biblical work ethic. Though these standards can be clearly portrayed through a painting's theme, we feel they equally apply to the visual language or technique used to illustrate it.

The renowned English scientist, Sir Isaac Newton, once said, "If I have seen further, it is by standing on the shoulders of giants." Of course, this humble declaration was made about the empirical process of compounding knowledge by building on the pre-established foundation. Though his statement clearly referenced scientific thought, the same notion is valid for the fine arts.

In first-year classes, we take a close look at the principles and techniques that have been established by generations of successful artists, and assign exercises and projects that help our students become proficient in those proven practices. For a young artist to adequately convey an emotion, theme, or narrative, they must first be grounded in a visual language that is clearly understood by all. Can these concepts be related through abstraction or expressionism? Indeed, some can. But in most cases, more efficient portrayals are conveyed through the mastery of pre-established skills such as proportional drawing, color theory, and compositional design in representational form. The beauty and aesthetic of creation are only by-products of the order and balance with which it was created. It is both complex and intelligent in its design; therefore, we try to emulate that great beauty through ordered drawing and painting methods.

As a faculty, we not only want our students to convey edifying themes, but we also hope they will understand the importance of preserving the time-tested techniques passed down to them. Just as salt preserves, the DBU Art Department is committed to teaching classical techniques so students can fully express themselves in all forms of visual communication (Matthew 5:13; Colossians 4:6).

Glorification

As an art faculty, we labor continually to integrate faith in learning, so when it comes to the three aforementioned principles, we submit that *the glorification of God* is the most important. This can be no better conveyed than through the Dallas Baptist University's Department of Visual Art's Mission Statement, which, as an extension of the University Mission Statement, seeks to prepare servant-leader art students for a professional career in the visual arts and to offer avenues of creative fulfillment for all students of the university. This aim is accomplished through pursuing excellence and artistic achievement within a Christian context.

To make clear our objectives as a department, a filter has been agreed upon so all three principles—the glorification of God being first and foremost—can be consistently maintained in the classroom, and as biblical Scripture is upheld by all of us as inerrant and infallible, no better filter can be constructed than that which is given in Philippians 4:8:

> Finally, brethren, whatever things are true, whatever things *are* noble, whatever things *are* just, whatever things *are* pure, whatever things *are* lovely, whatever things *are* of good report, if there *is* any virtue and if *there is* anything praiseworthy—meditate on these things (NKJV).

Working alongside our students, we live out this principle, leading by example, knowing it can be used as an optimistic and uplifting guidepost—a measuring stick by which to compare our self-expression. What, then, does the Christian artist do with the term self-expression, and how do we as art faculty adequately convey this concept to our students? As a foundation to all work created in class, we teach that our self-expression is a representation of Christ Himself. As Christian artists, we are more than just ambassadors; we have Christ living in us. Acts 11:26 states it was in Antioch that the disciples were first called "Christians." The word's Greek roots would imply that the apostles were literally referred to as *little Christs*. If Christian artists are, in fact, little Christs, then their self-expression[13] will innately reflect the attributes of Christ and His Word.

With this third and final objective explained, it gives clarity to the desire of DBU's Art Department mission, *to educate and train young artists in excellence and artistic achievement within a Christian context*. We are thrilled to know that when the glorification of God is foremost in our work, then the previous principles of edification and preservation will be naturally fulfilled.

Certainly, the future of visual art and art education is uncertain. The internet, social media, and artificial intelligence are quickly changing the face of commercial and fine art as we know it. In the midst of these changes, the DBU Art Department seeks to adapt its pedagogical styles, combining new and creative media with practical training so students can adapt and thrive in the contemporary art world. Just as importantly, we integrate biblical principles through faith in learning so the intrinsic quality of their work will stand out as examples of light and excellence.

Music Theory

In Deuteronomy 31, God is speaking to Moses at the end of his life. Leadership of the Israelites will soon pass from Moses to Joshua so God visits him and makes a prediction that the Israelites will begin to worship other gods. As a reminder to the Israelites that He has walked with them through the desert, God writes a song and exhorts Moses to teach it to the Israelite people. Throughout Scripture, music is created as a means of worship, communication, celebration, and remembrance. Here we see that God Himself is a composer of songs. That music is present in Scripture and an important means for expressing faith in God is undeniable.

Something much deeper integrates our Christian faith with learning about creative subjects like music and art. In the poetic account of

---

[13] John 1:1.

God's own creative act (Genesis 1), He created the light and saw that it was good. He created the seas and saw that they were good. He made plants and animals and saw that they were good as well. And finally, when His work was done, He looked at all of it and saw that it was good. God did not simply create the earth and all that is in it, but at every step of the process He observed and evaluated it. To create like our Creator, we must understand what we make, truly see it, and evaluate it. This idea is at the heart of integrated faith and learning in the arts—it is not just the creative act that is important but the ability to assess and analyze what has been created.

Case Studies in the Music Theory Classroom

Moving from the more philosophical and abstract ideas about faith integration to the more practical approaches to music curricula, the following section will focus on specific examples from music courses using the Holmes approach. Taking an Attitudinal Approach to faith integration is the first category in Holmes's approach. Here the instructor models Christlike attitudes in his or her treatment of students, management of the classroom, and evaluation of students' work. As an instructor and person of faith, this practice can feel almost instinctual. For many it would feel more challenging to divorce a Christian perspective from the relational work of teaching than to integrate it. This approach is also applicable in any classroom, secular or religious, as it focuses on the relationship of the instructor and student.

At the most basic level, integrating faith into the attitude of the course is done in developing fair policies for evaluating students and approaching students with kindness. Often the manner in which a student is addressed before an exam or performance in class can impact his or her ability to demonstrate skill development. Consciously speaking to students with kindness and patience can change how well they perform. Music courses often require students to perform music they have not practiced publicly in front of the class because this skill is critically important to the ability to work as a musician in any context whether it be teaching in a classroom, recording in a studio, or performing in a symphony hall. Students are also typically publicly evaluated on these performances. Treating all students with respect and providing helpful feedback that meets the student at the level of his or her performance is an important demonstration of love and care for the students. It is also important to encourage the attitude of Christ in the overall environment of the classroom. Creating an agreement for how students will respond to and encourage one another during these challenging public exams is a sound way to help students be aware of their attitude and make the connection to their faith.

Holmes states that Christianity makes no obvious difference in performance-oriented fields but that the Attitudinal Approach where the focus is on the faith-based perspective of the teacher and students is a clear way to integrate faith. To imply that skill-based fields do not have a philosophical or ethical component where students can think deeply about and incorporate faith is an unfortunate misunderstanding on Holmes's part. Though I disagree with Holmes's notion that there is no such thing as "Christian piano," the idea that students in fields with heavy focus on skill development should view that work as an important part of their vocational development and gifting from God is useful. Having a faith-oriented view of skill development can provide a larger purpose for returning to the practice room yet again, working on improving that one phrase of the music for hours, and developing the habits of focus and discipline that are critical to careers in music. For the Christian professor, this is developing relationships with students and classroom environments that are both rigorous and nurturing.

According to Holmes, the Ethical Approach to faith integration lives in a middle space between information and a godly response of justice and love. He poses the question about what purposes God had in mind when He created this area of human endeavor. This is an especially useful question to pose about music and composition. One obvious biblical purpose for music is the act of worshiping God through song. Many music students at faith-based institutions have the goal of working full-time in music ministry in a church. To limit the purpose of music to worship, however, would be a missed opportunity to see the many other God-given purposes music serves in our culture, in our society, and in our individual lives. Music-making can be an act of service, whether it is performing, teaching, composing, or any of the other musical activities. To help students connect music as a profession and music theory as a discipline to servant leadership, I introduce a piece of music to analyze in class that is written specifically for high school level percussion ensembles. This exercise meets several of our learning outcomes for the course—it exposes students to percussion notation, which is different than typical pitched notation and it allows students to focus specifically on rhythm without other melodic and harmonic components. But it also allows students to think more deeply about the act of composition as a service to other people. The composer of the percussion piece explains that many high schools have limitations such as lack of equipment, no access to unusual or extremely expensive instruments, and student performers who have varied skill levels. Much of the existing percussion ensemble music is either too simple, too difficult, or requires too much equipment and high school percussion ensembles struggle to find repertoire for performances. The composer saw the need and wrote a collection of pieces that can be played on instruments most school programs would own. It is designed to allow students to double-up on one instrument so many different students can be involved. Some of the parts are quite simple, catering to younger or less-trained students, while some of the parts are quite challenging for the more experienced players. I then challenge the students to discuss ways they can use their classroom knowledge as a service to a specific community. They first identify a community with a need of some kind, and then suggest ways they could help meet that need with things they learn in class. Activities like this help students exercise the muscle of service and of connecting their faith with their work.

Ethical faith integration is also a critical component of class discussion in my Jazz Theory course. The class involves traditional music theory tasks such as listening, demonstrating on a keyboard, and analyzing music, but it also introduces students to the distinctive style periods of Jazz and exposes them to music they likely have not encountered before. One cannot discuss jazz history or the music itself without discussing race. Jazz is a music that was predominantly created by black musicians and is the direct result of the mingling of the European music tradition with the African and Latin music cultures. Despite this, many of the earliest recordings and publications of jazz music were made by white musicians. Furthermore, many white musicians have appropriated the jazz tunes of their black colleagues without properly crediting them or even acknowledging their influence. One cannot understand the music without also addressing this history. In discussions about this, students must encounter the facts of the biased origins of the radio and music recording industry and then ask themselves what God's purpose is for such activities. Obviously, it is not to favor one population of people over another. Throughout the course students discuss questions such as, "What is an Ethical Approach to offering recording contracts to musicians?" or "What is the difference between appropriating a song and covering it? Or between appropriating a song and being inspired by the work of someone else?" These questions lead students to view the facts of the course from the perspective of a Christian ethic that seeks justice for all.

A Foundational Approach to faith integration places the course content into a larger historical and biblical context. In the music classroom, this means helping students connect the musical objects they study—whether it be written music, audio recordings, or primary source documents—into their correct historical context. Music history and the church are closely tied with one another, so much so that music notation and solmization—a pedagogical tool still used in classrooms today—all have their origins in the creation, teaching, and dissemination of music in the Catholic church. Until the 1700s, much of the music we have that was written down was composed for and preserved by the church. To understand the great masses of Palestrina, an important Renaissance composer, one must understand the Christian liturgy and important biblical texts. To analyze the Passions written by J. S. Bach, one must have knowledge of the biblical account of Christ's death and resurrection. It could even be argued that a true believer has a deeper and more personal understanding of this music than a secular academic. It is the Christian professor's responsibility to help students understand these connections and to encourage students to make their own faith a part of their music-making both in and out of the context of church.

It is commonly known that Johann Sebastian Bach was a person of deep faith and that he believed his work as a musician was to be done to God's glory. Many of his compositions were written for the church and are paired with liturgical and biblical texts. Composed across the span of two decades, his *Mass in B Minor* was such a work. The "Crucifixus," which is a part of the Credo in the mass, was some of the last music to be written.[14] Bach was a Lutheran, which makes this mass unique. Lutheran masses typically only contain the Kyrie and the Gloria, but Bach composed music to set the entire Ordinary of the mass. The "Crucifixus" appears in the Credo, which would commonly not have been sung, and depicts in music the portion of the Nicene Creed that states, "*Crucifixus etiam pro nobis, sub Pontio Pilato. Passus et sepultus est.*" (Translation: [He was] crucified for us under Pontius Pilate. [He] suffered and was buried.) Students are introduced to this work in their first upper-level analysis course. First, they must understand the mass and its parts, with special focus on how the Credo is compiled. Students must also have knowledge of the typical compositional practices of the late-Baroque, as well as the Renaissance style that preceded it. Bach sets this text using a technique called imitative counterpoint, which originates in the Renaissance and is governed by many rules about how each voice must enter—one at a time and at a particular distance from one another—and how dissonance must be managed. Sopranos enter first, singing "Crucifixus" on a descending half step motion that begins on the sixth scale degree. This is an unusual choice, made even more dissonant by the entrance of the altos on a note a tritone away. The interval of a tritone was considered one of the most dissonant sounds and was usually avoided in counterpoint like this. The tenors enter next, followed by the

[14] Christoph Wolff and Walter Emery, "Bach, Johann Sebastian," Grove Music Online, Oxford Music Online, accessed November 28, 2023, https://doi.org/10.1093/gmo/9781561592630.article.6002278195.

basses who outline a diminished chord—again, a very dissonant sound in this style of music.

As students begin to analyze the score, I challenge them to consider the historical context of the work asking questions like "what makes these imitative lines so unusual?" and "why would Bach write so much dissonance in a composition like this?" The answer is clear. Bach is depicting the pain and suffering of Christ in the crucifixion by using dissonance. "Crucifixus" is in E minor and sets the full text twice with a cadence in the middle of the piece. The second set of entrances on the word "Crucifixus" repeats the dissonant entrances from the beginning but makes them even more pronounced by adding notes that do not align with the harmony and emphasizing the tritone by having voices sing it simultaneously rather than one note at a time. Below the singers, the instrumentalists are playing a passacaglia pattern—a bass line that descends chromatically to the fifth scale degree and is repeated throughout the entire work. In the second section of the work, the text "he died and was buried" appears twice in succession. At the end of the first statement, the basses sweep down to the lowest note of the piece, one so low that some basses might even have difficulty singing it. Again, Bach is painting the picture of the text using the musical language. Christ is buried as low as the singers can sing. However, the piece does not end there. The repeated bass pattern begins one more time, this time burying the upper three voices in the bottom of their ranges. Harmonically, though, Bach paints a different picture. Rather than repeating the pattern and ending in E minor, he breaks the pattern and ends the piece in G major. For a piece about the death and burial of Christ, this may seem surprising, but Bach is foreshadowing both the next part of the text as well as the music. Christ does not remain buried, but will be resurrected from the dead. Bach ends the piece quietly in the lowest range of the voices, but the G major key change prepares the listener for the next page of music when Christ will rise from the dead and ascend to Heaven.

Many musical compositions depict religious texts and ideas in the way that Bach did in the *Mass in B Minor*. Requiem masses, for example, are often replete with compositional techniques that depict ideas of faith. Mozart's *Requiem in D Minor* sets the Domine Jesu portion of the Offertory text as a great fugue between all the voices and the orchestra. This text pleads with God to rescue His people from the pains of Hell as He promised Abraham. Fugues are compositions that originate in the 18th century and are governed by many rules. To an experienced listener of a fugue, they are both exciting and at the same time predictable. Because the form of a fugue is predetermined, anyone who has heard one senses an inevitability to the voices and where each one leads. At the same time, fugues expel a large amount of musical energy. It is not surprising that when Mozart set the text of God's great promise to Abraham to liberate the souls of man, he chose a fugue. Many exciting musical events may occur in the fugue but in the end, all of the voices will enter as expected and the promise of the original subject will be explored and fulfilled. Many composers that followed Mozart set this text in a similar manner.

Johannes Brahms wrote *Ein Deutches Requiem* (A German Requiem), using biblical texts rather than the traditional liturgical texts of the Catholic mass. Though the text of God's promises to Abraham does not appear, a similar text "*Der Gerechten Seelen sind in Gottes Hand und keine Qual rühret sie an*" (Translation: The righteous are in the hands of God and no torment shall reach them) does appear in a similar place in the mass. Again, we see the promises of God to spare His people. Just as Mozart and many others have done, Brahms sets the text using a fugue. This fugue, however, features a tonic pedal tone on the pitch D that sounds in the lowest voices throughout the entire fugue. No matter what pitches or harmonies change above the pitch, it remains steady in the bass voices of the orchestra. As a part of their analysis of this work, students are prompted to contemplate why Brahms would include this long pedal tone. Pedals themselves are not uncommon, but they typically last a few measures, not several minutes of music. The pedal tone is a beautiful depiction of God's hand supporting the rest of the voices, through consonance and dissonance, as He promised. It remains constant through to the very last harmony where it forms the perfect foundation for the chord.

Reading Bach's depiction of the crucifixion through the lens of historical context and music history or Mozart and Brahms's profound representations of God's faithfulness through their fugues is an excellent starting place for students to connect their knowledge of history and music theory with their understanding of biblical truths. On an even deeper level, examples like this can be used to help students think about their own creative output. How can they draw connections with their faith in the music they create? How can they use the understanding their faith provides about these critical texts to convey their true message to an audience through performance?

An important next step for students is to understand that it is not just biblical texts and composers who identified themselves as part of a Christian tradition that welcome interpretation through the lens of faith. An excellent example of this is the *Kaddish Symphony No. 3* by Leonard Bernstein. This piece, written for orchestra, narrator, choir, and children's chorus, is a setting of the Jewish prayer of kaddish, used as a way of mourning the death and celebrating the life of a loved one that has died. In the work, Bernstein's narrator comments on the text of the kaddish, at times angry and in denial, at times thankful and full of praise. The music is very innovative, featuring many new techniques that would have been surprising to a 1960s audience when it premiered, including sections where each part of the choir sings in different keys and tempos creating a feeling of chaos. This piece is uniquely Jewish in its origins, was written by a Jewish composer, and was composed for a secular audience. Still there is much of value to discuss in the way the text is set and in the purely instrumental sections as well. Students often find parallels to their own wrestling with faith in God, which opens the door for deep and valuable discussions on the relationship between music, worship, faith, and expression.

Bernstein's *Kaddish* provides an excellent transition to the Worldview Approach to faith integration. In this approach, there is no divide between sacred and secular and the professor is able to lead interdisciplinary discussions tying course content with other subjects. As just discussed with the Bernstein piece, the music theory classroom provides opportunities for students to analyze many different kinds of music and seek meaning and understanding from their structure and creativity. The most basic connection that can be made between the study of music theory and our faith in God is the science of pitched sound.

Acoustical physics teaches us that all pitched sound contains a fundamental pitch with many overtones that sound above it. These overtones help listeners to discern differences in pitch as well as timbre or tone color. In other words, without these overtones one cannot tell the difference between a trumpet, a flute, and a tenor. Scientists and mathematicians have been aware of these fundamentals and overtones for many centuries and music theory has its origins in the practice of measuring the mathematical values that distinguish one pitch from another. As students begin their coursework in Music Theory, I begin by teaching them about how sound is produced from a fundamental. But what is perhaps more interesting is that much of the structure of the music we create and how we notate it is built into the harmonic series of overtones. Even the order of the flats and sharps is built into God's design for sound. For many students this is the first time they have considered that there is no divide between divine inspiration and human creativity. In its most basic components of pitch, rhythm, and meter God created the structures we use to make music.

Conclusion

God is ever-present in the way we teach our students about the arts. From the visual arts to music and music theory, we see that faith provides a clear foundation for all we do. This chapter has provided a short overview of some of the many ways our professors seek to integrate faith into the classroom and teach students to do likewise in their own lives. Our hope is that our students learn to see the beauty of God's creation and find unique ways to share that beauty with the world around them. Whether they are glorifying God through painting, sculpture, graphic design, piano performance, or a vocal ensemble, we hope students will learn to integrate faith into every aspect of their creative lives.

Chapter 9

Integrating Faith in the College of Education

By Karla Hagan[1]

Introduction

The DBU College of Education (COE) trains those who will serve on the front lines of education in our undergraduate, graduate, and doctoral programs. Our educators in training become superintendents, principals, counselors, coaches, diagnosticians, and teachers who take Jesus Christ to the myriad of places they serve across this globe. We encourage and equip those called to the ministry of education in our coursework and in our conversations. As their professors, we have "tried to imagine a 'more excellent way' refus[ing] to separate the sacred from the secular, believing that the Christian faith must be woven through the life of learning so that there, as everywhere else, Jesus Christ is Lord."[2] The COE professors lovingly and strategically use the phrase: "missionaries cleverly disguised as educators" to articulate Plantinga's intent of integration. We believe that our commitment to Jesus Christ and the "way, truth and life" that has been offered to us all is the basis of our steps and fuels our strategy in the COE. Therefore, the COE seeks to integrate our faith in Jesus Christ into the message of our discipline and model that integration through the ways we serve our students.

---

[1] Karla Hagan is Director of Master of Education in Curriculum and Instruction program and Assistant Professor of Education.

[2] Plantinga, Jr., *Engaging God's World*, 123.

Beliefs on Integration

The DBU COE mission and vision statements were developed collaboratively by the faculty to further illustrate this focus and maintain alignment with the institutional mission, vision, and core values. As the DBU Mission Statement articulates, we strive to "produce servant leaders who have the ability to integrate faith and learning through their respective callings."[3] The purpose of the COE is to provide a Christ-centered, supportive learning environment in which our students develop as servant leaders to transform the lives of K–12 students to create a positive impact in their local and global community. We do this through the development of deep content and pedagogical knowledge, effective skills, and critical dispositions at the undergraduate, graduate, and doctoral levels. The COE is committed to developing reflective students through relevant field-based experiences who can integrate faith and learning as they implement and adapt effective instructional strategies to meet the individual needs of diverse K–12 students.

The Constructivist Theory of Learning is the foundation of these values and beliefs and is in alignment with our desire to integrate faith and learning. We want our students to understand those that they lead come to them with past experiences and prior knowledge upon which they can construct their own knowledge. Our students, training to become teachers or facilitators of learning, develop their abilities to know when to use hands-on learning, manipulatives, technology, and other research-based strategies. Our students, training to become educational leaders—whether that be a counselor, principal, coach, diagnostician, or superintendent—become more of a "guide on the side" to those they are serving and working to build the organization together in collaborative efforts. If our students encourage, utilize, and reward the value of everyone they serve in all that they do, the learning environment is enhanced. The focus is on the relationship between our students and the K–12 students and the cognitive, emotional, and spiritual development

[3] "Mission Statement," About DBU, Dallas Baptist University, accessed November 17, 2023, www.dbu.edu/about/.

that occurs when whomever they are leading "has to travel this road on his own two feet."[4] It is our role as professors to create these environments of learning as well through conversation around this intent and priority, and as we model this focus, our students capture the heart of our mission and carry the torch to those they lead.

COE Belief Statements

The philosophy for achieving the program's purpose is drawn from the nine COE core belief statements.[5] These belief statements direct our work and undergird our steps. As Christ-centered servant leaders, our students are prepared and equipped to live out this calling in the work before them as teachers, principals, counselors, coaches, diagnosticians, and superintendents. As we continue the work, we remain focused on excellence in education but also excellence in the calling rooted in these belief statements. These belief statements also apply to Holmes's Foundational, Worldview, Attitudinal, and Ethical Approaches to integration of faith and learning. Chronicled below is not only a few of the belief statements applied to Holmes's fourfold approach but also the stories of our students, adjunct professors, and faculty. Students highlighted are Dr. Beth Ray, Yiran Li, Hayley Briggs, Kaylee Jones, and Dr. Andru Gilbert. Dr. Gilbert also shares his perspective as an adjunct professor. Last, there are perspectives shared from my classes as well as Professor Ginger Earl, Dr. Pamela Brown, and Dr. DeAnna Jenkins. Theories, beliefs, themes, mission statements, and plans are important, but it is the result of this work that makes the difference. If all this conversation and planning does not achieve the intent, then we are just left with a myriad of words and a lot of great ideas. The test is the story, the life lived as a student or professor at Dallas Baptist University. These professors and students offer a glimpse into their experience at DBU, and clearly, they experienced the integration of faith and learning that equipped them for the calling ahead of them. While coming from dif-

[4] Lee Vygotsky, *Educational Psychology* (Delray Beach, FL: St. Lucie Press, 1992).
[5] See COE Belief Statement #1–9 at the conclusion of this chapter.

ferent backgrounds and purposes, Holmes's fourfold approach to the integration of faith and learning emerged through their experiences.

Holmes's Fourfold Approach

Foundational Approach

First, and in line with Holmes's Foundational Approach, the COE believes that all K–12 students can learn, and everyone is endowed with God-given, inherent value and talent on a journey of life-long learning and transformational development.[6] As educators, we embrace our calling to guide them on the journey and take a deep interest in the lives of each one. The time we take at the beginning of each semester to get to know our students is important as trust is developed during these moments. A common phrase in the COE is that they don't care how much you know until they know how much you care. In fact, we, in our faculty workshops, share the myriad of ways we have creatively done this through FLIP intros, M&M "get to know you" games, 2 Minute Masterpiece, etc.[7] This is always a rich time as we swap ideas and encourage each other to build these relationships with our students before we begin to build their knowledge base. Dr. Pamela Brown also builds this trust within each class time as she spends a moment, like many of our professors, sharing prayer requests and how her group of students can be a support to each other. She celebrates this time to give space for her students to take a breath and remember the community we are to each other and the support we can offer through our faith. In addition to time at the beginning of the course to discuss faith and prayer requests, Professor Ginger Earl weaves faith in the core of an introductory reading instruction course that she leads. She shares in her Phonics class (READ 4335) each semester that "when you teach a child to read, you are giving them the key to read God's holy, perfect words for themselves. You are giving them one of the greatest keys to experiencing God, learning about Him, and most of all having a relationship with

[6] COE Belief Statement #1.

[7] For further explanation of these activities and more, contact Dr. Karla Hagan in the DBU COE at karla@dbu.edu.

Him." She goes on to encourage them that in today's schools, you may not be allowed to talk openly about God's grace, but you can give them a key to knowing Him. You can provide for them the ability to hear God Himself speak. You can give them the power to read the book that has created such amazing change in so many lives. Earl says, "you may not be able to easily walk them through salvation in your public-school classroom, but you can prepare the soil so that when the seed of salvation is planted, it will thrive!" These are just a few examples of how we engage our students on a personal level and motivate them through our care and vision for learning.

Worldview Approach

Secondly, the COE believes to facilitate teaching and learning, our students must possess a strong knowledge base, essential skills, and dispositions critical for teaching. This includes a deep understanding of content and pedagogical skills based on current research, which is grounded in sound theory, and a passion for their subject and their K–12 students that will result in learners who are actively engaged in the learning process.[8] This deep understanding and passion stems from a Christ-centered approach to education founded on a biblical worldview that incorporates the integration of faith and learning to develop transformational servant leaders. This belief statement aligns with Holmes's Worldview Approach and can be seen in action in the classes we teach. For example, in EDAD 6312 (School Law), the students are asked to write case briefs about specific laws that have impacted education. Not only are they asked to write about the significance of the case for educators related to how it has changed the educational environment, services for students, roles of teachers, or policies, they are also asked to reflect on if/how this case might be viewed by or impact the educator who maintains a Christian worldview. The student must offer biblical/scriptural support for their response. Dr. DeAnna Jenkins, who leads this course, has students apply their Christian worldview to other assignments in the course as well as the School and Multicultural

[8] COE Belief Statement #3.

Society (EDUC 6308) course that she leads. In this course, students complete journal entries as a response to the texts read and connect this information to a biblical worldview as a Christian educator. Students in this course, like in others, can explore the content, and apply their faith into the very fabric of the course. Another example comes in the Field-Based Learning 2 classes (EDUC 4312 and 4314). Professor Martha Oldenburg and I lead students in these two classes as they serve in a Dallas Independent School District (ISD) school in the mornings on Tuesday and Thursday and then attend a course on Teaching Special Populations and a course on Best Practices in Teaching at DBU in the afternoon. It is a service-learning program that requires our students to apply their learning in classrooms across Dallas. We started the semester with the phrase "In him." I provided the first verse—"For in him we live and move and have our being" (Acts 17:28). I introduced the idea that as they move through the semester and their Dallas ISD classroom to adopt the mantra "In Him" and to look for ways to apply that in their steps of service this semester. We continued throughout the semester taking time at the beginning of each class to add verses as students would come upon a new one. We would talk through that new verse and its application to the day and the struggles they faced. Part of this course each Tuesday and Thursday is to walk through what they experienced in the classrooms that morning, so it was always a perfect time to remind them of our "In Him" mantra and how they weaved this belief in and through their day and the needs of the students they served. While we may not be able to publicly share that faith, we do so in action. We can seek Him in our quiet time and prepare our heart to serve our students. We can pray on the way to our schools or as we walk into the building. Kaylee Jones, a student in these classes, called that time an "anointing" and said that this was one more "occasion where I was reminded of the high calling of an educator. Throughout my time as an undergraduate student in the COE, I was directly immersed in an environment not only through the COE but also through my university, where I learned not only to be an effective, successful educator, but how to be an undercover missionary through the profession of an educator." This vision of seeing things from a Christian perspective is a key approach in one's integration of faith and learning.

Attitudinal Approach

Thirdly, we believe that biblical servant leadership, the foundation for all learning, is developed through service-learning experiences, which unite passion and calling that foster transformative local and global civic responsibility.[9] The teacher's attitude toward learning and providing these real-world experiences equips the students for their future steps. Their care for the student to become all God intends for them to be and supporting them along the way reflects Holmes's Attitudinal Approach. Dr. Andru Gilbert celebrated this care of one Ed.D. professor when he wrote that "her devotional thoughts, weekly emails, and prayer warrior spirit made us all feel we not only had someone in our corner, but someone who knew and cared for us intimately." Dr. Beth Ray also noted that the leaders in the Ed.D. program "believed in me before I believed in myself. This is something special about this place. From the interview to graduation of my doctoral degree, there was never a time that faith and learning was not integrated in my experience at Dallas Baptist University. The experience felt sacred from the beginning to the end." Dr. Ray remembers that she got lost on her way to the Ed.D. interview when applying for the program. She called the Ed.D. office and the student assistant for the doctoral program literally stayed on the phone with her until she arrived in the parking lot and then prayed for her before she got out of her car. Dr. Ray also remembers another moment in her dissertation journey when she had completed her first draft but had some significant issues to address. Both directors in the program spent time coaching her, validating her work, but also holding her accountable for the work still needing to be done. She remarks, "what the Lord had for me was to step up. They led me to these high expectations for myself while also showing support, love, and graciousness. They were concerned about my success and spent many hours after work time helping me to get there." An international

[9] COE Belief Statement #5.

student, Yiran (Ruth) Li said that "it was the example of the professors in my education courses that pointed me to God right from the start. When I came back to school after my grandmother's death, I realized how many professors had been praying for me. Even a professor that I did not know came up to me and asked about my grandmother. This showed me that the professors in the COE were a family, talking to each other, praying together, and reaching out to us as students and caring for our needs." Ruth is now a graduate assistant for the COE and hopes to instill in the students she now leads this same care and support. DBU has the privilege of welcoming and serving a strong population of international students. Coming from across the globe, they are interested in American education and learning the best practices in teaching and learning so they can return to their home countries and become leaders in education. Ruth was one such student coming from China and is now serving a group of Chinese students that are studying in the COE to become teachers. She notes that as these international students "are facing language and cultural barriers, professors are flexible and patient with each student. This is another way DBU shows their care for the success of every student both academically and spiritually." Each of these stories highlights the personal level that the COE professors connect with students and the impact this has made.

Ethical Approach

Lastly, and aligned with Holmes's Ethical Approach, we believe that teaching is a God-given calling, and our mission is to develop transformational, Christ-centered educators who will model the highest levels of moral and ethical character and critical dispositions as they respond to their call to teach.[10] The state of Texas publishes an Educator Code of Ethics as part of the Texas Administrative Code for educator certification. This code "provide[s] rules for standard practices and ethical conduct toward students, professional colleagues, school officials, parents,

[10] COE Belief Statement #9.

and members of the community."[11] This code of ethics is part of every introductory class in the undergraduate, graduate, and doctoral classes (EDUC 1017, EDAD 6300, and EDDL 7300). It is important at each level to remember the basis of our actions and use this code of ethics as a backdrop for the character of Jesus Christ calling us to these choices of conduct. Even in the interviews for our programs, we ask questions related to this Texas Code of Ethics and how our faith and belief in Jesus Christ impacts this. We are honest with our students that life in the world of education will be challenging at times. Our foundation of faith will be our strength and guide through the days of serving students, parents, teachers, and colleagues. Dr. Andru Gilbert, an adjunct professor in the COE, believes the students he teaches are:

> entering a workforce that will be challenging for them personally. Our public education system needs DBU educators. We need their spirit, and their faith based, Christ-centered outlook. I work consistently to pour into them the importance of living your faith, avoiding the teacher's lounge, finding the innermost part of their kids, and serving with the Lord's will.

Every semester, Dr. Gilbert invites his students to write their "gold key affirmation." Most classroom keys in Texas education are gold, and thus Dr. Gilbert wanted a symbol that would remind his students that on those days when the road is tough, the day is long, and they are feeling as though they are not making an impact—their work matters. A student in Dr. Gilbert's class, Mary Hill, believed this affirmation was and will be important to her future classes. She said, "I thought he did a great job of painting the picture of what it will look like in a public-school classroom. The crisis situations that will come are so small related to our greater call to be a teacher. He reminded us that the Lord has placed us in that classroom specifically for the purpose of loving on these students, and I am so grateful for this vision that Dr. Gilbert gave

[11] "Educators' Code of Ethics," Texas Education Agency, accessed November 27, 2023, https://tea.texas. gov/texas-educators/investigations/educators-code-of-ethics. A complete list of the Educators' Code of Ethics can be located here: Texas Administrative Code, Title 19, Part 7, Chapter 247, Rule §247.1 and §247.2.

to us." The Ethical Approach is important to remember in the world we live in and the K–12 students we will serve. We serve in a world marked by sin, and the faith that we bring as Christian educators reminds us of the greater purpose to live out our calling.

Conclusion

These stories above chronicle the experiences of full-time and adjunct professors, undergraduate and graduate students, international and national students, and continue to serve as a litmus test to our mission and purpose. Whether in faculty workshops, monthly COE meetings, curriculum planning meetings, accreditation discussions, or casual conversations, we are continually asking ourselves as faculty how to take the theoretical foundations of integration of faith and learning from our classroom at the university to the K–12 classrooms where our students teach, lead, and serve. As faculty, we are consistently considering different ideas of application related to content/curriculum, pedagogy/instruction, and assignments/products/assessments based on the model of Jesus. As graduate Haley Briggs remarks, "the experience and knowledge that I gained during my time of study in the COE has set me apart from others in many ways related to pedagogy and instruction, but most importantly, the DBU COE taught me that teaching is a God-given calling and that I should treat it as such throughout every situation." Seen through the stories above, these are just a few of the ways we are seeking to apply this focus of integration of faith in the COE. It is a work in progress and one that is a collaborative effort amongst the faculty. Dr. Pamela Brown, an adjunct professor that teaches Pedagogy of Language Arts (READ 4338) said it best:

> The students we serve are looking for a different learning experience when they walk through our doors. The integration of faith and learning is what sets us apart from another university where a student might be learning the core curriculum for their career. Whether it is through initial prayer requests, praise reports or writing reflections that are a part of each class, students are always provid-

ed an opportunity to see faith as an integral part of their daily lives. It is not a separate part of what I teach. Faith is the instrument by which we learn, grow, and do in order to become educators who will serve students who may need a light in their lives. There is no price that can be put on the experience of growing your faith while you learn!

COE Core Belief Statement

1. All Can Learn: "We believe that all children can learn and that each individual is endowed with God-given, inherent value and talent on a journey of life-long learning and transformational development."
2. Diversity: "We believe that all students should be valued, appreciated, and respected for their individual differences as they learn and work together in our local and global society, and we are committed to promoting and defending fairness and equal opportunity in the learning community."
3. Knowledge Base/Pedagogy: "We believe to facilitate teaching and learning, a teacher must possess a strong knowledge base, essential skills, and dispositions critical for teaching. This includes a deep understanding of content and pedagogical skills based on current research which is grounded in sound theory, and a passion for their subject and their students that will result in learners who are actively engaged in the learning process."
4. Assessment: "We believe that multiple forms of developmentally appropriate, outcomes-oriented assessments create critical self-reflection and accountability, foster responsive instruction, and promote a culture of continuous improvement."
5. Servant Leadership: "We believe that biblical servant leadership, the foundation for all learning, is developed through service-learning experiences, which unite passion and calling that foster transformative local and global civic responsibility."
6. Critical Thinking: "We believe developing the skills of critical thinking and problem solving enhances the teaching and learn-

ing process, resulting in informed decision making and reflective practice to meet the needs of each learner."

7. Technology: "We believe that the use of multiple resources, including current technology, should be modeled and appropriately integrated into effective instruction."
8. Community: "We believe that students learn best in a collaborative environment of communication, support, and involvement of all stakeholders in the teaching and learning process."
9. Behavior/Morals/Ethics: "We believe that teaching is a God-given calling, and our mission is to develop transformational, Christ-centered educators who will model the highest levels of moral and ethical character and critical dispositions as they respond to their call to teach."

Chapter 10

Integrating Faith in History

By Michael Whiting[1]

Introduction

The study of history encompasses everything under the sun in the development of cultures, religions, politics, economics, philosophies, the arts, literature, and more. It can truly be said that we cannot fully comprehend the world we live in without it. But *how* the study and teaching of history is to be done right or even whether it can truly be done at all has been the subject of academic conversation for at least 300 years.

By the 1700–1800s, a Christian interpretation of history according to the will and actions of divine providence and supernatural intervention was becoming predominated by more "scientific" quests to analyze natural and human causes. Then, by the later twentieth century, confidence in historical objectivity gave way to theories of postmodern relativism that criticized ideals of reconstructing the past as both an exercise of power over others and subjective to historical-cultural context and personal bias.

Where does the Christian faith fit in this discussion of the nature and methods of the professor's historical task? Does the Christian faith necessitate a providential interpretation of history modeled after the Bible? What use should Christian professors of history make of the critical and analytical tools of the modern discipline—of sociology, cultural

[1] Michael Whiting serves as Assistant Professor of Christian History and Leadership in the Gary Cook School of Leadership.

studies, source criticism, etc.?[2] How should our faith impact the way we teach history in the classroom? How do we avoid misconstruing the past in efforts to defend our values, and can we respect the particularity of historical contexts while also offering universal Christian theological and moral judgments?

The purpose of this chapter is to share my perspective on integrating faith into the teaching of history utilizing the Attitudinal, Ethical, Foundational, and Worldview Approaches outlined in Arthur Holmes's classic book, *The Idea of a Christian College*.[3] Illustrations, examples, and anecdotes will be drawn from my own experiences of teaching history at Dallas Baptist University. First, however, it is important to understand how the discipline of history and faith integration has developed over the last few centuries, at least since the Protestant Reformation. Framing this context is useful for appreciating both the contemporary challenges and opportunities for Christian historians and history professors as they honor the biblical worldview centered in Christ and render faithfully their study and account of the past.

The Integration of Faith and History (Since 1500)

During the divisive Protestant Reformation period of the 1500s and 1600s, history was used polemically in favor of a particular denominational group as "true Christianity," such as the Lutheran *A Catalogue of Witnesses to the Truth* (1556); John Foxe's English Protestant *Acts and Monuments* (1563), the Anabaptist *Martyrs Mirror* (1660), or the Roman Catholic *Ecclesiastical Annals* (1588–1607). In many ways, Christian history has been littered with theological polarization that has scarred the history of the west for 200 years.[4]

[2] For an example of sociology applied to the study of Christian history, cf. Rodney Stark, *The Rise of Christianity: How the Obscure, Marginal Jesus Movement Became the Dominant Religious Force in the Western World in Five Centuries* (San Francisco, CA: Harper, 1996).

[3] Holmes, *The Idea of a Christian College*, 45–60.

[4] Euan Cameron, *Interpreting Christian History: The Challenge of the Churches' Past* (Oxford, UK: Blackwell, 2005), 122, 131–42, 145.

Beginning in the 1700s, Christian historians became less polemical and more impartial toward denominations,[5] with Johann Lorenz von Mosheim, author of the *Institutes of Ecclesiastical History*, being considered the "father of church history."[6] The Mercersburg Seminary professor and father of American church history, Philip Schaff, authored the classic eight-volume *History of the Christian Church* and helped to establish the American Society of Church History in 1888. Several decades later, Kenneth Scott LaTourette published his multivolume *History of the Expansion of Christianity* (1937) to provide the discipline more global coverage (though still from a Eurocentric point of view).

New developments in Church history of the twentieth century by European and North American Protestants applied a social-cultural analysis (and critique) of Christianity's historical development vis-a-vis the New Testament ethics of the Kingdom of God. Examples include Christianity's synthesis with Hellenism in Adolf von Harnack's *History of Dogma* (1893) and *What is Christianity?* (1900), Christianity's capitulation to industrial capitalism in Walter Rauschenbusch's *Christianity and the Social Crisis* (1907), and Christianity's adaption to class and national divisions in H. Richard Niebuhr's *The Social Sources of Denominationalism* (1929).[7]

Centuries prior to this, in the 1700s, the modern divorcing of historical study from the Christian faith began. No longer the provenance of church ministers and theologians, the study of history was infused with new Enlightenment emphases on analyzing causes through rational and scientific methods. For the new philosophers of history such as Voltaire, there was no longer even a personal commitment to Protestant or Catholic Christianity, only theistic rational virtue, with history interpreted from the standpoint of the development of human reason, freedom,

---

[5] James E. Bradley and Richard A. Muller, *Church History: An Introduction to Research, Reference Works, and Methods* (Grand Rapids, MI: Eerdmans, 1995), 13; Cameron, *Interpreting Christian History*, 145–48.

[6] Bradley and Muller, *Church History*, 16–17; Cameron, *Interpreting Christian History*, 149–51.

[7] Cameron, *Interpreting Christian History*, 174–82, 199, 202–3; For an intriguing analysis of Christianity's diverse historical-cultural models, cf. Niebuhr, *Christ and Culture*.

and progress.[8] Then, historians in the nineteenth century began incorporating the new humanistic science of sociology to study the human past for deterministic patterns of natural law. Soon, however, even this methodology was considered inadequate for appreciating differences of historical context and the freedom of self-conscious human personality. Rather than analyzing history according to a universal ethical or philosophical ideal, building on techniques developed at the University of Göttingen with the influence of German Pietism and Romanticism, historians pursued a deeper and sympathetic study of past eras for their own sake. Known as "historicism," Leopold von Ranke (1795–1886) is considered the "father of history" in this sense. Ranke, a German Lutheran and political historian, dove deeper into archival documents to understand the development of nation states viewed from within their own relative contexts. For the historicist, knowledge of the past may help in understanding the present, but history is misused if the past is prejudged by the present or used to defend universal values, for guidance of present and future decisions, or to promote the interests and power of one group over another (i.e., propaganda). Interpretations of universal meaning in history may be the realm of the philosopher, ethicist, or theologian, but not *the historian*, whose primary job is to understand and describe things as they were. Historicism accentuated the importance of context for understanding the past on its own terms and paved the way for the narrowing of scholarly specialization, but it also neutralized the theological, philosophical, or ethical uses of historical study.[9]

Into the twentieth century, while some Christian historians continued to interpret the process of history with explicit reference to the purposes and providence of God, "technical" or "ordinary" history, devoid of any acknowledgement of divine intervention or supernatural activity,

[8] This was a secular-philosophical version of the biblical rendering of history as moving toward an ideal future, adapted later in the 1800s and early 1900s by Darwinian evolutionary theory, Hegelian dialectic, and materialist Marxism.

[9] John Tosh, *The Pursuit of History: Aims, Methods, and New Directions in the Study of History*, 6th ed. (New York, NY: Routledge, 2015), 6–9, 24–25, 151–52, 185. For an overview and critical analysis of the various historiographical models and approaches, cf. David Bebbington, *Patterns in History: A Christian Perspective on Historical Thought* (Grand Rapids, MI: Baker, 1990).

was becoming more fashionable in the new era and its emphasis on the authority of empirical science (as was happening in other fields, including historical criticism of the Bible). Historical study by this time had widened beyond the life of the Church, world religions and cultures were treated with increasing sympathy, and other factors for understanding the complexity of human motivation and the historical process were standardized, whether economic, cultural, political, or social, etc. Impartiality and objectivity meant marginalizing the previous favor shown to Christianity in the study of history and the exclusion of personal faith (a biblical worldview and moral judgment) from the interpretive task of the historian.[10] Historians who were Christians found themselves having to decide about which side to play on, and many chose to adapt to the new rules of empiricism while holding the principles of their Christian faith and belief in God's providence more implicit.

Christian historians Herbert Butterfield (1900–1979) and Christopher Dawson (1889–1970) developed a synthesis one might describe as Thomistic (grace completing nature). While acknowledging the first role of Christian historians as understanding the past and its natural and human causes, a providential view *supplements* technical-ordinary history. Moral assertions (not condemnation) can be offered but must be impartial (e.g., of both Catholicism *and* Protestantism, socialism *and* capitalism). The Christian faith provides the very theoretical framework for valuing the study of history as God's creation, in the sympathetic study of human personalities within their contexts, and in appreciation of the constructive role of religion (i.e., Christianity) in the history of culture.[11]

A more cautious, moderate view of integrating faith and history characterizes three notable evangelical professors of American religious

---

[10] Bradley and Muller, *Church History*, 20.

[11] William A. Speck, "Herbert Butterfield: The Legacy of a Christian Historian," in *A Christian View of History?* ed. George Marsden and Frank Roberts (Grand Rapids, MI: Eerdmans, 1975), 102–3, 105–9, 114–5; Robert Clouse, "Herbert Butterfield," in *Historians of the Christian Tradition: Their Methodology and Influence on Western Thought*, ed. Michael Baumen and Martin I. Klauber (Nashville, TN: B&H, 1995), 519–30; Carl T. McIntire, "Modern Pioneers: Herbert Butterfield," *Christian History* 72, no. 4 (2001): 45–47; Herbert Butterfield, *Christianity and History* (Glasgow, UK: Fontana Books, 1958); Christopher Dawson, *The Crisis of Western Education* (London, UK: Sheed and Ward, 1961).

history: Mark A. Noll, George Marsden, and Nathan Hatch. Although recognizing there are valid settings for practicing providential history, the first task of the historian is to strive for an accurate understanding of the past. For example, their book *The Search for Christian America* argues that a politically conservative agenda favoring the Moral Majority and Religious Right in the 1970s and 80s oversimplified and misconstrued the more complex religious and philosophical heritage of the founders of our Republic.[12]

Also, when it comes to establishing credibility with a wider audience of professional historians of the secular academy, they argue providential beliefs should be kept implicit with greater stress on a critical analysis of human causes. Even when made explicit, providential interpretations should be offered cautiously. While the Scriptures are written from an explicitly providential-theological perspective of history, historians since then do not operate with the same prophetic authority as the inspired authors of the Bible.[13] Like Abraham Lincoln's "Meditations on the Divine Will" (1865), written during a protracted American Civil War that claimed the lives of hundreds of thousands on both sides, Christian historians must refrain from making definitive interpretations of the mind and will behind God's providential hand.[14]

For evangelicals like John Woodbridge or John Warwick Montgomery, however, keeping faith implicit does not guarantee that Christian historians will be fully embraced by the mainstream secular guild, and since the Bible and most of history practiced a providential view, Christian historians who operate primarily in the field of ordinary history concede too much and do not integrate their faith into the study of history enough.[15] It was this very issue among evangelicals that led

---

[12] Mark A. Noll, George Marsden, and Nathan Hatch, *The Search for Christian America*, exp. ed. (Colorado Springs, CO: Helmers and Howard, 1989).

[13] See also Bebbington, *Patterns in History*, 168–88.

[14] Mark A. Noll, *The Civil War as a Theological Crisis* (Chapel Hill, NC: University of North Carolina Press, 2006), 88–90.

[15] Maxie B. Burch, *The Evangelical Historians: The Historiography of George Marsden, Nathan Hatch, and Mark Noll* (Lanham, MD: University Press of America, 1996). See also the conversation on faith and history, George Marsden and John Woodbridge, "Christian History Today," *Christian History* 72, no. 4 (2001): 50–53.

to the establishment of the Conference on Faith and History in 1967. The CFH (and its accompanying academic journal *Fides et Historia*) developed from the American Society of Church History (ASCH) and American Historical Association (AHA)—with which it was later formally affiliated—as a way for those of like-minded evangelical faith to fellowship together and discuss the distinguishing value that a Christian faith brings to the practice of historical research, writing, and teaching.[16]

Since the postmodern era of the 1960s and 70s, the objectivity of the historical task has been even more significantly deconstructed. It is widely accepted today that every historian operates from preconceived values and historical, linguistic, and cultural limitations that make a pure and definitive reconstruction of the past impossible. However, most historians today refuse to adopt relativism and instead emphasize the making of *probable* conclusions about the past,[17] which can be achieved through critical analysis of primary and secondary sources, self-awareness of bias, as well as solicitation of peer review from other historical experts.

In the decades of global decolonization and the rise of worldwide social-political liberation movements in the 1960s and 70s, centuries of historical methodology were also deconstructed as privileging the powerful few, whether in the documents written and preserved or in the way history was traditionally written, taught, and used—especially as predominated by white males of Anglo-European descent. Most people in history have been largely excluded or ignored, including women, slaves, ethnic minorities, native peoples, the poor, etc. Women and gender studies, the history of North American minorities (blacks, Asians, Jews, and Hispanics), and the study of cultural and religious history from the

---

[16] Darryl G. Hart, "History in Search of Meaning: The Conference on Faith and History," in *History and the Christian Historian*, ed. Ronald A. Wells (Grand Rapids, MI: Eerdmans, 1998), 71–75, 79–82. Among the goals stated in the Conference on Faith and History's Constitution, "Article II: Purposes," are: "To encourage scholars to explore the relationship between Christian faith and historical studies" and "To encourage and advance teaching and research informed by Christian faith commitments." "Constitution of the Conference on Faith and History," About CFH, Conference on Faith and History, accessed November 28, 2023, https://faithandhistory.org/about-chf/.

[17] Bebbington, *Patterns in History*, 9.

perspective of global native peoples has burgeoned to give much needed attention and dignity to voices and experiences of the historically neglected.[18] This has borne a new emphasis on people's histories, or efforts to view history from the perspective and experiences of the lesser empowered and privileged of the world.[19] In the area of church history and Christian history, these latter twentieth-century developments have positively broadened its historical and global scope to include the faith experiences of everyday and often oppressed people and to follow the shifting of the numerical strength of Christianity outside of Europe and North America.[20] This provides a fresh opportunity for faith to be integrated into the writing and teaching of history, through incorporating a more comprehensive study of all Christian people having worth in the eyes of God.

History and Holmes in the Christian College

In view of this background, Arthur Holmes's four-fold approach to the integration of faith and liberal arts learning provides a useful structure for thinking about the task and unique calling facing the Christian historian-as-professor in today's world. The remaining portion of this chapter will focus on how I view these approaches being applied to the teaching of history with some personal examples from courses I teach.

---

[18] Tosh, *The Pursuit of History*, 166, 169, 173, 175–76, 231–34, 239, 243–44, 246–48. John Fea, *Why Study History? Reflecting on the Importance of the Past* (Grand Rapids, MI: Baker, 2013), 88–89.

[19] Tosh, *The Pursuit of History*, 162–63. Howard Zinn, *A People's History of the United States*, Reissue ed. (San Francisco, CA: Harper, 2015). For criticism of Zinn, see Mary Graber, *Debunking Howard Zinn: Exposing the Fake History That Turned a Generation Against America* (Washington, DC: Regnery History, 2020).

[20] Bradley and Muller, *Church History*, 24. Cf. Diana B. Bass, *A People's History of Christianity: The Other Side of the Story*, Reprint (San Francisco, CA: Harper, 2010); A volume on Global Christianity appears in Denis Janz, *A People's History of Christianity*, 7 vols. (Minneapolis, MN: Fortress Press, 2014); Scott Sunquist, *The Unexpected Century: The Reversal and Transformation of Global Christianity, 1900–2000* (Grand Rapids, MI: Baker, 2015); Paul R. Spickard and Kevin M. Craig, *A Global History of Christians: How Everyday Believers Experienced Their World* (Grand Rapids, MI: Baker, 2001); Philip Jenkins, *The New Faces of Christianity: Believing the Bible in the Global South* (Oxford, UK: Oxford University Press, 2006).

Attitudinal Approach

The foundation of faith integration for Holmes is the "Attitudinal Approach," or the attitude of the professor and student toward the study of the arts and sciences, which is the "initial and perhaps most salient point of contact with the Christian faith."[21] As it relates specifically to the teaching of history, Christian professors model the integration of faith by approaching history as a worthy endeavor because the world and all of creation belong to the Lord (Psalm 82:8). This includes the study of biblical and Christian history specifically, for the foundation of the Christian faith *is* historical—the true life, death, and bodily resurrection of Jesus.

At the same time, since all nations are His, to pursue understanding of all peoples of the world He has made is to share in God's valuing of the world. While there continues to be a need for a narrower, parochial study of Christian history to serve the Church's memory and mission,[22] and modern secular history prejudicially minimizes and even disparages Christianity's historical and cultural contribution to world history, it is not necessary for a Christian professor of history to use history only in service to the Church or its faith. As God's providence extends over all the nations of the world, being a Christian professor of history can also mean providing a faithful narrative of Tibetan Buddhism or the life of Mahatma Gandhi. Creation is worth studying because God made it, and the Word of God in Jesus Christ became incarnate within history.[23] *One of the best ways to engage students with history in the classroom is by exhibiting a contagious passion and enthusiasm for its doxological value.*

A second attitude Christian professors of history should model for their students is *humility*. This includes, first, a humility in knowledge. Despite my many years of research, writing, and teaching, and despite earning graduate and postgraduate degrees, I have only come to discover more how little I actually know, how dependent I am upon the

[21] Holmes, *The Idea of a Christian College*, 45–47.

[22] Cf. Rowan Williams, *Why Study the Past? The Quest for the Historical Church* (Grand Rapids, MI: Eerdmans, 2005); David C. Steinmetz, *Memory and Mission: Theological Reflections on the Christian Past* (Nashville, TN: Abingdon Press, 1988), 17–34.

[23] See Mark A. Noll, *Jesus Christ and the Life of the Mind* (Grand Rapids, MI: Eerdmans, 2013).

work of other scholars, and how far removed I am in time, place, and worldview from the people and time periods I am investigating and teaching about. Recorded history alone literally includes the world and thousands of years. Several lifetimes could not make me an expert on all of it. The discipline of history has become increasingly specialized to the point that no single historian or history professor can be expected to speak authoritatively on every period.

Christian professors of history should be the humblest historians, especially when we compare our finite knowledge to the infinite, all-knowing character of the God they worship,[24] who knows the end from the beginning and has sovereign knowledge of all points and details in between down to the fall of each sparrow (Matthew 10:29). We can model for our students our own continuing inquisitiveness and lifelong learning of history, and rather than just teaching as experts *at* the students (though we will be further along down the path), we can design our courses as an invitation to be led along a journey of learning together.

Not only intellectual humility, but in the light of our universal need of God's mercy, moral humility should also be a distinctive trait of the Christian professor of history. The first task of the historian is to understand the strange and unfamiliar in history with the sensitivity of a cross-cultural tourist. I tell my students it is easy in hindsight to criticize the blind spots and moral failings of the past, but Christians must first seek to understand accurately and then be humble in their assessments. No one, and a Christian more than others should know this, is self-righteous and without sin to stand in a position of condemnation and judgment upon others (Romans 3:23).

In the introductions to my courses, I always encourage students as they approach the strange and oftentimes unrighteous past, to remember that some future day our own history will be written about. DBU is a university that stands downstream from the Protestant Reformation, and we can identify many glaring weaknesses with the medieval world,

[24] Donald A. MacPhee, "The Muse Meets the Master: Clio and Christ," in *A Christian View of History?* ed. George Marsden and Frank Roberts (Grand Rapids, MI: Eerdmans, 1975), 80.

but that does not mean we cannot also look for strengths since God was still at work. After all, universities are a legacy of the medieval world, as is our possession of the many ancient manuscripts that were hand-copied and preserved through the centuries in monastic libraries. No historical age is perfect even in the Church, as reading Paul's letters to the Corinthians makes evident. I urge students, as we approach the past, to consider what the future will say about us and how our generations have failed. A study of history can humble us by not only soberly reminding us of our finitude in the grandeur of the longer human story and exposing the historical origins of things we take for granted—like political democracy, literacy, and Bibles in our languages. We can also develop some empathy for the limitations and weaknesses of others in the past as we consider our own lives and the sin nature that we—even as Christians—share with the whole of humanity. We can certainly learn from mistakes of the past, but the past (simply because it is passed) should not be entirely viewed as all mistakes either, or what C. S. Lewis described as an attitude of "chronological snobbery."[25]

On the other hand, Christian professors should warn students about having an unrealistic nostalgia toward certain periods of the past that glosses over or whitewashes their problems, such as over-glamorizing the era of the Protestant Reformation, American colonial revivalism, or the morally conservative era of the 1950s, as if to forget that African Americans during this decade were striving to finally end Jim Crow segregation policies in the South and exercise basic legal rights (including the Voting Rights Act passed in 1965).[26] As discussed further below, the paradox of the human condition as made in the image of God and corrupted by the Fall means we will find some ugly as well as some good, true, and beautiful in successive ages of history.

---

[25] Clive S. Lewis, *Surprised by Joy: The Shape of My Early Life* (New York, NY: Harcourt Brace, 1955), 200; Cf. Clive S. Lewis, "Preface," in *Saint Athanasius' On the Incarnation*, trans. John Behr (Yonkers, NY: St. Vladimirs Seminary Press, 2012), 10–11.

[26] Tosh, *The Pursuit of History*, 15–17, 27–28.

Ethical Approach

The first principle of the Ethical Approach in Holmes's model of integration, as it pertains to teaching history, is intellectual integrity and honesty. Acknowledging the inescapable challenges of limited sources, changing contexts over time, and the biased perspective of the historian in reconstructing the past *definitively*, the honest study and teaching of history involves utilizing the best methods and tools of the historical discipline (discussed further below) to present history more truthfully and with greater *probability*.[27] Christian professors of history should be lovers of the truth and should encourage and model for students not to accept historical claims uncritically nor misconstrue the facts of history, a danger whenever history is manipulated to defend or support the interests of a particular group in a way that is dishonest to the past.

One example is uncritical praise of historical personalities such as the German reformer Martin Luther, exaggerating his positive traits and influence (i.e., hagiography) without acknowledging character flaws and adverse outcomes of his legacy as well—such as his vitriolic and hateful speech against Jews in Germany. The same could be said of teaching about movements like the Protestant Reformation more generally. Although important developments in religion on behalf of the common people in the sixteenth century should be highlighted, [28] it would be bad, or incomplete, history for a (Protestant) Christian professor not to acknowledge what was good in the Middle Ages or only focus on the positive intentions and outcomes of the Reformation. Significant divisions among Protestants as well as with Catholics that engulfed European nation-state church establishments in dogmatic conflict and religious war were the context for the response of secular rationalism in the Enlightenment.[29]

---

[27] Bebbington, *Patterns in History*, 2–9.

[28] Positively, Alister McGrath views the problem of Protestant pluralism as opening more creative religious expressions that have contributed to Christianity's global flourishing in diverse cultural contexts. Alister McGrath, *Christianity's Dangerous Idea: The Protestant Revolution—A History From the Sixteenth Century to the Twenty-First* (San Francisco, CA: Harper, 2007).

[29] Eventually, doubt in the objectivity of human reason and science even gave way to a movement of postmodern relativism. See Brad S. Gregory, *The Unintended Reformation: How a Religious Revolution Secularized Society* (Cambridge, MA: Harvard University Press, 2012).

Faith integration and an Ethical Approach to teaching history means coming to terms with moral inconsistencies in our most admired leaders of the past, including the well-known policymakers and founders who framed the American experiment in 1776 but who, either assertively or passively, maintained the systematic denial of equality and freedom to thousands of African slaves. In our teaching of history, in other words, we should strive to be fair and honest and, when choosing to be critical, impartial. We must be careful not to uncritically idolize historical persons (and on the other hand unilaterally demonize), and we should approach each historical person in every historical age with a sense of realism. As Reinhold Niebuhr asserted, sin has been a constant and pervasive element of the human condition.[30] Will Durant echoed this, noting that sin remains a constant force throughout history. Yet, for all the instances of human evil, there are also stories of its counterpart, stories of hope and charity.[31]

The moral use of history will be discussed further below, but as mentioned earlier, a historicist approach that developed first in nineteenth-century Germany rejected imposing present values and critical judgments on the past. This was viewed as the profession of the philosopher, theologian, or pastor, but not the historian whose primary and proper vocation is to understand the past on its own terms. Postmodern theory also rejected interpreting or judging history by a singular, universal metanarrative that stands outside and above the process of history, arguing that *all* reading (and teaching) of history is unavoidably relative, subjective, and influenced by a desire to embolden particular social, religious, or ethnic and cultural identities (ironically, they employ a metanarrative of the will-to-power in their study of history and historical criticism).

However, as *Christian* professors of history, may we pass over events like the Holocaust, apartheid in South Africa, or the genocide in

[30] Reinhold Niebuhr, *Man's Nature and His Communities: Essays on the Dynamics and Enigmas of Man's Personal and Social Existence* (New York, NY: Scribner, 1965), 24.

[31] Will Durant and Ariel Durant, *The Lessons of History* (New York, NY: Simon and Schuster, 1968), 41, (italics mine).

Rwanda without interjecting carefully thought out theological or moral assessments? Is refraining from moral judgment really objective and amoral? With faith in the Bible as the self-expression and revelation of God's character and will through the metanarrative of Creation-Fall-Redemption, Christian professors of history have an objective standard by which they can evaluate past ideas, choices, and systems, even those that have claimed to be Christian (2 Corinthians 10:5; 1 John 4:1).[32] This does not preclude the need for the exercise of humility in doing so, recognizing our moral fallenness and the finite limits of our knowledge and interpretation of people and events—we see through "a glass darkly" (1 Corinthians 13:12). Theological and moral judgments may not be the *primary* calling of a professor of history,[33] and many Christian historians may lack confidence or solid training in theological studies or moral philosophy. Yet the careful work of history is the vital foundation for making *informed* theological or philosophical and moral judgments about the problems of the past. History will be turned to inevitably for insight. The question is, will it be turned to correctly?[34] The nineteenth century drove a wedge between the professions of the moral philosopher, theologian, and the historian, but Christians who see all truth as essentially part of one whole must learn how to appropriately incorporate such reflection in interpreting the intellectual and moral problems of history, whether English Civil War of the 1640s, the French Revolution in the 1790s, or the Great Depression of the 1930s. One of my favorite assignments to review is end of the semester reflection papers, when my students have the chance to step back and consider the lessons of history *they* discovered along their journey through the course as it relates to enriching their personal formation and vocational development.

Foundational Approach

The Foundational Approach in Holmes's model of integration answers the "What," "Why," and "How" questions of each academic

[32] George Marsden, "What Difference Might Christian Perspectives Make?" in *History and the Christian Historian*, ed. Ronald A. Wells (Grand Rapids, MI: Eerdmans, 1998), 20–22.

[33] Fea, *Why Study History*, 55–56.

[34] Tosh, *The Pursuit of History*, 41.

discipline. It defines the building blocks of history, or what might be described as its grammar. Regarding the "What," it must be admitted upfront that history is lost to us. We cannot reconstruct the past perfectly. We can piece together sources of various kinds and try to make sense of them, but ultimately, the past is just that—passed: "The past does not exist, and all we have is a set of surviving traces of the past."[35] The further removed, the stranger and less familiar is the history we study. The closer we are in time to the past we are studying, the more challenging it is to view the whole forest from within the midst of the trees.[36] Ironically, as it relates to the Ethical Approach above, the greater awareness we have of our limitations, our biases, and the lack of sources available to us, the more objective (or at least probable) we can strive for a fair and honest treatment of the past. This will be dealt with further below under the "How" of historical study.

The Foundational Approach also deals with the "Why" question. What is the use or purpose of history? Why is it important that we preserve history at all? For the historicists, once history was understood, that was the end of that. To make present use out of it would inevitably distort history since no two periods of time are ever the same. What use can we make of a history anyway that, as Durant noted, is biased and twisted by historians whose motives are colored by their own political or religious lenses.[37] Yet the Christian historian, with a belief in God's providence (even if implicit) and a worldview shaped by the biblical story of sin and redemption, cannot but raise questions and reflect on the meaning and relevance of history's particularities. The Scriptures speak of the value of historical remembrance for Israel and the Church,[38] and preserving a collective identity through memory that would serve the faith and obedience of generations to come was the very reason for writing down and recording all the stories, prophecies, and teachings, from Genesis through Revelation.

---

35 Bradley and Muller, *Church History*, 35.

36 Ronald A. Wells, *History Through the Eyes of Faith: Western Civilization and the Kingdom of God* (Grand Rapids, MI: Baker, 1989), 6–7.

37 Durant and Durant, *The Lessons of History*, 11–13.

38 Exod. 13:3; Num. 15:39; Deut. 4:10; 9:7; 15:15; Ps. 78:42; Isa. 46:9; Heb. 19:32; Rev. 2:5.

However, we need to be careful that we do not always go to history expressly for something usable. Such a pragmatic-heavy approach to history can lead to misconstruing the past. The historicists were partly right in insisting that we should do our best to understand the past on its own terms, just as Christians might stress the importance of identifying authorial intent and context in biblical interpretation, but once that hard work is done, then the Christian professor of history can help students proceed to make the best, informed conclusions they can about the meaning and relevance of the past through a Christian framework. We can balance the perspective of the ancient philosopher Heraclitus (reality is plurality and change) with that of Parmenides (reality is one and permanent). Contexts undoubtedly change over time, so there are no perfect analogies. However, more fundamentally our human condition, problems, and struggles remain the same in the age between the Fall and the fullness of the future Kingdom of God, so it is natural for professors and students to observe and analyze patterns without adopting a purely cyclical view of history.[39]

One of the patterns in history I share with my students is the degree to which religious movements and reactions seem often, at least initially, to be extreme. This is not to simplify all of history through the lens of Hegel's dialectic, but there are indeed many evidences of a proverbial pendulum swinging back and forth.[40] In my classes, I bring attention to such patterns in history: how the worldliness of the Imperial Church motivated a burst of popularity for desert ascetic monasticism, an approach that is similar (though not identical) to the withdrawal of Anabaptist communities from the magisterial state-churches of the sixteenth century or the disengagement of Protestant Fundamentalists from mainstream American liberal and secular culture in the early twentieth century. We also discuss how a perceived emphasis on rational knowledge in medieval university scholasticism begat reactionary movements of spiritual mysticism and ethical humanism in the 1400s, which was not

---

[39] Marsden, "What Difference Might Christian Perspectives Make?" 35; Wells, *History Through the Eyes of Faith*, 2–3; Fea, *Why Study History*, 53; Tosh, *The Pursuit of History*, 32, 39.

[40] Cf. Cameron, "Constantly Shifting Emphases in Christian History," 58–102.

so altogether unlike how confessional Protestant orthodoxies in seventeenth-century Europe prompted the response of alternative emphases in Protestant Pietism and Enlightenment moral philosophy. Although the analogies between historical scenarios are never exact because of changing contexts, history is a laboratory for Christian professors and students to compare how people of different ages have approached substantive and relevant questions of church and state, religion and culture, and faith and ethics. One way to avoid continuing to fall into extremes is to be aware that this propensity of human nature exists, as is the tendency over time to corrupt noble ideas and intentions, and a long view of history provides countless illustrations that can raise awareness, caution, and greater balance.[41]

One fruitful area for using history to help students appreciate the complexity of enduring religious questions is through the practice of formal debates. Many students relate how they have never participated in a classroom debate, even though this was the cardinal methodology of medieval education in Europe's first universities. Group debate allows students a unique opportunity for collaboration and critical thinking and helps them think differently about a complex question for which they may already have a preconceived, but untested, stance. The question I often use is whether places of worship should be adorned with images of biblical saints. This was an issue of severe political and religious controversy in the medieval Greek East, and it also divides churches of the Catholic and Protestant worlds to this day. While some students come away firmer in their convictions, others after listening and weighing the theological and practical pros and cons come away less certain after their simplistic opinions have been challenged. Another issue we wrestle through is the ending of Christian persecution and the increasing freedom and favor of the Roman government toward the Church in the fourth century. Students role-play as church leaders who marshal evidence and make their case for the benefits versus problems of a closer

[41] Mark A. Noll, *Turning Points: Decisive Moments in the History of Christianity*, 3rd ed. (Grand Rapids, MI: Baker, 2012), 7–8.

union of Church and State—which prompts them to consider the complicated relationship of Christianity and politics today.

The teaching of history is also essential for helping students understand the world in which they live and are called to serve. I place a lot of stress on this point for my students. I explain and demonstrate how history can illumine where the global and denominational diversity of our faith came from and the centuries of people, circumstances, and stories—the threads—that connect the Book of Acts to our own contemporary experience. I emphasize how history leads to understanding our current moment, including the increasing religious pluralism and secularism of North America and Europe since the nineteenth century, the antagonism of Islam toward the West and its involvement in Middle Eastern politics dating back to the medieval period, or why former British colonies like India have so adamantly (and understandably) rejected Western Christian missions in the twentieth century.

History also spurs reflection on what degree the contemporary experiences and values we take for granted are shaped by New Testament Christianity or more by our social, political, or cultural contexts.[42] By traveling outside of our own time to study another, we can better perceive how much we are all shaped by our environments, and perhaps correct our course of thought and action or expose simplistic opinions or blind spots that we have neglected.[43]

We have many identities today that have been shaped by historical processes: Protestant, Catholic, Republican, Democrat, etc. By studying history, we come to realize that so many of the options surrounding us are historically conditioned. I encourage my students to put themselves in the mindset of the people in history and to see the world from the situational limits of their point of view. Did people wake up one day and believe they were suddenly in the "Middle Ages" or the "Reformation?" These categories are obviously loaded with assumptions created by later historians who named these periods—including an obviously Eurocentric frame of reference. I help my students to appreciate the

[42] Marsden, "What Difference Might Christian Perspectives Make?" 44.
[43] Lewis, "Preface," 10–11.

fact that all the varieties of denominations available to them today did not exist for most of Christianity's history. In the town where I live sits Episcopal, Lutheran, and Baptist churches all sharing the same street corner. Although medieval Catholicism was not as uniform as many assume, medieval Europe was still nowhere near the consumer marketplace that characterizes the diversity of North American religion.

There is much we take for granted about the world as we experience it—as if it has always been this way—that was simply not the case in the past. We may not be able to transcend being influenced by the context that we inhabit, but the more we allow history to show us the ways our worldview and language have been shaped by our environment, the more freedom we can exercise for influence within it.[44] One assignment I find useful as it pertains to appreciating the historical diversity of Christianity is to require my students to attend churches outside of their familiar tradition, as there is much even in the way they view how church and worship should be done that they take for granted as if it has always been this way or is simply the obviously biblical way—even though the age of many of their traditions are only 1–25% of the whole story of Christianity from ancient Israel to modern times.

This brings us to the "How" of teaching history. The historical process from within involves multiple levels of causal explanation, including human personalities, social motivations, and cultural realities. Given that absolute objectivity in historical study is always elusive, how do Christian professors of history approach the past ethically for more accurate understanding, meaning, and judgment? The distinctive domains of history are many, and as each new domain came to prominence in modern historiography the specializations of historians became narrower. With biography, religious history, and intellectual history, there was joined cultural history, social and economic history, political history, and gender and ethnic history. Of course, these domains might be helpful for the purposes of historical analysis, but in the actual past they were not separable, and to claim that a full and accu-

[44] Tosh, *The Pursuit of History*, 28.

rate history has been written that only considers one of these domains is wrong—as is the case with a Marxist view of history that interprets history singularly as economic and social class conflict.

As you can see, the task before the Christian professor of history in faithfully reconstructing the past for our students in all its human dimensions is massive. This is also true of the primary sources studied: autobiographies, legal documents, treatises, literary correspondence, journals, media and art, and oral testimony. Guiding students to step into the past through engagement with primary sources is critical, but we must acknowledge that we do not have access to all the sources of the past, and even as we choose and select sources based on our own teaching preferences and interests, the sources left behind are biased themselves in what was recorded and how it was recorded.[45]

Nevertheless, with humility, as Christian professors of history we must do our best to tell the truth about the past, as Herbert Butterfield in his *Whig Interpretation of History* (1931) warned against the partisan-politicizing of history. To help, the 5 C's of historical study should guide the Christian professor in his or her presentation of history to avoid the following: oversimplification, false generalizations, anachronisms (not appreciating differences between past and present contexts), and misconstruing history to justify a particular group's values in the present. These do not guarantee an infallible historical interpretation, but as Christians operate under the same limitations of historical study,[46] these are a significant step in the right direction:

- History is never equivalent but *changes* through time.
- C*ontext* is key to understanding the past on its own terms.
- Events should be studied for multiple, intersecting *causes*.
- The historical process from the perspective of human intentions and decisions should be seen as *contingent* rather than as predetermined or necessitated by their outcomes.

[45] Ibid., 15–16, 159–60.
[46] MacPhee, "The Muse Meets the Master," 81.

- The past is a *complex* web of causal and contextual factors that defies absolute and definitive interpretations.[47]

Next, what role should distinctively *Christian* professors of history give to discerning the mind and intentions of God's providence as we engage the process of history?[48] The Bible models interpretation of history in terms of divine blessings and judgments, and it presumes God's intervention with and through human decisions and their consequences—as well as the activities of Satan. This way of interpreting history may appeal more to majority world cultures such as Africa or Asia where there is still a vivid cognizance of the activities of spiritual beings and that are less dominated by a worldview of scientific secularism. In the West, to interpret history from the perspective of the spiritual realm and convictions of faith is unscientific. Even the Book of Job challenges any equivocal correspondence between our experience of history and definitive knowledge of God's intentions—whether divine favor and our prosperity on the one hand or divine displeasure and our sufferings on the other (see also Psalm 73). A belief in divine providence should neither discount the reality of God's use of ordinary means of human agency in history, as Jonathan Edwards explained about the experience of revival and later Baptist William Carey defended in his call to mission efforts against British hyper-Calvinism.[49]

Christian professors of history do need to avoid speaking authoritatively for God's mind, intentions, and plans,[50] remembering that Job's friends were chastised for misinterpreting what they observed (Job 42:7–9). As C. S. Lewis said, history is written with "the fingerprint of God, but do we have the text"?[51] We must exemplify for our students a humility and caution in identifying the providential workings of God or oversimplifying the historical process as the actions of exclusively good

[47] Fea, *Why Study History*, 6–15; Tosh, *The Pursuit of History*, 161–62, 164–65.

[48] Marsden, "What Difference Might Christian Perspectives Make?" 38–40.

[49] Ibid., 46.

[50] Wells, *History Through the Eyes of Faith*, 4–5.

[51] Cf. Philip I. Mitchell, "Written by the Finger of God: C. S. Lewis and Historical Judgment," *Mythlore: A Journal of J. R. R. Tolkien, C. S. Lewis, Charles Williams, and Mythopoeic Literature* 38, no. 2 (Spring/Summer 2020): 5–21.

or evil spiritual forces. The story of Joseph from the Old Testament and the crucifixion of Jesus give evidence that appearances are not always what they seem. For example, in teaching about the birth of the American Republic, the benefits of the establishment of religious freedom in the United States are celebrated as the providence of God that allowed Christianity to flourish in distinctive ways, but we must also acknowledge that among founding leaders and politicians of the time included a number of men influenced by the Enlightenment and unorthodox religious Deism who were vigorously critical of Christianity and the organized churches of Britain and Europe. Also, our democratic principle of religious liberty from government control created unforeseen challenges for the Christian faith three centuries later in competition with increasing numbers of Americans of other faiths, or no faith at all, who desire equality of representation and influence to shape the moral values of our society, including through the media and state-supported public education.

Furthermore, an uncritical providential approach to teaching history can often lead to whitewashing those persons and events who are considered God's instruments to bring about the heritage of our own spiritual identity.[52] For Christian professors of history, this means we need to seriously admit the failures and problems of the churches, including those seen as pioneers of our denominational traditions. This could include not minimizing the moral blight of the Crusades, pro-slavery and racist attitudes in American churches, and even understanding that movements that were originally celebrated by churches as the blessing of God and seemed intent on advancing human culture and society, like the Protestant Reformation or the Industrial Revolution, had a mixture of positive as well as harmful outcomes. The Christian professor of history, especially, "with such knowledge that man is capable of being both the crown and the scum of the universe, views man's cultural achievements in this perspective."[53] The grandeurs and claims

[52] Hart, *History in Search of Meaning*, 85–86.

[53] Marsden, "What Difference Might Christian Perspectives Make?" 41, 48; Marsden and Woodbridge, "Christian History Today," 52.

of human achievement in every age can be eyed with a sense of caution and realism that history involving fallen humans is not a steady march in progress, as is symbolized by the Tower of Babel in Genesis 11.[54] This is especially true as technological change continues to outpace moral reflection, most recently as we begin to experience the prospects and problems of Artificial Intelligence.

On the surface, the tools and methods of the Christian professor of history will resemble the secular historian in many ways. Yet the Christian professor should not marginalize the role of religion and the spiritual motivations of people among the many causal layers of historical events, and although they have the additional perspective of biblical faith, they should make judgments about the past with humility and refrain from speaking *authoritatively or definitively* for God's providential intentions or identifying selective parts of the historical process as the actions of exclusively good or evil spiritual forces.[55] Along with humble theological and moral assessments of the past, what uniquely characterizes every Christian who integrates faith into his teaching of history should be what MacPhee describes:

> ...the qualities to be cultivated and cherished most by the historian are intellectual *honesty* in searching the truth about the past; intellectual *humility* regarding the limits of human insight and understanding; *judiciousness* in making assessments; a healthy *skepticism* of sources; painstaking workmanship; a *compassionate* spirit; and a sense of *balance* and proportion.[56]

[54] For a realist critique of the liberal and optimistic view of historical progress, cf. Reinhold Niebuhr, *Moral Man and Immoral Society: A Study in Ethics and Politics*, 2nd ed. (Louisville, KY: Westminster John Knox Press, 2013); Reinhold Niebuhr, *Faith and History: A Comparison of Christian and Modern Views of History* (New York, NY: Scribner, 1949); Reinhold Niebuhr, *Beyond Tragedy: Essays on the Christian Interpretation of History* (New York, NY: Scribner, 1937).

[55] Bebbington, *Patterns in History*, 187.

[56] MacPhee, "The Muse Meets the Master," 84 (italics mine). Cf. Bradley and Muller, *Church History*, 49.

Worldview Approach

To conclude, Holmes's fourth approach of faith integration is Worldview.[57] Rather than undermining a scientific study of the past, the Christian faith really provides the only theoretical basis for approaching the study of history as an intelligible whole. Contrary to a postmodern view of history with no ultimate unifying reference point in the past or future, a Christian professor of history understands from biblical revelation that history is the story of the human condition in relationship to God with an introduction and a conclusion. The Creation-Fall-Redemption narrative allows Christian professors of history to ascertain what is good, true, and beautiful in every stage of history under God's common grace as well as the co-existence of the shameful and evil in the present age, even among those who profess faith in Christ. In fact, with greater objectivity, a Christian professor of history has the point of view from which to consider all historical ideas, systems, cultures, and religions (including the Christian past) from the perspectival truth that "there is no one righteous" (Romans 3:10 [NIV]), and perfection awaits a promised future when God will be "all in all" (1 Corinthians 15:28 [NIV]). Until then, we can expect that the best of humanity will always fall short, and sins will be mixed with virtues. It is the uniquely Christian view of the world that, in Bebbington's view, unites the best of historiographical perspectives in a realism that appreciates the paradox of history as "about human beings who are like God yet habitual wrongdoers…who are the shapers and yet also the victims of history."[58]

This includes even the Church, made up of citizens of heaven who are yet outwardly subject to the process of history, as I share with students through the life of the north African bishop Augustine and in his book *City of God*. Coming to terms with the Germanic attack on Rome in 410, the tragedy that befell the center of the young "Christian" Em-

---

[57] The most helpful books I have read on the Christian worldview are Walsh and Middleton, *The Transforming Vision*; Plantinga, Jr. *Engaging God's World*; J. Richard Middleton, *A New Heaven and New Earth: Reclaiming Biblical Eschatology* (Grand Rapids, MI: Baker, 2014); N. Tom Wright, *Simply Jesus: A New Vision of Who He Is, What He Did, and Why He Matters* (San Francisco, CA: Harper, 2018).

[58] Bebbington, *Patterns in History*, 168.

pire by invading pagan armies invoked questions from Roman people about "Where is God?" It challenged any optimistic correlation in the here and now between God's favor on the Church and the welfare of the State and pointed to the Kingdom of God as heavenly and future. For Augustine, the lust for power upon which all earthly cities post-Fall are built and expanded (Rome's glory included), and the mixture of the righteous (the city of God) among the unrighteous (the city of man) in the Church and the world until the end of history negates placing any permanent hope in the present world and comforts our despair in the face of temporal tragedy. This is a lesson worth repeating in every age when Christians suffer the decline or loss of former privilege or prosperity.

A Christian worldview helps us as professors of history to moderate our appraisal of events and movements in history even as we consider our current generation and the future outcomes that remain to be known. In my sessions dealing with the end of persecution under Emperor Constantine, we discuss how this moment viewed from one point of view was triumphally acclaimed by the fourth-century bishop and church historian Eusebius who celebrated the increasing imperial favor of Christianity.[59] However, looking back we can also acknowledge that it created space for a more nominal faith to grow among the Roman masses and led to the development of a hierarchical institution of clergy possessing increasing amounts of temporal power and control over church rituals and liturgy throughout the medieval period—as well as church-sanctioned support of state violence against heretics and schismatics.[60] In other sessions, we discuss how the Protestant Reformation made personal access to God and the direct authority of His Word more equitable for more people, but soon, differences in reading and interpreting the Bible also created spiraling divisions between a host of new churches and sects that harmed Christian unity and ignited confes-

[59] Eusebius, *History of the Church: A New Translation*, trans. Jeremy M. Schott (Oakland, CA: University of California Press, 2019), Books 9–10. Cf. Everett Ferguson, "The Problem of Eusebius," *Christian History* 72, no. 4 (November 2001): 8–12.

[60] John D. Roth, ed. *Constantine Revisited: Leithart, Yoder, and the Constantinian Debate* (Eugene, OR: Pickwick, 2013).

sional hostilities in the sixteenth and seventeenth centuries. Elsewhere, we analyze how the decline and fall of monarchies and rural aristocracy in early modern Europe allowed for the development of urban bourgeoise capitalism, distributing political power and economic wealth more democratically than ever before, fueled in part by a new Protestant work ethic. Yet, it also led to another form of aristocracy and slave labor that developed under rich business oligarchs and tycoons of the Industrial Revolution. Federal regulations in child labor, wage earning, and work hours responded to agitations against injustice in urban factories and the challenges of socialist, religious, and political philosophy for a more just and equitable distribution of meaningful work and economic flourishing. Such softer ideals were implemented with revolutionary force to horrific lengths of oppression and brutality in Communist Russia, demonstrating that neither unbridled capitalism with a strong priority on the individual nor government-mandated socialism with strong priority on the collective are perfect systems when established and carried forward by fallen human beings. Thus, the Christian worldview enables us as professors and students of history to understand why the best of human intentions and efforts are marked by successes and failures, and why there is good and evil mixed up in the historical process, and why we must not be too quick to either hope or despair in our current moment of history from our limited point of view.

Conclusion

I share with my students that human history in all its political, social, economic, and religious dimensions can be seen as a story of tension between extremes of unity and diversity—between uniformity and tyranny on the one hand and division and chaos on the other. This is fundamentally the fracturing and breakdown of humankind made in the image of a Triune God: three distinct but equal persons who exist in perfect union and harmony through honoring and loving each other.[61]

[61] I believe a Trinitarian worldview for interpreting the problems and complexities of political, economic, cultural, and religious history is one of the most untapped and fruitful areas for future Christian historians to consider.

Any hope of restoration then for human society is with individuals *freely, mutually, and generously* living for one another, which is modeled perfectly in the eternal Trinity. A Christian professor of history uniquely believes that the paradox of the human condition not only reflects the *corruption* (not negation) of a world originally created good by a Triune God but also points to the universal longing and pull out of sin toward the *shalom* that characterizes the promised perfection of the Kingdom in the age to come actualized with the return of Jesus Christ. Until then, the Christian professor of history leads students to approach the whole story of humanity expectantly in our cultural, social, and political relationships as the story of struggle, sin, success, virtue, and failure through a beautiful but fallen world, of the personal and collective sin of marred and half-redeemed images of God—a beautiful mess.

Chapter 11

Integrating Faith in the Study of Religion

By Brent A. Thomason[1]

Introduction

Integrating faith and learning in the study of religion should not be hard, or at least one would think. However, many institutions of higher education approach the study of religion in general, or even a designated religion specifically, from a purely literary perspective. Wielding the executioner's blade of unbelief, they dissect the genres, demythologize the miracle stories, and decapitate any religious text that dares rear its head to make a truth claim. My brother sat under the tutelage of one such executioner during his college years. He attended a large state school known for its mechanical engineering program. As an elective, he enrolled in a seminar on the New Testament. To his shock, the professor was not a Christian nor was the curriculum taught from a perspective of belief in the claims of the Bible. Rather, the professor approached the subject matter of the New Testament as a sacred religious text from antiquity. The text was sacred not because it had come from God nor because the professor actually believed its contents; it was sacred only because the Judeo-Christian communities of the first and second century revered the texts as such and preserved them for the generations for millennia to come. Consequently, claims about the afterlife were dismissed and stories of miracles were likened to fairy tales

[1] Brent A. Thomason serves as Dean of the Graduate School of Ministry and Professor of Biblical Studies at Dallas Baptist University.

ad nauseam. So, while integrating faith and learning in the study of religion cannot be assumed at every institution, it can be assumed at Dallas Baptist University (DBU).

Answering the Objections

But before we endeavor to exegete how this is done at DBU, we first need to define some terms and answer a few objections. The word "religion" in the title and throughout the chapter should be understood in the context of the DBU catalog of course offerings. Classes related to the study of the Bible, Church history, Christian doctrine, etc. are under the domain of RELI, or religion. So, for instance a class on the Gospels is RELI 4307, a class on Christian Ministry is RELI 1310, a class on Ethics is RELI 3301, and a class on the History of Christianity is RELI 3383. It is within this realm of religious studies that the chapter explores the intersection of faith and learning. Consequently, the term "faith" is understood as the Christian faith experienced from the position of Orthodox Christianity. It is a perspective of belief in the sacred texts taught, the principles drawn from the Bible, and the subsequent worldview formed from the tenets of said faith. Integrating faith into a Christian curriculum believes what is being taught, teaches it truthfully from conviction, and invites the students to do the same. In this way, it can be assumed that faith is integrated in learning at DBU because religion is taught from the perspective of a life changed.

Is there any real added value to the teaching of religion when faith is integrated? I maintain that the student is best served, and not at the sacrifice of the curriculum, when the professor believes the content and models for the student the very curriculum taught. It is at this deepest level of congruence between message and messenger, between subject and schoolteacher, that faith is integrated in learning. This is the fertile ground of deep learning because the professor does not teach from a position of study but from a posture of surety. She believes what she teaches and from that *quelle* of conviction her impassioned content takes root in the minds of students. Who are the best teachers from your past?

Those whose pedagogy was fueled by their passionate belief in what they taught. Value is added to the teaching of religion when faith is integrated in the fabric of the curriculum.

But are we not infringing on a student's beliefs when we teach religion from a particular faith persuasion? In the "cancel" culture of today, many define infringement as any presentation of ideas contrary to the worldview of the listener. Under such a definition, only the scenario by which the professor and pupils' worldview align perfectly would it not be an infringement. And yet that is not the type of learning that higher education has fostered for thousands of years. Instead, higher education is a realm where students are presented with all manner of truth claims in a variety of disciplines and then are taught how to think critically for themselves and synthesize valid truth claims into an integrated worldview for life. The fact that the professor believes what she is teaching no more infringes on a student's worldview any more than the Mathematics professor who believes 2 + 2 = 4 and teaches it as such infringes on the student's belief in relative truth. In this way, it is the very duty of the professor to present truth claims to students, but to do so in a way that asks the students to critically analyze those truth claims for themselves. If this is what we ask of professors in Mathematics, should this not also be what we expect of our professors in Religion?

Laying the Foundation

The basis on which we integrate faith and learning at DBU stems from our reading of Scripture. The Bible portrays the character of God and the standard by which we measure our lives. From it, we derive a responsibility to love learning and to teach charitably. Consequently, the foundation of integrating faith and learning in religion includes (1) the Genesis account, (2) the greatest commandment, (3) the commission of Christ, and (4) the example of Ezra.

The biblical account attributes creation to the work of God. It is in His nature to create, and it is His desire for His creatures to learn about Him through what He has created (Romans 1:20). The book of

Genesis records that God created humanity for the purpose of ruling over the creatures of the earth (1:26) and that after having created them, He gave them the first command to subdue creation (1:28). Subduing and ruling require a level of learning about the fish and birds and living things over which they were to exercise dominion, not to mention the plants, trees, and seeds that were given to them for food (1:29). Learning about creation was a means of exercising faith in the God who created and entered into relationship with them. Thus, from the genesis of time and life itself, learning and faith were inseparable. So indivisible were they that they comprised all those first humans knew of their religion. They simply learned from a position of faith out of obedience to their religion. At DBU, faith and learning are like the treble and bass clefs on the sheet music of religion, together harmonizing in a spiritual song of pedagogy.

The Gospel of Mark records the story of a scribe asking Jesus to identify the greatest commandment. But Jesus, the greatest teacher, weds two commands in one: "The foremost is, 'HEAR ISRAEL! THE LORD IS OUR GOD, THE LORD IS ONE; AND YOU SHALL LOVE THE LORD YOUR GOD WITH ALL YOUR HEART, AND WITH ALL YOUR SOUL, AND WITH ALL YOUR MIND, AND WITH ALL YOUR STRENGTH.' The second is this, 'YOU SHALL LOVE YOUR NEIGHBOR AS YOURSELF.' There is no other commandment greater than these" (Mark 12:29–31 [NASB]). The scribe would have immediately recognized this first commandment from his own sacred texts. As a Jewish boy, he would have grown up hearing and reciting the *Shema* from the book of Deuteronomy (6:4). But a careful inspection by our modern eyes reveals that Jesus added, or rather drew out, a component part of the holistic expression of love for God. He said, "With all your *mind*." Imbedded in the *Shema* was the idea of loving God intellectually, and yet Jesus perceives the need to remind this scribe, this "teacher" of the Law, that love of God includes an intellectual expression as worship. For Jesus, the greatest commandment is to love God holistically, an expression that includes engaging the mind and activating the intellect. I am sure for the scribe of the Law this was a sobering reminder, if not slight rebuke, from the brightest rabbi explaining the greatest commandment that intimately weds loving God with intellectual pursuit. Dare we say this is evidence from the Master Teacher Himself of a level of such deep integration of faith and learning that it finds expression in love of God? At DBU, we think so.

One of the final commands of Jesus before His ascension into Heaven is known as the Great Commission: "Go, therefore, and make disciples of all the nations, baptizing them in the name of the Father and the Son and the Holy Spirit, teaching them to follow all that I commanded you" (Matthew 28:19–20a [NASB]). Standing atop a mountain in Galilee the carpenter suggests to His fishermen several ways to express their religious conviction. The litmus test that they are truly His disciples is if they reproduce, if they make other disciples of Jesus. Then having made such disciples, they are commanded to teach those disciples obedience to the statutes and standards of their Savior. Once again, we see here the integration of faith and learning in the expression of religion. The disciples express their faith through teaching. But numbness to the intellectual enterprise is not their goal. Rather it is a persuasion, a plea yielding obedience to the commands of Christ both within the teacher and the taught. The recipient of such impassioned religious teaching receives the faith channeled through the learning of all that Jesus commanded. Our goal at DBU is nothing short of obedience to Christ, fulfilling His commission in our classroom.

In the Old Testament, we learn of a scribe named Ezra living in exile in Babylonian captivity who longed to return to Jerusalem to restore the city of Zion to its former glory. The scribe was a priest "skilled in the Law of Moses" (Ezra 7:6 [NASB]) teaching the commands of God to anyone ignorant of them, according to the edict of the king no less (Ezra 7:25). Yet it was not hubris that characterized this priest, but humility for the book of Ezra states, "Ezra had set his heart to study the Law of the Lord, and to do it and to teach his statutes and rules in Israel" (Ezra 7:10 [ESV]). Before the thought ever occurred to Ezra to teach others, he first set to learn for himself. Then having studied, he determined to model the message he taught by practicing it religiously.

Ezra authors the manual for integrating faith and learning in religion. His faith drove him to learn for himself. His faith compelled him to teach his religion to others. And his teaching became a seamless woven fabric of religion; one could not ascertain where the learning ended, and the faith began. Ezra's example sets the tempo and the tone for religion professors at DBU. Like Ezra, those who teach religion must demonstrate unquestionable Christian character and a Christ-like attitude. They must be an active member in their local church. Consequently, they are exercising their spiritual gifts and serving their fellow man both within the church and beyond to the community. They are seeking to study and purposing to practice their religion sufficiently before attempting to teach it to students. And like Ezra, their faith informs their teaching of religion in such a way that the pupil learning the religion is persuaded to believe.

Applying Holmes's Approach

Of all the disciplines one might teach in a setting of higher education, religion courses house the greatest potential to employ Arthur Holmes's fourfold approach to the integration of faith and learning. Holmes's Attitudinal, Ethical, Foundational, and Worldview Approaches have as their goal the holistic engagement and change in every dimension of the student's life and character, until every intellectual segment on the learning continuum is supersaturated by faith-infused teaching. Using DBU as a case study, this section will investigate practical ways to integrate faith and learning using Holmes's approach in the classrooms of religious studies.

Attitudinal Approach

The Attitudinal Approach is explored first since the professor's attitude is likely the first point of contact between a student and Christianity in the study of religion. The attitude of the professor walking into the classroom broadcasts to the students in a trailer-teaser format the study of the religion. The continued performance of that attitude throughout the semester solidifies the students' star ratings of religious studies, as it is played out in this reality TV format that we call the classroom. To be successful, complete congruence between the professor's attitude and the curriculum's content is necessary. Luckily for us, the very content the professor teaches calls for such an attitude.

For instance, in the RELI 4307 Gospels course, we trace the life and ministry of Jesus of Nazareth. Because this course is designed for fourth-year college students, we explore exhaustively the characteristics of Jesus, one of which is the person of Jesus as a teacher, a master teacher. Throughout the fourfold Gospel, Jesus modeled the message He taught. The same Rabbi who taught that God the Father functions like a shepherd pursuing a lost sheep (Luke 15:3–7), Himself took time, even going out of His way, to show compassionate care for the marginalized in society (John 4:4–7). The same Teacher who explained a terrifying final judgment of unrighteousness in the eschaton (Matthew 24–25), Himself zealously drove out with a whip the unrighteous from the Temple (John 2:13–17). The congruence between the messenger's actions and the message itself is unparalleled. Learning from His example, the professor of RELI 4307 adopts the approach of Jesus and showcases the message via his own attitude. And since the message of the RELI 4307's content is "Come to Me, all who are weary and burdened, and I will give you rest" (Matthew 11:28 [NASB]), the professor's attitude is one of tender concern for the well-being of the student. Part of Holmes's Attitudinal Approach is consequently achieved when there is no disconnect between the content being taught and the Christian teaching it. In this case, faith is integrated in the teaching process via the attitude especially, because the curriculum itself demands that such faith emanate from the one teaching it.

But this is only part of the attitudinal goal. While the professor can integrate faith in the teaching, the Attitudinal Approach is fully achieved when the student learns the content from a faith-infused position. This does not necessarily mean the student must believe the curriculum at the same level as that of the professor's faith in order to achieve true integration, though that might be the case. Rather, it means the student learns the content from an attitudinal perspective that is consistent with the manner in which it was taught. Assuming that the teacher has modeled the message, the approach is realized when the student's attitude toward learning synchronizes with both the faith of the professor and the curriculum's content. This means for RELI 4307 that the student's attitude in learning aligns with the Gospel's calling toward Christlikeness. As we have explored above, that Christlikeness includes viewing the intellectual enterprise as a way to express love. Considering the Attitudinal Approach only comes full circle after the student has caught what we have taught, we can measure the success of our approach when the student's learning of the religious content becomes a means of their loving others better.

Ethical Approach

When teaching religion courses at DBU, the Ethical Approach can be addressed from two vantage points: first is the ethical conduct of the professor and second is the cultivation of ethics in the student. Regarding the latter, the survey courses (RELI 1301 and RELI 1302) are a prime opportunity to raise awareness of moral dilemmas and begin crafting within the student a cohesive and comprehensive response to ethical situations. The Old Testament Survey course encounters any number of critical issues such as genocide and just war theory, polygamy and sexuality, abortion and welfare, capital punishment and anarchy to name a few. In the New Testament Survey course, we broach subjects like discrimination and nepotism, harassment and personal vengeance, lawsuits, and bribes for instance. These are extremely complex topics. Though we wish we could forge a simple answer, we often walk away having merely scratched the surface. They are emotionally personal to us. While remaining objective throughout the discussion is ideal, it is often unrealistic. But then again, our goal is not to have the moral matter resolved at the end of the discussion; rather our goal is to expose the student to the inherent morality of so many subjects while helping the student begin forming a coherent response to these issues. And the formation of that response must come from the curriculum itself—the Bible. Thus, faith is integrated into learning since the curriculum raises awareness of the ethical issue while it simultaneously provides the answer to the moral dilemma.

In these Survey courses, inevitably the professor will have to deal with the subject of death, final judgment, and the afterlife. A professor disproportionately concerned about her standing on *Rate My Professors* might shy away from teaching the unsavory news that those who reject God perish in an eternal hellfire. Far from gaining favor among students who disagree, it might have a direct negative effect on her ratings. And yet the morality of the professor that bids her extrapolate the full gamut of the subject including the positive benefits and negative consequences of the matter, fashions within the student an ethical mindset to treat the whole matter honestly for faithfulness to the subject, rather than shirk for fear of man. The Ethical Approach takes the two threads of (1) the ethical conduct of the professor and (2) the cultivation of the student's moral framework and weaves them together on the loom of faith and learning forming an ethical tapestry that cannot be unraveled; unhemming the former forfeits the latter.

Foundational Approach

When teaching religion courses at DBU, the Foundational Approach requires the least exegesis among Holmes's fourfold approach due to several belief thresholds: the Bible is true, humans are created in the *imago Dei*, God desires a relationship with humankind, that relationship drives humans to excel. This is not an exhaustive list, but it does serve as a framework from which to begin our discussion. Because we start our classes based on belief in the Bible, we explore its contents in the religion courses to give meaning to life, direction on decision making, accurate accounts of historical events, description of our roles on earth, etc. The self-disclosure of God from within the contents of the Bible forms the foundation of all other disciplines we study. If we did not believe the Bible, all other subject matters would be suspect. For example, we explore history (RELI 4370–4373) highlighting the cultural, scientific, artistic, and other societal contributions by prominent historical figures whose Christian faith and belief in God propelled them toward advancement and human flourishing. This foundational lens by which we train students to view history even led us to create a course (RELI 4360) and write a book[2] on the church reformation figure Martin Luther and his advancements to law, economics, church-state relations, and music among others. This example is merely one offshoot of integrating faith and learning in religious studies when we approach the subject from Holmes's foundational perspective.

Worldview Approach

In religious studies, the prior three approaches are certainly imbedded within Holmes's final, Worldview Approach. But the Worldview Approach itself moves further still toward a comprehensive perspective in the study of religion. Developing the worldview in the mind of the student is so valued in the Religion Department, we have classes whose purpose is to explore the biblical worldview against the backdrop of other religions. For instance, the Christian Worldview course (RELI 3374) lays the foundations of biblical themes such as creation, fall, and redemption. Then building upon those foundations, the course explores their implications to every aspect of life including family, education, and the arts. In essence, the course puts students through a spiritual refraction test. Then having measured their vision, it prescribes corrective biblical lenses through which the student can see the world and all its interconnectivity. With this new set of God glasses, students consider how the biblical worldview compares to and differentiates itself from other religions in Christianity in a Pluralistic World (RELI 4345). There, we explore the intersect of these religions and how our faith speaks into the others. This is integration of faith and learning at the rudimentary level. By investigating the basic worldview questions of various faiths, students begin to understand how faith informs all of life, not the least learning about life!

For Christians, this should not come as a shock. The book of 1 Corinthians commands the early church believers to glorify God "whether

[2] David Cook, ed., *Luther on Leadership: Leadership Insights From the Great Reformer* (Eugene, OR: Wipf and Stock, 2017).

you eat or drink, or whatever you do" (10:31 [NASB]). If something so elementary as eating or drinking should be conducted in a way that glorifies God, how much more the complex matters of life. In fact, 1 Corinthians perceives there is no real or potential act committed at the exclusion of faith's infusion. If all can be done in a way that glorifies God, then nothing is exempt from faith integration. Moreover, the book of Romans commands a mental makeover for believers: "Do not be conformed to this world, but be transformed by the renewing of your mind" (Romans 12:2 [NASB]). In our religious studies courses, we apply this text through the Christian Doctrine (RELI 2304) and the Systematic Theology (RELI 4350) courses. Through these courses, students are learning a new way to think, a transformative way of thinking biblically.

But it is not just the upper-level courses specifically designed for worldview exposure that accomplish Holmes's Worldview Approach. It occurs on the granular level of the genre and category specific courses we offer, which acclimate students to various *Weltanschauung* questions. From the interaction in these courses, students begin building a framework for life and purpose and beginning and end. The professor teaches a holistic approach to the Bible forming a biblical worldview, an approach that begins connecting Paul to the Pentateuch, or the Gospels to the Major Prophets, or the Historical Books to the General Epistles. The approach demonstrates a grander metanarrative of God's plan for humanity, a plan that bids the student participate. By echoing that call through his teaching, the professor's faith inundates the learning process, thereby making the student the blessed beneficiary of the Worldview Approach.

Reaping the Benefits

At this point you might be wondering, "How do I know if I'm successfully integrating faith and learning?" and, "How would I even measure that?" Over the past eight years of teaching religion courses at DBU, I have discovered two metrics, both initiated by the student, that help gauge the success of faith/learning integration: post-lecture informal inquiries and formal mentoring requests. Both of these metrics might be tracked quantitatively with semester-to-semester percentages demonstrating an uptick (or reversal) in student inquiries and mentoring requests, but I have just measured them anecdotally over the years. Allow me to explain. I am more prone to consider a lecture "successful" based upon the immediate, post-lecture questions I get from students as I am transitioning from the end of one class to the start of another. I have found that in these settings, students are mostly, genuinely interested in the follow-up question or conversation they initiate. None of their peers are around to impress. And they know per my syllabus I do not give extra points, so that eliminates any possibility of schmoozing for bonus points. Additionally, given the way I organize assessments in my classes, these types of questions posited by students are not about assignments, rather they orient around the implementation and application of the material studied. To use Holmes's nomenclature, their questions speak to the Ethical and Worldview Approaches. The higher the frequency of such questions from any particular student and/or the greater number of questions from multiple students are for me a certain measure of successful integration of faith and learning.

In addition to this are the formal mentoring requests I receive from students. This metric is less helpful than the former given the restraints I impose on it: I mentor at most two students per semester, and I do not mentor the student who is currently enrolled in my class—he must wait until the following semester to be mentored. So, tracking this metric quantitatively poses more difficulties. Still, the volume of students who ask and the subsequent follow-up after the semester ends so we might begin our formal mentoring relationship helps me see that Holmes's Attitudinal Approach hit its mark on two grounds: (1) the student desires to learn further from the professor who modeled the message and (2) the student himself adopts the attitude of loving via learning.

The above measurement tools track the benefits of integrating faith and learning in religion courses but from a professor's perspective. So, I thought it would be helpful to hear from student stories as well. Their first-hand testimony would either corroborate my observations or overturn my conclusions. After interviewing three of them, thankfully, it was the former. To gain these perspectives, I interviewed three students who recently took my New Testament Survey class. I specifically chose them to interview because they represent a broad range on the continuum of exposure to the Christian religion generally and the New Testament particularly. One was a practicing Hindu from India. It was her first semester in the U.S.A. studying at DBU. While in India, she had practically only heard whispers of the Christian faith. This course was her first real introduction to Jesus. The second student had, only the semester before, made a profession of faith and became a Christian. While he received some introduction to Christianity in the past, it was equivalent to the biannual pilgrimage to church for Easter and Christmas services. This class served as his "crash course" in Christianity. The third student was further along in her faith journey. She grew up Lutheran and had recently come to DBU. The semester prior to my class, she began taking her faith seriously. Accountability groups challenged her, and she found herself desiring to "go deeper" and flesh out the implications of her faith in daily life. This course was the biggest influence on her life to take her faith to "the next level."

The goal of my interviews was to ascertain if the way I had taught the curriculum compelled them to believe the content itself, resulting either in salvation for the skeptic or sanctification for the saint. In other words, had I integrated faith and learning? Did some combination of my use of Holmes's fourfold approach to integrating faith and learning resonate with the student? And in their own words, what did that look like?

From my interview with the first student, I concluded that the Attitudinal Approach was most effective. The fact that I taught with conviction and belief in the curriculum itself impressed this student to listen and learn. Back in India, if a student were to ask a teacher about Christianity (which rarely happened), the teacher would google the question and simply read the answer from the internet. This student commented, "You would read from the Bible, and would rather us read the Bible ourselves, to answer questions because you believe what the Bible says." At the conclusion of the semester, this student did not believe the New Testament content. But she respected what it said because she had learned it from someone who modeled what it taught.

Based upon the second student's responses to my questions, I would say that the Attitudinal and Ethical Approaches struck a chord. Throughout the interview, the second student often compared my lectures to sermons, my communication style to preaching, and my responses related to questions about "life issues" to the responses given by his pastor. In fact, he confessed that most of the deep learning that took place for him in the classroom was when I would go "off script" to address life application questions or current cultural concerns. Interestingly, he made a comparison between the classroom and chapel services: "The purpose of chapel is to develop the spirit and soul and that is what was happening in the classroom." And yet, a glance at the course description of New Testament Survey reveals that is not its purpose.[3] What can we conclude from this? This student was being exposed in the classroom to the same Christianity he received in the church. To him, there was no disconnect. The same ethical admonition he heard in the church from his pastor was echoed in the classroom by his professor. This is a sign that teaching in the classroom went beyond dissemination of information; it struck the very heart of the intersect of faith and learning.

Lastly, it was clear from the third student's reflections on the class, the Worldview Approach was front and center. From her perspective, I spent more time talking about "life issues" than I did the lecture notes over which students were examined. In fact, she remarked that "sometimes the emphasis on how to live your life and apply it could be a bit overbearing." That comment, though perhaps with a negative connota-

[3] "A survey of the literature, events, and message of the New Testament, including the organization and basic geography of the New Testament. Students will also be exposed to the key events in the life of Christ, the historical context of the intertestamental period, how the promise of the Old Testament Messianic hope is fulfilled in the New Testament, and the progression of the Gospel through the life and ministry of Paul." "RELI 1302 (3–3–0) New Testament Survey," Catalog Fall 22—Summer 23, Dallas Baptist University, accessed June 19, 2022, https://archive-catalog-dbu-22-23.coursedog.com/undergrad/courses/reli.

tion, has "Worldview Approach" written all over it. But if that sounded like a criticism, her next comment was an encouragement: "New Testament Survey was the biggest influence on my life of understanding the Christian faith." This combination of understanding both the tenets of the Christian faith and their application to daily life is a sure indicator of successfully integrating faith and learning via the Worldview Approach.

Conclusion

The professor of religion has an important task in imparting both knowledge about the Bible and in modeling how to have faith in God and His Word. As opposed to professors at secular universities, who may teach the Bible merely from the standpoint of literary criticism, we believe it is vital that DBU professors integrate their faith into the very teaching of the Bible as God's inspired Word. The role our religion professors play is critical, as it teaches students not just how to study the Bible, but how to live it out in their daily lives. Our great hope is that this integration of faith and learning leaves a lasting impact on the students who take our religion courses.

Chapter 12

Integrating Faith in General Education

By Mary K. Flickner[1]

Introduction

Perhaps you have read the oft-quoted epigraph attributed to Greek philosopher Archimedes: "Give me a lever long enough and a fulcrum on which to place it, and I shall move the world." This ancient wisdom is reflected in a less erudite story of a farmer and his horse. One day a farmer was cajoling his stubborn horse to get into a trailer. Much time had passed, and many tactics had proven ineffective. The farmer, now emotionally charged and physically exhausted, was stomping, sweating, and swearing. Meanwhile, an old man was passing down the road while munching on an apple. And he, being full of wisdom born out of life experience, tossed his apple into the trailer and continued on his way. With his back turned and a smile breaking across his face, he listened to the steady clop of horse hooves on the metal ramp leading into the trailer. Whether you prefer highbrow Greek philosophy or commonplace farmer tales, the underlying message is the same—work within the nature of a thing and you can move the unmovable.

In this brief introduction, I have used some stories to prime your imagination for a picture I will now paint. Imagine this. You are teaching a general studies course. This means students at your institution *have to* take your class in order to complete a degree, but the course is

[1] Mary Flickner serves as Director of General Education and Assistant Professor of Developing a Christian Mind at Dallas Baptist University.

not explicitly connected to that degree. It is nonvocational. You pass out the syllabus and look at a sea of faces and you know what they are thinking: tick the box, jump through the hoop, get in and out and move on. Those of us who teach general studies courses are confronted with indifference, which often manifests as deep resistance to learning.

Educator Eva Brann acknowledges the reality we face in our classrooms. Often our young people are "obscured by *accidie*,"[2] or apathetic indifference. But, Brann poses a counterbalance to this reality: "teachers know and gamble on [their students'] underlying love of learning."[3] In other words, when we teach, we say with Aristotle that "all human beings by nature desire to know."[4] Although we may face a classroom full of young adults who are like the stubborn horse, unwilling to engage with the ideas we put before them, we are going to move the unmovable by leveraging a certain understanding of the human person as a learner.

In the pages that follow, I hope to cast a vision for general education that is in essence what Black intellectual William E. B. Du Bois called the "drawing out of human powers," but place that educative work within a biblical epistemology.[5] First, I will survey the origin and purpose of general education. For those who teach and administrate in this space, it is helpful to know the perennial value (and robust history) of the general education tradition, historically derived from the liberal arts. Second, I will explain what is meant by a biblical epistemology and how this undergirds our approach to general education at DBU. Finally, I will share the story of one general education class that has shaped our institutional approach to the integration of faith and learning. By the conclusion of these pages, I hope your own imagination considers fresh ways to design courses and teach students. As a Christian academ-

---

[2] Eva Brann, *Paradoxes of Education in a Republic* (Chicago, IL: University of Chicago Press, 1979), 49.

[3] Ibid., 59. The context for this statement is Brann's consideration of a paradox: liberal education is both a good end in itself *and* a means to the end of living a good life. Liberal education is therefore a utility, but not *merely* a utility.

[4] Aristotle, *The Works of Aristotle*, vol. 8, *Metaphysics*, ed. and trans. David Ross. (Oxford, UK: Clarendon Press, 1963).

[5] William E. B. Du Bois, *The Education of Black People: Ten Critiques, 1906–1960* (New York, NY: Monthly Review Press, 2001), 25.

ic community, may we intentionally work in response to God as the Creator and Redeemer of learners and learning.[6]

The Purpose of General Education

There is a consensus that American colleges and universities aim to prepare persons to live and lead well in society. We could trace this historical purpose to the fourth century B.C.E. on the steps of Plato's Academy, but I will assume that timeline would be too cumbersome for our purposes here. Instead, let's begin on the shores of North America. Prior to America's founding, King George III petitioned wealthy Englishmen to send funds to the colonies to finance colleges because of the needed education and skills higher education provided.[7] The colonies did indeed found colleges. By 1781, two years prior to the Treaty of Paris and King George's surrender, the institutions we know as Harvard, William and Mary, Yale, Princeton, Columbia, Brown, Dartmouth, Rutgers, and the University of Pennsylvania had opened their doors.[8] These colleges existed to form persons who would live well in the world and lead their communities.

This commitment to whole person formation has persisted, but there has never been agreement on how that formation is best achieved. In our pragmatic American society, we often equate living well in the world with securing a lucrative job or possessing vocational skills that advance society. Take for example the burgeoning higher education landscape of the early 19th century. As industrialization and Progressive ideals swept the country, a smattering of new institutions populated the landscape. From large research institutions to smaller religiously affiliated colleges and historically Black colleges, Americans reimagined what constituted living well in the world and how greater numbers of Americans could access the type of formation postsecondary education

---

6 Todd C. Ream and Perry L. Glanzer, *The Idea of a Christian College: A Reexamination for Today's University* (Eugene, OR: Cascade Books, 2013), 11.

7 As cited in Frederick Rudolph, *The American College and University: A History* (Athens, GA: University of Georgia Press, 1990), 12–13.

8 John R. Thelin, *A History of American Higher Education*, 3rd ed. (Baltimore, MD: Johns Hopkins, 2019), 1.

promised.[9] Often the elite, aristocratic liberal arts approach was pitted against an education better suited to the world of research and work.[10] Herein lies a perennial tension in our cultural understanding of what college is supposed to do. On the one hand, we view higher education as contributing to the formation of a citizen. On the other hand, we view higher education as preparing that citizen to work.

To underscore this tension, consider the very public debate between Booker T. Washington and William E. B. Du Bois. Both men passionately argued for Black Americans to assume full citizenship following their emancipation from slavery. Washington, as demonstrated at his Tuskegee Institute, valued vocational training and economic independence, stating that "the opportunity to earn a dollar in a factory right now is worth infinitely more than the opportunity to spend a dollar at an opera-house."[11] In vehement opposition, Du Bois advocated for liberal arts training of Black leaders and argued that full citizenship required "self-development and self-realization in all lines of human endeavor."[12] Both men sought to articulate the type of formation best suited to living well in the world, particularly as a free citizen with full access to the rights and responsibilities of citizenship.

In her *Paradoxes of Education in a Republic*, Eva Brann takes up a similar idea, exploring the relationship between the rights of citizenship and education.[13] Brann sets forth two types of education: utilitarian and liberal. Utilitarian education is that which serves a desired end. Consider the example of Washington and Du Bois. Washington advocated

---

[9] For a robust account of the expansion and diversification of higher education in the 19th century, see Chapter 4 "Captains of Industry and Erudition: University-Builders, 1880 to 1910," in ibid.

[10] For two refutations of this idea that liberal arts learning is only for the elite, cf. William Damon and Margarita A. Mooney, "Every Child Has a Spark: The Tandem of Internal Motivation and Co-Learning," in *The Love of Learning: Seven Dialogues on the Liberal Arts*, ed. Margarita A. Mooney (Providence, RI: Cluny, 2021); Angel A. Parham and Anika Prather, *The Black Intellectual Tradition: Reading Freedom in Classical Literature* (Camp Hill, PA: Classical Academic Press, 2022).

[11] Booker T. Washington, *Up From Slavery: An Autobiography* (New York, NY: Doubleday, 1901), 224.

[12] William E. B. Du Bois, *The Education of Black People: Ten Critiques, 1906–1960*, ed. H. Aptheker (Millwood, NY: KTO Press, 1977), 5.

[13] Brann, *Paradoxes of Education*, 60.

for vocational training that would ensure economic independence. In this sense, one's education is a utility—it enables the ultimate end of economic independence. Brann argues that practicing education as a utility is "narrowly industrial, insofar as the worker does not realize his own ideas but by a mere routine produces a useful object."[14] Vocational training may equip a worker to gain economic independence, but is he fully formed as a free citizen if he has not formed his own ideas?

In contrast, liberal education is "free from the bonds of utility."[15] It is not education to some end; it is education as its own end. In *The Idea of a Christian College* Holmes defines liberal education as an "open invitation to join the human race and become more fully human."[16] Liberal education does not equip you to *do* something, but rather to *be* something—a better human![17] Brann argues that citizens in the American Republic must have a liberal education.[18] She concedes that one might live life and experience liberty without the intellectual development achieved through liberal learning, but to develop the human capacity to pursue happiness, to make accurate judgments of what is good and to pursue that goodness, liberal learning "is a near essential preparation."[19] In other words, a free person cannot pursue happiness if they do not know how to choose what is good, that which ultimately leads to happiness.

Understanding this distinction between utilitarian and liberal education is important because it helps us understand something about our institutions and something about our students. First, our institutions, particularly in America, have been shaped by this tension between utilitarian and liberal approaches. You may even hear remnants of the Washington-Du Bois debate in committee meetings at your institution as departments vie for funding and make their case for how students

---

[14] Ibid.

[15] Ibid.

[16] Holmes, *The Idea of a Christian College*, 35.

[17] Ibid., 29.

[18] Brann sets her argument inside America's founding document that promises life, liberty, and the pursuit of happiness.

[19] Brann, *Paradoxes of Education*, 63.

are best prepared for a successful life after graduation. In large part, colleges and universities have attempted to resolve this tension through their general studies requirements.[20] In 1947 the Truman administration published a *Report of the President's Commission on Higher Education*, making an appeal for general education:

> Today's college graduate may have gained technical or professional training in one field of work or another, but is only incidentally, if at all, made ready for performing his duties as a man, a parent, and a citizen...
>
> The crucial task of higher education today, therefore, is to provide a unified general education for American youth. Colleges must find the right relationship between specialized training on the one hand, aiming at a thousand different careers, and the transmission of a common cultural heritage toward a common citizenship on the other...
>
> "General education" is the term that has come to be accepted for those phases of nonspecialized and nonvocational learning which should be the common experience of all educated men and women.
>
> ...general education is not sharply distinguishable from liberal education; the two differ mainly in degree, not in kind...General education is liberal education with its matter and method shifted from its original aristocratic intent to the service of democracy. General education seeks to extend to all men the benefits of an education that liberates.[21]

In other words, colleges and universities may train students for vocations, but they also have a particular duty to prepare whole persons who handle their liberty well. In his defense of liberal arts learning,

[20] According to Derek Bok, *The Struggle to Reform our Colleges* (Princeton, NJ: Princeton University Press, 2017), 22; David Schejbal, "The Core and the Adult Student," in *The Great Skills Gap: Optimizing Talent for the Future of Work*, ed. Jason Wingard and Christine Farrugia (Stanford, CA: Stanford University Press, 2021), 132. American institutions have maintained a commitment to some form of liberal arts learning, or general studies requirements.

[21] George F. Zook, ed., *Higher Education for American Democracy: A Report of the President's Commission on Higher Education*, vol. 1, *Establishing the Goals* (New York, NY: Harper, 1947), 49.

Richard A. Detweiler clarifies this duty as "serv[ing] the higher, common good—the needs of both the individual and society—through the formation of a responsible adult."[22] Liberal learning is the *raison d'être* for general education—that set of required courses that every student takes and that set of required courses that are uniquely tasked with developing responsible adults.

In addition to helping us understand our institutions, and how general education fulfills a primary duty of higher education, differentiating between liberal and utilitarian learning is also valuable because the distinction helps us understand something about our students. Remember the picture I painted in the introduction? Our students are looking at us and many are thinking: tick the box, jump through the hoop, get in and out and move on. They are thinking these thoughts because they see each class as a utility. They see their degree as a utility. Many hold what Harvard researchers Wendy Fischman and Howard Gardner call a transactional mental model of college, meaning "one goes to college and does what (and *only* what) is required to get a degree and then secure placement in graduate school and/or a job."[23] Yet utility is not at all the point of general education! General education requirements are aimed at capacity building such that our students gain what the often-quoted Yale Report of 1828 called sufficient "*discipline* and *furniture* of the mind."[24] Northeastern president, Joseph Aoun uses similar language when advocating for higher education that is robot-proof. He speaks of education as "is its own reward, equipping us with the mental furniture to live a rich, considered existence."[25] Fischman and Gardner argue that all college graduates should develop "the capacity to attend, analyze, reflect, connect, and communicate effectively," that the purpose of college is "to *create or amplify intellectual capital that ideally should*

[22] Richard A. Detweiler, *The Evidence Liberal Arts Needs* (Cambridge, MA: MIT Press, 2021), 36.

[23] Wendy Fischman and Howard Gardner, *The Real World of College: What Higher Education Is and What It Can Be* (Cambridge, MA: MIT Press, 2022), 121.

[24] Yale College, *Reports on the Course of Instruction in Yale College: By a Committee of the Corporation, and the Academical Faculty* (New Haven, CT: Hezekiah Howe, 1828), para 8.

[25] Joseph E. Aoun, *Robot-Proof: Higher Education in the Age of Artificial Intelligence* (Cambridge, MA: MIT Press, 2017), xvii.

last and be drawn upon for a lifetime."[26] This mental shift from education as a utility to education for freedom requires a certain conversion of thought, habit, and affection. But in order do this, we have to move our proverbial stubborn horses from the field of "education as utility" to the field of "education as person formation." Where is our apple?

Biblical Epistemology

To move the unmovable, we must know the nature of the thing. We also must understand the system we are operating inside of and leverage the resources available to us within that system to affect change. As Christian educators, we understand the system we operate inside of *and* the nature of our students, those immovable things, via a biblical epistemology. Several of my colleagues allude to this term in their chapters, so it is a common theme running throughout this book. I like the definition of epistemology that Mark Cook uses in his chapter on leadership: "Epistemology is the branch of philosophy that tries to make sense out of knowledge, rationality, and justified or unjustified beliefs."[27] Cook brings this into a common vernacular: "epistemology has to do with what 'counts' as knowledge."[28] For the Christian, this means we will "count" something as true knowledge within the parameters of reality as set by the revealed Word of God, the Scriptures.

Let me use a familiar story to illustrate this idea. In Genesis, we are privy to interactions between the Creator God and created man. These interactions tell us something about what "counts" as true knowledge in the material world. In the first vignette, we find God instructing Adam: "You may surely eat of every tree of the garden, but of the tree of the knowledge of good and evil you shall not eat, for in the day that you eat of it you shall surely die."[29] There is knowledge of good. There is knowledge of evil. There are also pathways of discerning what is good and not good, two to be precise. One of those pathways is false and will lead

[26] Fischman and Gardner, *The Real World of College*, 67.

[27] Moreland and Craig, *Philosophical Foundations*, 17.

[28] In the current work, Mark Cook, "Integrating Faith in Leadership Studies."

[29] Gen. 2:16–17 (ESV).

to death. This false way of "counting" what is true knowledge involves Adam orienting himself to the material world via the material world by taking fruit from the forbidden tree. This way aligns with Charles Taylor's understanding of our lives as taking place within a self-sufficient order where human reason judges accurately and this present time is all that *really* exists.[30]

The second pathway of knowing can be seen in the next vignette when the Creator God parades animals before Adam to make Adam aware of the not good: "It is not good that the man should be alone… there was not found a helper fit for him." [31] Here we see good and not good both present in creation. But how are good and not good discerned? It is God's wisdom that determines good and not good. It is important for us to see that God uses Adam's faculties of observation in the material world, but it is God's wisdom that ultimately makes moral sense of those observations. Incidentally, this vignette ends with God giving Adam a "helper fit for him." Her name is Eve, which plays off the Hebrew word for life-giver.

At DBU, we want to discern reality based upon the Scriptures. We want to observe the world around us but look to our faith commitments to make moral sense of those observations. As David Naugle wrote in his 2002 commentary on our DBU Mission Statement:

> Given the fundamental religious nature of human persons, DBU recognizes that education is not undertaken in an unbiased, objective manner, but is always governed by the previous commitments and control beliefs embraced by the scholarly community…there is not such a thing as presuppositionless scholarship, teaching, or learning…
>
> Thus, for DBU, the phrase "integrating faith and learning" refers to the scholarly activity in which the fundamental doctrines of the Christian faith—God, creation, humanity, sin, and redemption—serve as the theological and philosophical starting points by which the various disciplines are studied, appreciated, critiqued, and developed. The

[30] Taylor, *A Secular Age*, 542–43.
[31] Gen. 2:18, 20 (ESV).

> integration of faith and learning, which may be better termed the "integration of Christian theology and learning," is the pursuit of academic study within the framework of the assumptions and presuppositions of the biblical worldview.[32]

In other words, we are going to count as true the parameters of reality as communicated in the Scriptures. As we consider the specific aims of general education programs and courses, and as we devise pedagogies that will convert our students to embrace liberal learning, we are wise to think inside a biblical system. Just as Archimedes moves the world by thinking inside a physical system and just as our farmer moves the stubborn horse by thinking inside a system of equine psychology, so we will best engage our students when we educate "persons as persons," or in accord with how God has created human beings to live, learn, and act in the world.[33]

A Biblical Foundation for General Education

If education at its core is concerned with drawing out human powers, as Du Bois said, or with developing persons as persons, as Holmes said, how are we to understand the essence of a person? In his treatise, *Education at the Crossroads*, French philosopher Jacques Maritain argues that "education needs primarily to know what man *is*, what is the nature of man."[34] He further explains that defining a person scientifically cannot inform the education process because science relies upon observation and measurement. The entirety of a person cannot be observed via the senses or finitely measured. Therefore, Maritain argues, a person must be understood scientifically, philosophically, and religiously. The human person must be understood "in relation to God and the special gifts and trials and vocations involved."[35]

32 Naugle, "Commentary," 8.

33 Holmes, *The Idea of a Christian College*, 27.

34 Jacques Maritain, *Education at the Crossroads* (New Haven, CT: Yale University Press, 1943), 5.

35 Ibid., 6.

Holmes captures a holistic view of persons when he defines them as reflective, valuing, and responsible agents in the world. A person is reflective because she observes the world, looks for connections, and systematizes her understanding. A person is valuing because he has a sense of justice, an eye for beauty, and an instinct to delineate between right and wrong. These reflective and valuing capacities form a person to act responsibly in the world. To use an earlier example from Genesis, Adam observes the animal kingdom and assigns names, presumably that capture different qualities and distinguish different species. He also observes his own lack of a female partner. In this instance, Adam is using his reflective capacities. But to say a lack of a female partner is not good is a valuing task. Still further, to live well, Adam will be responsible for the ways in which he relates to the material world, to his partner Eve, to future children, and to God Himself. A person is therefore reflective, valuing, and responsible. The nature of one's personhood then shapes one's interaction with the world.

Holmes's idea coincides with the biblical concept of humans being created in God's image, or *imago Dei*. Much print has been spent and many hairs split to interpret this rich concept, but I have found Walsh and Middleton's definition from their text, *The Transforming Vision*, to be the most helpful. They write, "Our creation in the image of God is related to two important biblical notions: our dominion or rule over the earth, and the religious choice of serving God or idols."[36] When we combine Holmes's description of persons as reflective, valuing, and responsible agents with Walsh's and Middleton's idea that persons are made for dominion and religious choice, we see how important Christian education is to God's human project. Humans are made for responsible action in the world, but that responsible action is impossible without the formation of reflective and valuing capacities that are rightly oriented to God as the source of all truth. God has created the human person for dominion in the world. Rightly understood, human dominion is akin to stewardship. God has created the human person

[36] Walsh and Middleton, *The Transforming Vision*, 53.

for stewardship in the world and we can either steward the world well or poorly based upon the quality of our reflective and valuing capacities. For Christian educators, this is a compelling reason to advocate for robust and intentional core curricula! If general education is that which "forms a responsible adult" who will "serve the higher, common good—the needs of both the individual and society," then helping our students see that their general education experience is equipping them for effective stewardship is essential.[37]

Learning as Stewardship: Developing a Christian Mind

At DBU, we want *every* student to integrate faith and learning. We must therefore equip our students in the general education space with a framework for that integration and opportunities to practice. Throughout this book, you have had the opportunity to see how the integration of faith and learning plays out across academic disciplines, but it is important also to share how we provide our students with an initial framework for this integrative work in the general studies space.

Since 2004, DBU students have taken a course called "Developing a Christian Mind," known around campus as DCM, to learn a framework for their integrative practice across all their curricular and co-curricular experiences. A major aim of this course is to explore the biblical metanarrative of creation, fall, and redemption with our students so they might practice identifying themselves inside the biblical story. This story includes a fundamental understanding of persons as made in God's image for stewardship in the material world lived out under God's authority. We want our students to see that this view of the world and themselves in it will necessarily conflict with their cultural context. Yet, that tension is not at odds with biblical faith but rather a sign of biblical faith.[38] DCM supports students as they form an identity that both withstands pressures to conform to cultural norms as well as acts responsibly in the world for cultural renewal.

---

[37] Detweiler, *The Evidence Liberal Arts Needs*, 36.

[38] This idea of tension is beautifully explained in Michael W. Goheen and Craig G. Bartholomew, *Living at the Crossroads: An Introduction to Christian Worldview* (Grand Rapids, MI: Baker, 2008), 134.

As we explore the biblical story together, we build connections between the Bible's view of human identity and its teachings on work and purpose. We highlight passages like Genesis 1:28 where God's original design for the human project is revealed. But we also consider Jeremiah 29 when God's people find themselves in exile and Ephesians 2 when the gospel empowers our good works in the world. We make note of Jesus' prayer in Matthew 6, that He urges us to pray for God's will to be done on earth, in our midst, and not merely in Heaven. What does it mean to live inside of God's kingdom now even as we wait for God's kingdom to come later? DCM provides students an opportunity to ask this question and practice thinking about it inside the biblical story. The course further supplies students with an opportunity to think about their work as a vocation, as connected to their faith practice rather than a necessary part of life under the sun.

Perhaps you have noticed something about the design of this course and perhaps you are considering a unique strength of *Christian* general education. Recall that general education has been plagued by a perennial debate: are students prepared for life and leadership via liberal arts learning or via career development? Is a citizen one who thinks well or works well? The Christian looks to her epistemology and says, both. The Christian counts as true that she cannot live and lead well in the world apart from spiritual formation and this requires more than preparing specifically for a career. But the Christian also counts as true that he is made for work and his work will be a place of service to God and others.

Integrating faith and learning in the general studies space is the secret mojo of Christian institutions for two reasons. One, this integrative work connects the various academic disciplines that are part of the required core. As a result of his research into liberal arts learning, Detweiler noted that the value of "understanding the full range of knowledge" is diminished "unless one also understands connections among areas of knowledge."[39] A biblical epistemology that espouses God as the

[39] Detweiler, *The Evidence Liberal Arts Needs*, 83.

Creator of all things supplies a robust connection indeed! Second, this integrative work imbues general education courses with explicit purpose for students. Former Harvard president, Derek Bok lamented that too frequently students do not see relevance between a required course and their lives.[40] When we teach our students about the biblical story, how God has created them to learn and how essential learning is to their formation as whole persons working in a whole world, they start to see relevance.

Let me share an example. I was teaching a section of the DCM course and growing frustrated with disengaged and unprepared students. I assigned reading. My students were not reading, at least not with sufficient attention to then discuss ideas during class. I asked questions. My students answered the questions, sometimes, but with overly simplistic terms or unrelated ideas and illogical claims. In an attempt to show them what they were capable of as learners, I pulled out Bloom's Taxonomy and explained that learning *begins* with the recollection of basic facts; it does not *end* there. Several days later a student came to my office hours wanting help to become a better learner. She sat down, looked me in the eyes and said, "Bloom's Taxonomy convicted me. I am just doing what I need to do to scrape by. I now see there is so much more I can be doing. Otherwise, I'm not using the opportunity God gave me to prepare for life." Wow! My student was acquiring a new way of thinking by connecting her love for God with her study habits. Suddenly, I felt less like the frustrated farmer and more like the old man who threw an apple into the trailer and the stubborn horse walked up the ramp. My student engaged with her learning because she saw her identity and her work inside the biblical story.

[40] Bok, *The Struggle to Reform our Colleges,* 171.

Conclusion

Because this book is concerned with Holmes's rich description of the integration of faith and learning, it is appropriate to close with his statement that "Liberal arts education is the education of responsible agents for the vocation of life itself, life in all its parts and as a whole."[41] In their re-examination of Holmes's text for this new century, Todd Ream and Perry Glanzer remind us that God, Creator of all things, has invited us to join Him in His creative process, and this creating should extend into the realm of seeing seemingly mundane tasks as curriculum development.[42]

General education is broadly tasked with equipping students for life; this should be an area of intentional design for those of us working in Christian institutions. Our world is rapidly changing. We are wise to respond to those changes and prepare our students for meaningful participation in a global, technological, and complex world. We are wise to prepare our students for work. But we also recognize that preparing students for work necessarily involves their spiritual and moral formation. This is hard work. Our students have utility on the mind and often think we are wasting their time with general education requirements. As Christian educators, we just might find that the integration of faith and learning is the apple we need to engage our students with their own learning, with their own ethical development, and with a world that needs them.

---

[41] Holmes, *The Idea of a Christian College*, 38.
[42] Ream and Glanzer, *The Idea of a Christian College*, 36.

Part 2

Integrating Faith in the Broader Learning Environment of a Christian College

Chapter 13

Integrating Faith in Student Affairs and the Student Experience

By Jay Harley[1]

Introduction

For many college students, their university experience is marked by experiences outside the classroom. At Dallas Baptist University, the Student Affairs team views the time spent outside of class as pivotal moments in the lives of students. The time a student spends on campus while not in class can be leveraged for significant spiritual growth, academic development, leadership training, career development, and life skill growth. Learning by college students while on the university campus does not only occur in a traditional classroom but "occurs horizontally, across experiences in and out of the classroom, as well as vertically within majors and disciplines, and in ways that are necessarily cumulative."[2] At colleges and universities all over the United States, student development is often enhanced by programming and services that occur alongside or outside of the traditional classroom environment. Higher Education leaders recognize the value in the experience outside of the classroom and invest heavily in programs, services, events, and opportunities for students that are not for class credit. Colleges allocate these valuable financial, human, and facility resources toward supporting stu-

[1] Jay Harley serves as the Vice President for Student Affairs at Dallas Baptist University.

[2] Richard P. Keeling and Richard H. Hersh, *We're Losing Our Minds: Rethinking American Higher Education* (New York, NY: Palgrave Macmillan, 2012), 21.

dent life outside the classroom as they acknowledge the importance of providing a rich and fulfilling college experience. High school students also report they are interested in a school that has much to offer them outside of the classroom.[3] At the typical American college and university, full departments, offices, services, and programs exist to enhance a student's experience at the college or university. From the Christian college or university perspective, these programs and services should not only be about meeting the whims of prospective students and families but be intentionally connected to the school's mission and purpose.

These functional areas of the university may be identified by different names but share a similar hopeful outcome which is to engage the student in growth and development opportunities. For the purpose of this chapter, the term "Student Affairs" will be used as a primary name for the programming, services, and event functions at the University that are designed to support student development. The Student Affairs area at a university can serve as a crucial support system and resource hub for students, encompassing a wide range of services designed to enhance the overall student experience and promote their personal, academic, and professional growth. Its primary purpose is to foster a vibrant campus community, providing students with opportunities for engagement, leadership development, and meaningful connections with peers, faculty, and staff. Student Affairs strives to create a supportive environment where students can thrive by offering services such as counseling, career guidance, health and wellness programs, housing assistance, student organizations, and campus activities. At the Christian college or university, the Student Affairs area can also provide significant opportunities for student spiritual growth. Additionally, Student Affairs plays a pivotal role in advocating for student needs and ensuring their voices are heard within university life. By addressing students' holistic well-being and offering comprehensive support, Student Affairs plays a vital role in shaping a fulfilling and successful college journey

[3] Karen D'Souza, "Many High School Seniors Prefer High-Amenity Colleges, Survey Shows," News Update, Ed Source, June 22, 2022, https://edsource.org/updates/many-high-school-seniors-prefer-high-amenity-colleges-survey-shows.

for each student. The Student Affairs areas should be viewed as integral to the overall effectiveness of an institution of higher education. The important role of Student Affairs throughout the second half of the twentieth century and now into this century was identified as important by Dungy as she traced the historical engagement Student Affairs professionals have with students. She asserted, "With institutional mission as a foundation, and educating the whole student as a basic principle, student affairs has had a key role in addressing the perennial challenges facing higher education."[4]

As core to the higher education experience at the Christian college or university, a student should be exposed to and participate in coordinated and dynamic programs, ministries, and events that promote the values of a Christ-centered life. Student Affairs should promote the values and ideals of Christian discipleship, service, leadership development, cross-cultural experiences, physical wellness, and academic integrity and excellence. Focused programming in those areas will allow for holistic student development within the framework of the Christ-centered institution. The programs, events, services, and ministries of Student Affairs should be viewed as steps to seeing all students reaching maturity.

For students, the college years are a significant time of development where beliefs and values are formed, changed, abandoned, or solidified. The full college student experience encompasses more than just what occurs in the classroom. Students spend the majority of their lives outside of the classroom, and it is also likely that many of their significant relationships are with individuals who are not their professors. Student Affairs staff and leaders at Christian institutions should envision their roles as intimately connected to their work with students. A 2020 study of Student Affairs leaders at Christian colleges and universities discerned this from extensive research on Student Affairs leaders

[4] Gwendolyn J. Dungy, "Students and Student Affairs: Facing Perennial Challenges in Ever-Changing Contexts," *Change* 50, no. 4 (October 2018): 61.

at Christian institutions.[5] Through this research, it became clear that Student Affairs leaders recognized the vital role they played in helping students grow spiritually, and therefore, integrating Christian faith into their work occurred.[6] The research confirmed the work of Student Affairs leaders by stating, "All in all, this process involves teaching students to think, speak, and live theologically with a focus that relies upon God and not the ability to articulate the latest academic theory of cultural movement in higher education."[7] Therefore, a significant opportunity exists for student development outside of the classroom. According to this research, "At Christian universities SALs (Student Affairs Leaders) in particular are charged with bearing God's image and imitating Christ by modeling individual and corporate virtues, such as God's sacrificial love and mentoring, and discipling students to do the same."[8] Throughout the professional field of Student Affairs at Christian institutions of higher education, the professionals who work in these areas appreciate their place in the integration of faith and learning.

Is an Emphasis on Spirituality Needed on the College Campus?

Spiritual growth and development are not only the foci of religious institutions exclusively; many colleges and universities provide some component of spiritual development for students. With the present-day emphasis, the spiritual development and maturation of college students has been an important aspect of the college experience throughout the history of higher education. One of the earliest statements of practice and values for Student Affairs professionals in the United States was released in 1939 and represented the commitment to develop the whole person, which included the spiritual component.[9] While a spiritual focus

---

[5] Perry L. Glanzer, et al., *Christ-Enlivened Student Affairs: A Guide to Thinking and Practice in the Field* (Abilene, TX: ACU Press, 2020), 103–04.

[6] Ibid., 104.

[7] Ibid., 113.

[8] Ibid., 69.

[9] Arthur Sandeen and Margaret J. Barr, *Critical Issues for Student Affairs: Challenges and Opportunities* (New York, NY: John Wiley, 2014), 5.

is viewed as important across the Student Affairs profession, spirituality within higher education may not be synonymous with a Christian expression. Even with the devaluing of Christianity within higher education, higher education continues to be a place of spiritual searching, questioning, and maturation for students. During the late 19th century, a major transformation occurred within higher education in America that would seriously alter the Christian influence on the college campuses. Institutions were changing from the Christian liberal arts colleges to larger, research-focused universities. These changes affected the spiritual focus of the college campus as the Christian faith became less important and less broadcast in the classroom and on the campus.

In the earliest days of American higher education, the Church was the major controlling force on colleges and universities. However, during the 20th century, the university began to hold a more prominent place in society, replacing the local church as the most influential organization in America. These changes, therefore, obviously altered the religious focus of American colleges and universities, and faith was pushed to the margins or completely away from the campus.

Most schools of higher education were founded by church or denominational groups, and therefore, the spiritual component of higher education was built into the educational setting. Most of the earliest American colleges would have followed a model of truncation where the pious Christian faith was placed as the foundation and channel of all educational endeavors. Often, subjects that were not directly related to the Christian faith were not included in the early curriculum. "In nineteenth-century America, educational and theological orthodoxy almost always went together."[10] In the earliest days of America, "Each of the eight other colleges founded prior to the American Revolution shared the same broad sense of dual purpose as that enunciated by Harvard, namely, educating civic leaders and preparing a learned clergy."[11]

---

[10] Laurence Veysey, *The Emergence of the American University* (Chicago, IL: University of Chicago Press, 1965), 24.

[11] Christopher J. Lucas, *American Higher Education: A History* (New York, NY: Palgrave Macmillan, 2006), 105.

Students at these schools recognized the need for spiritual development outside of the classroom and started the earliest campus ministries in America that were known as Student Christian Societies. Examining these groups, "The interesting thing here is that students began to organize their own religious societies despite the fact that the first colleges themselves were founded by church bodies in the interest of providing resources to educate the clergy."[12] The reasons for the development of these groups were unknown by historians.[13] It should also be noted that during this same time period at Oxford University in England, John and Charles Wesley founded their Holy Club, which appeared to share many similarities with the early student Christian societies in the United States.[14] The lasting result of these societies was the American world missions movement.[15]

Spiritual Struggle of College Students

Higher education changed, and faith became unessential to the purpose of many modern American universities. Strategic plans, campus programming, and academic programs may have devalued a spiritual component, but research showed that students continued to wrestle with issues of spirituality. A significant study in this area, Bryant and Astin explored spirituality among college students and through their findings, specifically identified a phenomenon among college students that they called "spiritual struggle." Even though this study was conducted before the global pandemic of 2020 and 2021, the results provided needed insight for higher education leaders on religious faith and college students. The authors of the study defined spiritual struggle and stated, "Spiritual struggle is an experience familiar to many students whose college years are marked by reflections on faith, purpose, and life meaning and by efforts to understand the preponderance of suffer-

[12] Donald Shockley, *Campus Ministry: The Church Beyond Itself* (Louisville, KY: John Knox Press, 1989), 13.

[13] Samuel Sanford, *Baptist Campus Ministry at Crossroads: A Historical and Philosophical Perspective on Its Diamond Anniversary* (Franklin, TN: Providence House, 1997), 20.

[14] Shockley, *Campus Ministry*, 13.

[15] Sanford, *Baptist Campus Ministry at Crossroads*, 22.

ing, evil, and death in the world."[16] The specific focus of the broader study was the relationship between spiritual struggle and certain typical college environments or representative events in college students' lives. The results proved that a considerable number of college students indicated they faced spiritual struggles. As higher education leaders pushed spirituality away, college students are considering spiritual matters consistently.

Vital knowledge concerning the need for the spiritual development of college students was found from this study. One-fifth of the students in the study answered that they frequently struggled with issues concerning evil, suffering, and death, 18 percent specified that they frequently question their religious/spiritual beliefs, and 40 percent had occasionally felt angry toward God.[17] Some common themes existed among students with the highest amount of spiritual struggle, and examples of these behaviors or experiences were: converting to another religion, being on a spiritual quest, discussing religion/spirituality with friends, and discussing politics.[18] College students' understanding of God was also directly related to their amount of spiritual struggle. Bryant and Astin noted this result, "Individuals who perceive God as 'teacher,' 'divine mystery,' or 'universal spirit' (implying a more elusive, unknowable God) are more inclined to struggle, whereas students who identify God as 'beloved,' 'protector,' or 'part of me' (indicating a close and secure relationship to the divine) or whose perceptions of God do not fit with those indicated on the survey ('none of the above,' suggesting little interest in God) experience less struggle."[19] In an additional study, college students indicated a strong attentiveness to spirituality, and the research noted that 80 percent of college students expressed this interest, 75 percent stated they believed in God, and 66 percent relied

[16] Alyssa Bryant and Helen Astin, "The Correlates of Spiritual Struggle During the College Years," *Journal of Higher Education* 79, no. 1 (January-February 2008): 1.

[17] Ibid., 12.

[18] Alexander W. Astin, Helen S. Astin, and Jennifer A. Lindholm, *Cultivating the Spirit: How College Can Enhance Students' Inner Lives* (San Francisco, CA: Jossey-Bass, 2011), 101–14. Chapter 7 discusses in broad detail the factors that cause religious skepticism and struggle among college students.

[19] Bryant and Astin, "The Correlates of Spiritual Struggle During the College Years," 15.

upon their religious beliefs.[20] This data overwhelmingly demonstrates the case of spiritual development opportunities among students.

Bryant and Astin also discovered results that showed a direct relationship to the events, programs, and ministries of a Christian university integrating faith into programming outside the classroom education. They found an important result: "Conversely, students demonstrating marked levels of religious engagement (i.e., attending religious services, reading sacred texts, joining a religious organization on campus, etc.) show *lower* levels of spiritual struggle than do students who are less engaged."[21] Therefore, the involvement of institutional staff and programming assigned to enhance the spiritual development of students could prove to facilitate a decrease in students' spiritual struggles. All the more, the integration of faith into all aspects of university life could provide an environment where spiritual conversation, growth, and exploration is celebrated as students come to embrace their Christian faith.

Students at Christian colleges and universities can also experience spiritual struggle. The Bryant and Astin study discovered that students at Christian colleges were not immune to spiritual struggle and attending a religious college did not mean that students did not have spiritual struggles. The study affirmed, "Counter to the expectations of the second hypothesis, students who attended Evangelical, Roman Catholic, or other Christian church-affiliated institutions are more inclined to struggle spiritually than are students attending public or private nonsectarian institutions."[22] The authors revealed they believe this could be related to additional questioning and examination of religious beliefs at the church-affiliated institutions, or this could be related to a student's questioning of the norms and beliefs presented at the institutions.[23] The Christian college and university may have concern that their students experience "spiritual struggle." It is clear from this research that college

[20] Astin, Astin, and Lindholm, *Cultivating the Spirit*, 3.

[21] Bryant and Astin, "The Correlates of Spiritual Struggle During the College Years," 14.

[22] Ibid., 13–14.

[23] Ibid., 14.

students, especially those at the Christian college or university, are exploring spiritual ideas, talking about their faith, and learning together. This research creates a greater need for the Christian college and university to integrate faith into all parts of university life, not just through academics. Therefore, the integration of faith into the programming and services outside the classroom can be an essential place for spiritual growth for the Christian college or university. Faith integration has been shown to support student development and learning in holistic ways.[24]

College students will explore spiritual matters, and this has held true since the earliest days of higher education in the United States. For the Christian college and university, the importance of the outside of the classroom experience should not be lost on higher education leaders. The integration of Christian faith into the outside of the class experience can enhance the student experience.

What Is Student Affairs?

Student Affairs at DBU is a group of professional staff that "provide students the support needed for spiritual, intellectual, physical, emotional, and social development to enable them to become Christian servant leaders throughout the world."[25] The Student Affairs division functions in various ways among colleges and universities with varying organizational structures. Considering these assortments of priorities and designs, three main components are primary functions of Student Affairs: student services, student development, and student learning.[26] Through these broad categories, the whole function of Student Affairs can be more accurately understood. Student services would be the broad collection of services provided to enrolled students at an institution of higher education such as housing, counseling, health, accommodations, and

[24] Jennifer Capehart-Meningall, "Role of Spirituality and Spiritual Development in Student Life Outside the Classroom," *New Directions for Teaching and Learning*, no. 104 (Winter 2005): 35.

[25] "Mission Statement," Student Affairs, Dallas Baptist University, accessed November 27, 2023, www.dbu.edu/student-affairs/.

[26] George D. Kuh, Jillian Kinzie, John H. Schuh, and Elizabeth J. White, *Student Success in College: Creating Conditions That Matter* (San Francisco, CA: Jossey-Bass, 2010), 45.

dining. Student development functions would include opportunities such as service-learning, leadership development, career development, and at the Christian college or university, spiritual development. Finally, student learning would encompass areas such as tutoring, internships, orientation programs, and at-risk student interventions.[27] While an institution will organize a Student Affairs division to best fit the needs of its students, these basic functions provide explanation of the work of Student Affairs within higher education. Understanding these categories demonstrates that Student Affairs plays a crucial role in higher education by providing comprehensive support and services that contribute to the overall well-being, personal growth, and academic success of college students. The existence of and functions of Student Affairs shows a recognition that a student's experience extends beyond the classroom as institutions of higher education have established dedicated departments and professionals within Student Affairs to address the diverse needs and challenges students encounter during their college journey.

In summary, the purpose of Student Affairs is to create a holistic and enriching environment that nurtures the development of students, both academically and personally. It goes beyond academic instruction, aiming to support students in their transition to college life, provide opportunities for engagement and involvement on campus, and to help students to foster a sense of belonging within the campus community. At DBU, the Student Affairs division also integrates Christian faith into its daily operation and work with students. Therefore, the integration of faith and learning extends beyond just classroom teaching and into student activities, the housing environment, campus programming, and individual appointments with students. As a Christian college or university such as DBU where faith is paramount to the University's mission, faith is not separated from the functions of Student Affairs but exhibited through each individual staff member and area of responsibility.

[27] Ibid., 43–45.

Applying Holmes's Approaches to Student Affairs

In his formative work entitled *The Idea of a Christian College,* Holmes identified four tactics to the integrating of faith and learning. Holmes's tactics can be applied to the work of Student Affairs and is specifically seen through the work of Student Affairs at DBU. It is important to recognize that Holmes did not claim that faith integration was ever fully completed or accomplished when he said, "Integration should be seen not as an achievement or a position but as an intellectual activity that goes on as long as we keep learning anything at all."[28] The Student Affairs leader must consistently strive to ensure that faith integration is occurring throughout the services and programming offered. Using Holmes's approaches, faith integration practices by Student Affairs leaders will be explored and discussed.

Attitudinal Approach

Holmes described the Attitudinal Approach as the first task of faith integration with an individual's attitude and motivation as crucial to accomplishing effective faith integration.[29] Holmes affirmed that the attitude and approach of a student will be a major determining factor in the student's success academically and with faith integration. The attitude and approach of the Student Affairs staff may also directly impact the attitude of a student toward their academic endeavors. Holmes believed that true faith integration was not limited to the mere inclusion of religious activities or programs on campus but encompassed an individual's overall attitude and worldview. Student Affairs professionals should strive to foster an environment that recognizes and respects the spirituality of students, while also encouraging open dialogue and exploration of faith-related questions. Supportive and caring spaces can be created where students feel safe to express their beliefs, engage in meaningful conversations, and grapple with the complexities of faith and spirituality. By adopting Holmes's Attitudinal Approach, colleges can nurture an inclusive and intellectually stimulating environment that

[28] Holmes, *The Idea of a Christian College,* 46.

[29] Ibid., 49.

allows students to explore their faith journeys while also fostering a deep sense of community and mutual respect.

Student Affairs leaders can support students by guiding them to approach their Christian education appropriately and affect the attitude of the student toward their academics and faith integration. Holmes confirmed the connection of academic success and the spiritual commitment of the student when he said, "Somehow or other the student must realize that education is a Christian vocation, one's prime calling from God for these years, that education must be an act of love, of worship, of stewardship, a wholehearted response to God."[30] The Student Affairs staff can serve as a primary encourager of students and help a student see their potential for academic success. In *Relationship Rich Education: How Human Connections Drive Success in College,* Felten and Lambert discuss the importance of relationships on student success. They summarize the needs each student has for these positive and encouraging relationships and how these relationships impact their attitudes toward academic success:

- Every student must experience genuine welcome and deep care.
- Every student must be inspired to learn.
- Every student must develop a web of significant relationships.[31]

Therefore, Student Affairs personnel at DBU view themselves as relational influences that can positively impact the attitude of a student. Student Affairs staff can demonstrate the Attitudinal Approach through how they relate to students, which will likely improve the attitude of students toward their learning and the integration of their faith into their learning.

Ethical Approach

Holmes's Ethical Approach to faith integration in higher education emphasizes the importance of students moving beyond the rote learning of facts and into the world of understanding values through critical

[30] Ibid.

[31] Peter Felten and Leo Lambert, *Relationship-Rich Education: How Human Connections Drive Success in College* (Baltimore, MD: Johns Hopkins, 2020), 17.

thinking.[32] Faith integration should lead to students considering the ethics and values of a matter that guide their actions and decision-making processes. From Holmes's perspective, the Christian college or university is not effective if a student just learns the correct information but finds success in a student processing information and making a value judgment on a specific topic.

Tim Elmore is a prominent voice regarding the characteristics and traits of Generation Z. The current college students belong to this generation, and Elmore provides a practical encouragement for the advancement of critical thinking among this generation. In agreement with Holmes, he emphasizes the importance of critical thinking especially for this generation of college-aged individuals. Recognizing the rapidly changing job and employment market for young adults, he espouses the importance of young adults learning to critically think as they "may likely find a job after graduation that doesn't even exist today."[33]

The programming sponsored by the Student Affairs division should also support ethical thinking by students. While there is need for student activities, which exist for students to have fun, Student Affairs should plan activities that impact student thinking and values in a deeper way than only having fun. Student Affairs events, activities, ministries, and services can often be learning and development occasions for students and can increase their ability to think critically. The importance of critical thinking and moving learning beyond just the understanding of facts was not just identified by Holmes but has roots in educational philosophy not connected to Christian foundations. Higher education leaders that endorse this type of educational environment for college students outlined practical principles, which contributed to college students broadening their understanding of ethics, values, and diverse perspectives. In modern higher education, certain experiences are "indicators of the development of broader perspectives and sensibilities in a college education:

[32] Holmes, *The Idea of a Christian College*, 51.

[33] Tim Elmore, *Generation Z Unfiltered: Facing Nine Hidden Challenges of the Most Anxious Population* (Atlanta, GA: Growing Leaders, 2019), 266.

- Learning about people from other cultures as an important part of college education.
- Having frequent serious conversations with others who are very different in terms of their religious beliefs, political opinions, or personal values.
- Discussing issues such as peace, justice, human rights, equality, and race relations with other students."[34]

By incorporating an ethical dimension into programming, events, and services, Student Affairs can foster this type of development among students. Even outside of the classroom, ethical decision-making can be a focus, preparing students to become leaders and engaged citizens in an increasingly complex and diverse world. An example of this approach through DBU Student Affairs is exhibited through the four living-learning communities administered through Student Affairs. These programs have an intentional focus on Christian discipleship and leadership development and expose the student participants to various speakers and topics that enhance ethical and values-based thinking by students.

The DBU living-learning communities are connected through University Housing in Ford Village. Holmes's Ethical Approach is seen even in the description of the overall living-learning community program at Ford Village:

> At DBU, however, we established Ford Village uniquely to house students from a variety of academic pursuits who share a common purpose—developing the knowledge, character, and application of Christ-centered servant leadership principles into every professional endeavor.
>
> In both the Pedersen Residential College and the Gunn Hall Global Scholars Program, each housing unit is led by a faculty mentor who arranges planned activities throughout the course of the college journey. Residents and their mentors engage in weekly and monthly Bible studies, community meals, travel study trips, guest lectureships, and guided discussions.

[34] Detweiler, *The Evidence Liberal Arts Needs*, 90.

> An intimate community within a larger University setting, Ford Village is a unique place on the DBU campus to grow academically and spiritually alongside other students with a vision to become Christian servant leaders to serve the world in the next generation.[35]

Foundational Approach

In the Foundational Approach, Holmes argues that education should be historical and connected. Since academic subjects have historical roots and are connected, the Christian college or university should demonstrate these connections to students. Holmes identifies that faculty should understand their discipline historically and its connection to other disciplines and classes. Holmes laments the lack of "interdepartmental interaction."[36] The Christian institution of higher education should recognize the value of multiple disciplines and helping students embrace a broad understanding of learning and the connection of academic disciplines to each other. Therefore, from Holmes's perspective, all academic disciplines should be consistently intertwined with each other, historical foundations, and the Christian faith.

The Foundational Approach by Holmes may appear to have little to do with the function of Student Affairs. The Foundational Approach appears to be more about the classroom and academics rather than what takes place outside of the classroom. However, Student Affairs should not become disconnected from student learning. While students will be graded and evaluated by faculty in the classroom, learning and personal, spiritual, and emotional development occurs in all aspects of life. Student Affairs is a significant part of this for students. Glanzer, Cockle, Jeong, and Graber advocate for what they call, "Student Affairs with Substance."[37] This model of Student Affairs demonstrates multilayered faith integration with Student Affairs leaders occurring primarily in relationships with students. As students make the connections among their academic disciplines, history, and with their faith, Student

---

[35] "A Living Learning Community Preparing Servant Leaders," John and Nita Ford Village, Dallas Baptist University, accessed November 27, 2023, www.dbu.edu/housing/ford-village/.

[36] Holmes, *The Idea of a Christian College*, 56.

[37] Glanzer, *Christ-Enlivened Student Affairs*, 103.

Affairs staff can guide them in making these connections outside of the classroom so students can see that their faith, decisions, vocation, and relationships are connected. Faith is not left out of these interconnected aspects of life but is the central catalyst. Within Student Affairs practice, faith is always there. An example of "Student Affairs with Substance" was through how one Student Affairs leader described career guidance:

> You walk into our career office, and you're not just getting a resume review or just a "Here's how to look for a job." But you're having a fuller conversation about how Christ calls us to certain places and things and how do we discern that in our lives? And there's a richness in those conversations that you wouldn't find at non-faith-based institutions.[38]

The engagement of Student Affairs with students can help foster the connections between faith, life, and academics, and demonstrates how Holmes's Foundational Approach is applied within the framework of Student Affairs.

Another example of Holmes's Foundational Approach expressed within DBU Student Affairs is within the Center for Career and Professional Development department's mission and invitation to students:

> Our mission in the Center for Career and Professional Development at Dallas Baptist University is to provide you with quality services to help you find and fulfill God's call on your life as a servant leader. From the day you start at DBU, we are committed to connecting transformational education with your vocational calling. We will provide you with career-related advising and resources while assisting you in making connections between your academic experience and career path.[39]

The merging of faith, career preparation, and professional resources to serve students is vital to faith integration in career development type work with college students.

---

[38] Ibid., 104.

[39] "Helping Students Find and Fulfill Their Call," Center for Career and Professional Development, Dallas Baptist University, accessed November 27, 2023, https://www.dbu.edu/ccpd/.

Worldview Approach

Holmes affirmed the importance of the worldview, and he stated when defining the Worldview Approach to faith integration, "The most embracing contact between Christianity and human learning is the all-encompassing world and life view."[40] Every college student has a worldview that may still be under development, and the Christian college or university should be guiding the student in this worldview development. The current generation of college students (Gen Z) has specific worldview characteristics that influence their decision making. Gen Z, the generation born between the mid-1990s and early 2010s, is often known as well-intentioned and holds a unique worldview shaped by the digital age in which they have come of age. Growing up in a highly connected and technologically advanced world, Gen Z exhibits a global mindset and an inherent comfort with digital platforms and social media. They are more likely to value diversity, inclusivity, and social justice, and are passionate about making a positive impact on the world. Gen Z tends to be socially conscious and actively engages in social and political issues, leveraging the power of technology to advocate for change. They are open-minded, adaptable, and have a strong desire for authenticity and transparency. Gen Z is characterized by a blend of skepticism and optimism, influenced by the challenges they face, such as economic uncertainties and environmental concerns. Overall, Gen Z's worldview reflects a generation that is highly informed, globally connected, and motivated to shape a more inclusive and sustainable future.[41]

Holmes describes a worldview as holistic, exploratory, pluralistic, and confessional/perspectival.[42] The holistic worldview is supported by Student Affairs through programming that helps students connect the seemingly different parts of life. The exploratory aspect of worldview

[40] Holmes, *The Idea of a Christian College,* 57.

[41] Elmore, 25–34. Chapter 3 in *Generation Z Unfiltered* provides an overview of the characteristics of Generation Z.

[42] Holmes, *The Idea of a Christian College,* 58–59.

development is supported by Student Affairs by providing opportunities for students to discover new perspectives, cultures, and ideas.

As Christian institutions approach worldview development, they do so from a confessional/perspectival approach since worldview development at the Christian institution starts with the premise of Christian belief and doctrine. Certainly, not every student at the Christian college or university holds to a Christian faith. It is important for Christian worldview development to occur within a framework where Christian belief and practice is the basis for programming and policies. For the Student Affairs area, this is an important framework as it informs areas such as housing guidelines, codes of conduct, and other standards of behavior. Christian worldview development occurs best in the environment that begins with a clear affirmation of the priority of the Christian faith. For example, if a housing guideline or code of conduct allows behavior discordant with Christian belief, this creates an obstacle to integrating faith in other areas of Student Affairs. Within DBU Student Affairs, policies and guidelines for students are crafted and prescribed in a way that facilitates an environment among the student body where faith is a part of each aspect of campus life and faith principles are expected among the actions of the student body.

Conclusion

Research validated the importance of the spiritual development of college students during their years enrolled in a higher education institution, and even showed that spiritual growth positively impacted of the student's life academically, psychologically, relationally, and in other ways.[43] With the enormous influence that a Student Affairs division has on the everyday lives of students, it is imperative that faith is integrated into the diverse functions of typical Student Affairs. The Christian college or university cannot just teach in the classroom from a Christian perspective but must also integrate faith into the experience for students that occurs when they are not in class yet still on campus. By inten-

[43] Astin, Astin, and Lindholm, *Cultivating the Spirit*, 115.

tionally infusing Christian values, principles, and perspectives into the various functions and services of student affairs, Christian colleges have the opportunity to create an environment that not only fosters academic growth but also nurtures students' spiritual, moral, and ethical formation. Ultimately, the integration of Christian faith in the student affairs area of a Christian college serves as a powerful tool in fostering a transformative college experience where students are equipped to impact the world with their knowledge, faith, and values.

Chapter 14

Integrating Faith in Title IX Compliance

By David D. Cook[1]

Introduction

As we explore the topic of integrating faith into the learning environment of a Christian college, it might be easy to overlook the area of Title IX compliance. When we talk about integrating faith into the classroom, as we have done in previous chapters, the tone is quite hopeful: we are helping to transform minds for Christ! This is rightfully so, for we have the chance as educators to help mold future generations who will be Christ's healing "hands and feet" to a hurting world. But in educating college students who are necessarily imperfect human beings, we also have to face the brokenness of sin head-on. We know that, even for the strongest Christian, life is a journey of sanctification where we struggle against sin and allow the Holy Spirit to make us look more like Christ every day. As Paul reminded the Early Church, "Therefore, I urge you, brothers and sisters, in view of God's mercy, to offer your bodies as a living sacrifice, holy and pleasing to God—this is your true and proper worship. Do not conform to the pattern of this world, but be transformed by the renewing of your mind" (Romans 12:1–2 [NIV]).

But on that journey of sanctification, we can sometimes stumble. Even the great biblical writer Paul himself noted,

---

[1] David D. Cook serves as the Senior Legal Counsel to the President. In this role as an attorney, he provides administrative and legal oversight for all Title IX cases at the University, working with DBU's Title IX Coordinator on these cases.

> I do not understand what I do. For what I want to do I do not do, but what I hate I do...So I find this law at work: Although I want to do good, evil is right there with me. For in my inner being I delight in God's law; but I see another law at work in me, waging war against the law of my mind and making me a prisoner of the law of sin at work within me. What a wretched man I am! Who will rescue me from this body that is subject to death? Thanks be to God, who delivers me through Jesus Christ our Lord! (Romans 7:15, 21–25 [NIV]).

So, as we engage in the ministry of Christian higher education, we know that, just as Paul reminded us, we are still dealing with students who have not yet been made perfect (Philippians 3:12). If even a Christ-follower as strong in his faith as Paul stumbled at times, we know that our students, too, will continue to struggle with sin. And that means part of our job as Christian educators is to help them grapple with sin in a way that honors Christ and challenges them to "put off [their] old self...and to put on the new self, created after the likeness of God..." (Ephesians 4:22–24 [ESV]).

Sometimes that means helping students overcome a personal addiction or teaching them how to escape destructive cycles. At other times, when their brokenness leads to wrongdoing that harms others, it means stepping in to hold students accountable for how their actions cause harm to others. And sadly, even on a Christian college campus, there are times where we are called as Christian educators to discipline students whose sinful choices damage another person who is made in God's image. Handling such cases is never pleasant, but it is an important part of our call to serve and protect the students God has entrusted to us.

One area of sin that can be quite difficult to grapple with is the area of sexual sin. For this reason, it is a weighty responsibility for Christian educators to step into darkness and adjudicate these types of sexual misconduct cases. This responsibility is even more important because of the myriad federal and state regulations governing this area, the most important of which is a federal regulation called Title IX. With that in mind, this chapter will explore what it looks like for Christian educators to integrate faith even into this dark area. We will investigate what it means for Christian educators to see such cases as an opportunity to serve the oppressed, call wrongdoers to account, and shine God's light into very difficult circumstances.

The Theological Foundations for Integrating Faith Into Title IX Compliance

As we look at what it means to integrate faith into the administration of justice in Title IX cases, the foundation for our efforts comes from the character of God Himself as a God who loves justice. Throughout the Bible, one can see that God clearly cares deeply about the cause of justice. From the Old Testament to the New Testament, we see that He is constantly teaching His people what it means to be "just" and calls them to be just as He Himself is just.[2] As Psalm 9:7–8 NIV explains, "The Lord reigns forever; he has established his throne for judgment. He rules the world in righteousness and judges the peoples with equity." We see throughout the Old Testament that God sets up judges and leaders to implement justice in God's name and help train the people's hearts toward justice. God Himself gave the people the Ten Commandments and set forth Levitical laws that provided a framework for justice amongst His people. Many of these laws were quite radical—both at the time and even for modern-day sensibilities—as they sought to instill a heart of justice in His people that was rooted in a love for God and a love for one's neighbors.[3]

---

[2] Examples include Exod. 22:21–24; Lev. 19:9–10; 23:22, 33–36; Deut. 24:19–21; 25:15; 27:19; Ruth 2:1–23; Ps. 9:8; 82:3; Prov. 11:1; 16:12; 20:10; 21:3; 28:15; 29:4; Isa. 1:17, 23; 30:18; Jer. 23:1–4; Ezek. 45:10; Mic. 6:8; Zech. 7:9–10; Mal. 3:5; Matt. 3:7–12; 5:3–10, 21–48; 6:1–4; 18:15–20; Luke 11:37–54; 15:11–32; 18:1–14; 20:20–26; John 2:13–25; 4:1–26; James 1:27.

[3] For example, many of the Levitical laws that mandated redemption, gleaning, and a Year of Jubilee where debts were canceled went well beyond the norms of the time and provided welfare and protection for the poor that showed God's desire for economic justice. See Exod. 22:21–24; Lev. 19:9–10, 33–34, 36; 23:22, 25; Deut. 24:19–21; 25:25; 27:19; Ruth 2:1–23; Ps. 82:3; Prov. 11:1; 20:10; Isa. 1:17; Ezek. 45:10; Zech. 7:9–10; Mal. 3:5; James 1:27.

As a part of this call for justice, God implored common people to be just in their own personal dealings,[4] and Jesus echoed this call for personal justice in His Sermon on the Mount.[5] But God, in His wisdom, also created positions of trust within society so certain leaders could help administer justice and formally serve as God's servant in the adjudication of disputed cases. God knew His people and that their sinful, selfish hearts would not be able to enact His justice without guidance and admonition.[6] As James Madison famously noted in more modern times, "If men were angels, no government would be necessary."[7] Thus, God created a system of earthly justice that was meant to mirror His own heart of justice.

His leaders were to be "servants of the Lord," who would steward justice in His name. The first of these lawgivers/judges was Moses, who administered justice in contested cases from "morning till evening,"[8] leaving him weary and spent. Quickly, his father-in-law, Jethro, wisely noted that this breakneck pace would be "too heavy for you," and he implored him,

---

[4] "He has shown you, O mortal, what is good. And what does the LORD require of you? To act justly and to love mercy and to walk humbly with your God," (Mic. 6:8 [NIV]); "To do what is right and just is more acceptable to the LORD than sacrifice," (Prov. 21:3 [NIV]).

[5] As a part of this sermon, Jesus first implored His disciples to be merciful, pure in heart, and to be peacemakers (Matt. 5:7–9). Thereafter, He called them to a higher order of holiness as He gave them admonitions against anger, lust, oaths, and personal retribution (Matt. 5:21–42). The culmination of Matthew 5 is Jesus' admonition to "love your enemies and pray for those who persecute you, that you may be children of your Father in heaven…Be perfect, therefore, as your heavenly Father is perfect" (Matt. 5:44–45, 48 [NIV]). In many ways, He was calling His disciples not just to mere adherence to the strict letter of the law, but to live their lives with the spirit of the law at the forefront. Thus, they were to be just in a way that honored the spirit of God's laws and honored His Lordship over all areas of their lives—even their economic and legal transactions.

[6] Zech. 7:11–12 states, "Your ancestors refused to listen to this message. They stubbornly turned away and put their fingers in their ears to keep from hearing. They made their hearts as hard as stone, so they could not hear the instructions or the messages that the LORD of Heaven's Armies had sent them by his Spirit through the earlier prophets" (NLT).

[7] James Madison, "The Structure of the Government Must Furnish the Proper Checks and Balances Between the Different Departments," in *The Federalist* 51 (February 1788), accessed November 27, 2023, https://guides.loc.gov/federalist-papers/text-51-60#s-lg-box-wrapper-25493427.

[8] Exod. 18:13.

> ...look for able men from all the people, men who fear God, who are trustworthy and hate a bribe, and place such men over the people as chiefs of thousands, of hundreds, of fifties, and of tens. And let them judge the people at all times. Every great matter they shall bring to you, but any small matter they shall decide themselves. So it will be easier for you, and they will bear the burden with you (Exodus 18:21–22 [ESV]).

In this way, not only Moses, but other respected leaders would administer justice in God's name. In later generations, God appointed other prophets and judges to perform similar functions,[9] always seeking to draw His people back to repentance and a heart of true justice. While the people time and again selfishly walked away from God and His justice, God continued to raise up leaders whose task was to draw the people back to His character of justice. In this effort, He even used foreign leaders to bring justice on the Israelites themselves when they became unjust.[10] Sadly, the people constantly wavered back and forth, at times living in accordance with God's call for justice, and at other times flagrantly living in their own sin. Thus, the culmination of God's plan to bring justice was found in the prophecy that one day, a Messiah would come who would make all things new. In Ezekiel 34, where God decried the leaders of Israel who had not administered God's justice (He likened them to "shepherds of Israel who only take care of yourselves" verse 2), He also gave a beautiful promise:

> I myself will search for my sheep and look after them. As a shepherd looks after his scattered flock when he is with them, so will I look after my sheep. I will rescue them from all the places where they were scattered on a day of clouds and darkness. I will bring them out from the nations and gather them from the countries, and I will bring them

[9] The entire biblical book of Judges is a narrative about the exploits of God's appointed judges such as Deborah, Gideon, and Samson. Likewise, 1 Samuel recounts the lives of Eli and Samuel, who were likewise appointed as prophets and judges for the people.

[10] For example, Hab. 1:5–6: "Look at the nations and watch—and be utterly amazed. For I am going to do something in your days that you would not believe, even if you were told. I am raising up the Babylonians, that ruthless and impetuous people, who sweep across the whole earth to seize dwellings not their own" (NIV).

> into their own land...I will search for the lost and bring back the strays. I will bind up the injured and strengthen the weak, but the sleek and the strong I will destroy. I will shepherd the flock with justice...I will place over them one shepherd, my servant David, and he will tend them; he will tend them and be their shepherd (Ezekiel 34:11–13, 16, 23 [NIV]).

This prophecy was fulfilled when Jesus, in John 10:11, proclaimed, "I am the good shepherd. The good shepherd lays down his life for the sheep" (NIV). As Jesus taught His disciples, He consistently called them to be agents of peace in the world around them,[11] and He promised that He would one day return.[12] This return would fulfill with finality the prophecy from Ezekiel 34: "For the Lamb at the center of the throne will be their shepherd; 'he will lead them to springs of living water.' 'And God will wipe away every tear from their eyes'" (Revelation 7:17 [NIV]). At that time, God would rule in justice in a world where He was "making everything new" (Revelation 21:5 [NIV]).

But in the intervening time between Jesus' resurrection and the Second Coming, it is clear that His plan was still to use earthly leaders to be agents of His to administer justice for all peoples. In 1 Peter 2:13–15, believers are counseled to respect government officials who are "sent by Him to punish those who do evil and to praise those who do good" (ESV). And Jesus Himself admonished His followers to "turn the other [cheek]" (Matthew 5:39 [NASB]) and "love your enemies" (Matthew 5:44 [NASB]) with the knowledge that God would administer justice on their behalf in due time.[13] During this intervening time between Christ's resurrection and the Second Coming, Paul instructed Christ-followers to be "subject to the governing authorities...For the one in authority is God's servant for your good...They are God's servants, agents of wrath to bring punishment on the wrongdoer" (Romans 13:1, 4 [NIV]).

---

[11] Matt. 5:9; 28:16–20; Luke 10:1–24; John 16:33.

[12] Matt. 24:1–31; Luke 21:34–36; John 14:1–3.

[13] "Beloved, never avenge yourselves, but leave it to the wrath of God, for it is written, 'Vengeance is mine, I will repay, says the Lord'" (Rom. 12:19 [ESV]).

As we can see from this brief review of Scripture, God calls His people to justice repeatedly, and sets rulers over them to administer justice for their good. How does this play into our role as administers of justice in Title IX cases? First, if we believe we are to be "subject to the governing authorities" in the form of our national, state, and local government officials, then we have a duty to follow the laws they promulgate for our good.[14] As Christians, we are to be model citizens, complying with not only the letter of the law but the spirit of the law, as well.[15] And this means that, at an institution like DBU, we are called to comply with a bevy of federal, state, and local regulations that are specific to higher education. One of these regulations is Title IX of the Education Amendments of 1972. In essence, Title IX is a federal regulation that prohibits discrimination based on sex and includes federal mandates on investigating and adjudicating allegations of sexual misconduct that occur on college campuses. Thus, we are tasked with complying with these mandates in a way that honors God and honors those involved in these types of cases.

Second, since we have a delegated role from the government to investigate and adjudicate sexual misconduct cases on our campus, we feel a responsibility to be stewards of God's justice as we handle these cases. Thus, as Colossians 3:17 reminds us, "And whatever you do, in word or in deed, do everything in the name of the Lord Jesus" (CSB). This includes even our roles as investigators and adjudicators in Title IX. We realize that we can be "salt and light" in these difficult cases as we handle them in a Christ-like spirit with excellence, efficiency, care, and compassion. And the starting point for that is we understand each party involved in these cases is made in the *Imago Dei*, and thus they have inherent worth.[16] No matter what they have done, they deserve

[14] As Jesus Himself noted: "Give to Caesar the things that are Caesar's, and to God the things that are God's" (Mark 12:17 [CSB]). Thus, we are, in general, to follow the laws of the rulers God has placed in positions of responsibility over us unless their decrees contradict God's commands. Cf. Acts 5:29, "We must obey God rather than human beings!" (NIV), where Peter and the apostles defied the governing authorities when they were ordered not to preach the Gospel.

[15] Rom. 13:1–5; Titus 3:1.

[16] "So God created mankind in His own image" (Gen. 1:27 [NIV]); "For you created my inmost being; you knit me together in my mother's womb" (Ps. 139:14 [NIV]).

respect, fairness, and equity because they are created in the image of God. Just as the Lord commanded the prophet Zechariah to "administer true justice, show mercy and compassion to one another,"[17] we feel a deep call to show kindness, respect, compassion, and mercy to all parties, even as we are ultimately seeking justice for any wrongs that may have been committed. We seek to do so in a spirit of humility, as God directs in Micah 6:8 when He calls His followers to "act justly and to love mercy and to walk humbly with your God" (NIV).

The rest of this chapter will thus focus on how we practically answer this dual call to serve our government and serve as God's stewards of justice in the cases we are asked to adjudicate. We will look at how the theological underpinnings for this endeavor provide a unique way of looking at our roles, and how this radically changes the way we treat this responsibility. While these cases can be difficult, we understand we have a unique opportunity to serve on mission with God as we seek to administer justice in our small sphere of influence.

Practically Integrating Faith Into Title IX Compliance at DBU

Attitudinal Approach

The starting point for DBU's distinctive way of seeing its Title IX responsibilities lies in the belief that we are stewards of God's call for justice. The attitude of serving God and serving justice in His name is one that comports well with Holmes's Attitudinal Approach to the integration of faith into the learning environment. Because we see ourselves as God's servants in these types of difficult cases, we carefully select some of the best faculty and staff available to be a part of our Title IX team. This includes our Title IX Coordinator, Deputy Coordinators, faculty, and staff who sit on the Hearing Panel, those who serve as Advisors, and those who serve in a variety of other roles. Each year, we intentionally pray about who should be involved in these cases, and we seek people who mix justice and mercy in the right measure in their

[17] Zech. 7:9 (NIV).

daily lives. This selection process is so important that the President of our institution himself reviews all selections carefully to ensure that we have the most fair, equitable, and just team possible.

One of the core elements of our attitude is that we prayerfully seek wisdom on each and every case that comes before us. Not only do we have prayer before every hearing, but our Title IX staff regularly prays for both the complainant and respondent involved in each case. As the Title IX Coordinator notes, "The Title IX process is costly and tremendously difficult for all involved, but it also offers the 'yet even now'[18] possibility of mercy and hope…My prayer, in each case is that discipline leads to repentance and blessing." As another staff member on the Title IX team noted,

> A standard of loving God and loving one's neighbor is desired for students, faculty, and staff alike [in Title IX cases]. In order to uphold the vision of building a university that is pleasing to God, DBU's Title IX personnel address the reality of sin through administration of justice where this standard is not met. However, these same personnel show mercy through their conduct, behavior, and support in working with the parties involved.

Another element of this Attitudinal Approach at DBU is to seek excellence so we work as unto the Lord.[19] With that in mind, we go above the minimum standards required by Title IX and provide additional resources to parties in each case. One example of this is the fact that each party is offered a free Confidential Consultant for the duration of the case. These Confidential Consultants serve a mission of compassion for the parties. They are available to pray with the party, serve as a listening ear, assist them in seeking counseling or medical care, help them understand the process before them, and serve as a general guide during this difficult journey. Because each party, whatever they may

[18] Referencing Joel 2:12–13, "'Even now,' declares the LORD, 'return to me with all your heart, with fasting and weeping and mourning. Rend your heart and not your garments. Return to the LORD your God, for he is gracious and compassionate, slow to anger and abounding in love'" (NIV).

[19] Col. 3:17.

be accused of doing, has inherent dignity and worth, DBU offers these Confidential Consultants to both parties to help them through the case. One of DBU's Confidential Consultants had this to say about her role:

> Students I have worked with on Title IX cases initially come to me with expressed feelings of depression, anxiety, shame, and fear. Coming from a mental health perspective, I have seen both complainants and respondents also struggling with self-worth and feelings of being "less than" due to the experience of being involved in a Title IX case. They have responded to the integration of faith with deep gratefulness and humility resulting from being treated not only fairly, but with respect and compassion by those involved in investigating and making final decisions on the cases.

This attitude of excellence also manifests itself in keeping detailed records, developing a 70+ page checklist to ensure the proper handling of cases, and the creation of model templates that ensure each case is handled with proper legal formalities. Our Title IX team reviews DBU's Sexual Misconduct Policy annually to determine ways to better serve parties in these cases, and we provide annual training to all our team members so they are equipped to do their jobs with excellence. Our hope is that, in creating a robust system for these cases and going above the minimum standards required by law, we can cultivate a process that provides equity and fairness to all parties.

Ethical Approach

A second way that we integrate faith into Title IX cases is using what Holmes's would label the Ethical Approach. Knowing that we are held to a high standard not only because of the many federal and state laws relating to this area, but also because of God's call for justice, we seek to operate in a way that goes above and beyond the minimum ethical standards for these cases. One of the strategic ways we sought to ensure fairness in our cases was choosing to use a jury-style Hearing Panel system rather than a single investigator/adjudicator model. Up until a few years ago, the single investigator/adjudicator model, which was less time-consuming, was the predominant model used at many other colleges. Yet DBU has chosen since 2016 to use a very robust jury-style Hearing Panel model that involves anywhere from 3–10 hearing panelists who decide a case. This decision was made to ensure the maximum amount of fairness and reduce the chances of a single adjudicator showing bias, prejudice, or conflict of interest.

Likewise, since 2020, when federal regulations provided the option for colleges to allow parties to use an Informal Resolution Process, DBU has made the voluntary choice to create a robust Informal Resolution Process as an alternative means for the parties to mediate their cases. This took considerable effort to create, but we have seen repeatedly that this type of model promotes a more conciliatory environment, which leads to less trauma for both parties involved. As one of our Informal Resolution Facilitators (who serves in a mediator-style role in these cases) noted,

> I have found that forgiveness is a topic that is sometimes explored during the process of the Title IX cases. There have been times when it was important to the respondent to offer an apology and seek forgiveness. I have seen students navigate a difficult discussion and the end result is that forgiveness is extended to the respondent. This is not forced or coerced and it does not change the consequences of the action. It is important to note that it is the student's choice to offer an apology and the student knows it may or may not be accepted. However, in the context of our university, students often want to integrate their faith into the process.

While this process is merely voluntary, DBU went to great lengths to create this system so parties could have a redemptive and restorative process to engage in should they desire that type of outcome.

Likewise, to ensure fairness in all cases, we have an attorney serve as the Hearing Officer to ensure that hearings are balanced, equitable, and procedurally sound. This attorney not only serves as an important ethical arbiter during the hearing, but also crafts a detailed Charge to the Hearing Panel that is similar to an official jury charge in court cases that ensures the Hearing Panels considers all issues fairly and correctly. Hearing Panelists receive training each year and serve for multiple years to ensure that they are well-versed in the law and have experience adjudicating these cases. As one attorney representing a party in a previous case noted,

> Title IX cases are never easy, and they often involve very difficult situations. I believe those investigating and deciding these cases mix justice and mercy because they make every effort to gather evidence that is relevant to both sides. The investigators and deciding officials have been fair and impartial throughout the process.

As a previous Title IX Coordinator at DBU noted,

> Just recently I had a former student contact me who was the respondent in a case three years prior. The outcome of the case was not favorable to the respondent; however, during the conversation he expressed his gratitude for the way he was treated during his case. In another case, the hearing was running into the evening. Instead of rushing to get the hearing completed, all of the respondent's witnesses were given the time needed to be heard and interviewed in order to be fair to everyone involved. Although the outcome was not favorable to the respondent, the respondent's parents expressed their gratitude that the time was taken and not rushed for all the witnesses to be heard.

One of the Hearing Panelists for a recent case summed up this Ethical Approach well when she said:

> We try to treat each one with kindness and respect, while also attempting to get to the truth of the situation. We genuinely want to do the "right" thing, which includes treating individuals with respect, but also confronting the offense and providing appropriate consequences.

Foundational Approach

Another key element of integrating faith into Title IX cases is what Holmes terms the Foundational Approach. Thus, we integrate faith into the Title IX process by continually discussing why we do what we do in light of the biblical mandate for justice. In trainings, policy review sessions, and before hearings, we focus on the idea from Micah 6:8 that we are to "act justly and to love mercy" as we handle each case. This balancing of justice and mercy in the right measure becomes a foundational concept for each of our Title IX team members as they investigate and adjudicate cases. As a former Title IX Coordinator noted: "Our gracious heavenly Father is both just and merciful; therefore, it is important that we seek the whole truth and administer justice through fair and appropriate sanctions when warranted."

Another foundational concept that undergirds our deliberations is the *Imago Dei*. We believe that each person involved in the case—whether a party, witness, or parent—is made in the image of God and deserves respect, kindness, and fairness. This means that, as the case is progressing, we not only provide a Confidential Consultant to pray with and for the parties, but our Investigators and Hearing Panelists pray for the parties, as well. When parties have questions during the process or want to dispute a claim, we spend the time to make sure we are hearing the whole story. In a case last year, our Investigators spent dozens of hours talking to over twenty witnesses in order to hear the full perspectives of all sides. As the Title IX Coordinator overseeing that case noted:

> The investigators and adjudicators at DBU begin their work in each Title IX case with the central belief that every human being is made in God's image and deserving of respect but also with the belief that every human being is born a sinner and in need of mercy. With this as the overarching framework, investigators seek justice by being thorough and impartial in their interviews and by making sure that both the complainant and respondent are treated equally and have the opportunity to present any witnesses for the investigation that they believe will provide important information for a fair decision to be made. Adjudicators also approach their role with impartiality and seek justice by searching for the truth in each investigative report they read and through each witness that testifies at the formal hearing.

Finally, another foundational concept that underlies our process is the idea that every perspective is valuable and important in a case. This ties in with the concept of the *Imago Dei*, for if each person in a case was made in God's image, their perspective on events deserves respect. Our goal is to listen intently and ask for wisdom to discern the truth of the matter; of course, this can be difficult at times. Sadly, some witnesses do not tell the whole truth, or attempt to bend the story toward their advantage. At other times, witnesses legitimately differ in their subjective perspectives on the events in question. We believe it is important for us to discern the objective truth of what really happened, but in listening for the truth, it is important to hear the lived perceptions and experiences of each individual involved. As one author noted about this "critical realist" approach, the truth is like an iceberg that is partially submerged in water: while we operate on the assumption that the true dimensions of the iceberg can objectively be found, there is still great value in listening to observers from different vantage points describe their perspective, as those underneath the waterline may be able to share an important perspective that those above the waterline may not see, and vice versa.[20] In giving each witness respect and the opportunity to share their perceptions, while then balancing those against the totality of the evidence from all angles, our Title IX team members attempt to wisely discern the objective truth of what happened in each case.[21]

---

[20] Geoff Easton, "Critical Realism in Case Study Research," *Industrial Marketing Management* 39, no. 1 (January 2010): 118–28.

[21] As Christians, 1 Corinthians 13:12 provides a foundation for the importance of critical realism: "For now we see only a reflection as in a mirror; then we shall see face to face. Now I know in part; then I shall know fully, even as I am fully known" (NIV). As Alister McGrath, a proponent of critical realism, noted in describing the sovereignty of God and His creation, Christians are "confronted with something so great that we cannot fully comprehend it, and so we must do the best that we can with the analytical and descriptive tools at our disposal," Alister McGrath, *Dawkins' God: Genes, Memes, and the Meaning of Life* (Oxford, UK: Blackwell, 2004), 158. Thus, while God created an objective reality, it is still important for investigators to understand the subjective perceptions individuals have of the world and the shared stories they tell that help them try to understand that reality. Cf. N. Tom Wright, *The New Testament and the People of God* (Minneapolis, MN: Fortress Press, 1992).

Worldview Approach

A fourth way we integrate faith into Title IX cases at DBU is through what Holmes terms the Worldview Approach. This starts with our belief that we are to be "peacemakers" in the world around us. In Matthew 5:9, Jesus revealed that "Blessed are the peacemakers, for they will be called children of God" (NIV). This concept of peace, which runs throughout the Bible, is the idea of bringing the very fullness of God's character to the world around us.[22] Bringing the *shalom* of God does not mean merely settling disputes, but actively injecting the love, compassion, mercy, justice, faithfulness, kindness, and joy of the Lord into every situation around us.[23] This holistic worldview causes us to see the whole realm of human life under the Lordship of Christ.[24] And this means not just the holy sides of our lives, but the sinful broken parts of our lives, as well. Throughout the Gospels we see that Christ Himself confronts sin head-on, as He calls people to repentance while still loving them and healing their wounds.[25] In much the same way, we are called not only to build up our students' best qualities, but also deal with their deepest sin issues. Within the learning environment, our goal is to holistically transform them spiritually, mentally, emotionally, and physically for Christ during their time at DBU, and that means grappling with all aspects of their lives—even those that are less than wholesome. As a former Title IX Coordinator noted,

---

[22] Num. 6:24–26; 25:12; Judg. 6:24; Ps. 29:11; Isa. 9:5–6; 26:3; 66:12; John 14:27; Eph. 2:14; Phil. 4:7.

[23] "In the Old Testament, 'peace' carries the fundamental meaning of welfare, prosperity, or wholeness as well as the absence of hostility. The term is frequently used as the antithesis of harm…" Joshua M. Greever, s.v. "Peace," in *The Lexham Bible Dictionary*, ed. John D. Barry (Bellingham, WA: Lexham Press, 2016): "There is further the sense of *šālôm* as state of being, as in contentment or tranquility. Isa. 32:17 draws a parallel between 'peace' and 'quietness and trust forever' as the results of righteousness." Daniel L. Smith-Christopher, s.v. "Peace," in *Eerdmans Dictionary of the Bible*, ed. David N. Freedman, Allen C. Myers, and Astrid B. Beck (Grand Rapids, MI: Eerdmans, 2000), 1021: "The Hebrew concept of *shalom* [is] the positive condition of personal or communal wholeness, integrity and well-being." Stanley J. Grenz and Jay T. Smith, *Pocket Dictionary of Ethics*, IVP Pocket Reference Series (Downers Grove, IL: IVP, 2003), 86.

[24] As the famous Dutch theologian Abraham Kuyper once noted, "There is not a square inch in the whole domain of our human existence over which Christ, who is Sovereign over all, does not cry 'Mine!'" James D. Bratt, ed., *Abraham Kuyper: A Centennial Reader* (Grand Rapids, MI: Eerdmans, 1998), 488.

[25] Mark 7:1–23; Luke 12:1–12; 15:11–32; 19:1–10; John 4:1–26; 8:1–11.

> We are all sinners in need of the saving grace of Christ. If we are truly Christ-followers, we will treat everyone we encounter with the same love and mercy with which we have been treated...[One component of this is] stopping behavior now before he or she continues down a path that could lead to even more destruction and devastation in their life and the lives of others that they encounter.

Thus, if we see our mission as a holistic endeavor to bring students closer to Christ in every aspect of their lives, our role as a Title IX team is a vital component in seeking to prevent sinful sexual misconduct and bring justice when that misconduct does occur.

One aspect of this holistic Worldview Approach is seeking true restorative justice in every case. In Western jurisprudence, there have been several strands of legal theories on punishment, including retribution, incapacitation, deterrence, and restoration.[26] While modern American jurisprudence has tended to focus on the first three, our goal is to incorporate a biblical concept of restoration into these cases, as well. This does not mean glossing over wrongdoing or lowering standards in deciding sanctions, but instead means that we make our decisions in light of the ultimate goal of seeking to restore the student to a right relationship with God and with his/her fellow students. As one attorney involved in a recent case noted, "While some of these cases involve bad decisions and bad acts, the team at DBU makes every effort to practice a restorative justice that supports the students rather than alienates them." In many cases, this means changing the way we view sanctions, and deliberating in ways that consider the holistic development of all parties. A previous Title IX Coordinator put it this way,

> It is important that we seek the whole truth and administer justice through fair and appropriate sanctions when warranted. If a respondent is found responsible for violations by the hearing panel, sanctions including removal from campus housing, removal from extracurricular activ-

[26] "The Purposes of Punishment," in *Criminal Law* (Minneapolis: University of Minnesota Libraries, 2015), accessed November 27, 2023, https://open.lib.umn.edu/criminallaw/chapter/1-5-the-purposes-of-punishment/.

> ities, suspension, and/or expulsion could be administered. However, also included in the final decision are sanctions, which reflect the mercy and the love of Christ, which allows the Title IX investigation and hearing to also be a redemptive process hopefully allowing the respondent to reflect, change, and grow into the young man or woman the Lord has called them to be. These sanctions could include assigning the respondent a campus mentor, requiring counseling through the DBU Counseling Center, or by paying for off-campus counseling.

In this effort to fairly decide cases while also seeking restorative justice, our goal is to deal with sin issues head-on so God can begin His process of sanctification in each of the parties' lives. As the current Title IX Coordinator noted,

> Here at Dallas Baptist University, we strive to treat each and every party involved in a Title IX case equally. We meet each party in their need, making every effort to serve their emotional, physical, and educational needs. We also work hard to balance love and justice. True restoration must include both. We make sure every individual's perspective is heard and considered and then with prayer and wisdom our decision makers move on a ruling, one that is made with the parties' overall welfare in mind.

Conclusion

While Title IX cases can be difficult for all involved, even in these situations, there is a great opportunity to work "as unto the Lord" and bring the fullness of God into the case. As agents for God's justice, it is important that Title IX officials mix justice and mercy in the right measure, always looking at how to structure a disciplinary process that seeks truth and metes out punishment in a God-honoring way. What we see is that, even amidst allegations of sin, hurt, pain, and harm, there is an opportunity to treat parties with respect, seek justice in all we do, and provide a process that is fair, equitable, and just. At DBU, our goal is for our Title IX officials to serve God and the interests of justice in such a way that we bring the very fullness of His character into even the darkest of situations.

Chapter 15

Integrating Faith in Athletics

By Blake Flickner[1]

- "You PLAY to WIN the GAME!" — Herm Edwards
- "It's not whether you win or lose, it's how you play the game." — Grantland Rice
- "Do you not know that in a race all the runners run, but only one receives the prize? So run that you may obtain it" (1 Corinthians 9:24 [ESV]).

Introduction

In week eight of the National Football League (NFL) season, the New York Jets fell to the Cleveland Browns. After achieving a record of 10–6 in 2001, the Jets' players, coaches, and fans were hoping for even more the following year. However, in 2002 the Jets were off to a disappointing start. With a record of 2–5 and five losses in their last six games, Jets Coach Herm Edwards was trying to find a way to move the team in a different direction. That week, Judy Battista of the New York Times asked Coach Edwards if he had talked to his team about not giving up. Coach Edwards responded with one of the most memorable rants in NFL history. The famous line, "Hellllllo? You play to win the game!" has been turned into a popular meme, and Coach Edwards'

[1] Blake Flickner serves as the Head Basketball Coach at Dallas Baptist University and as an adjunct faculty member.

passionate speech is a favorite of coaches in every sport when they feel their team needs a spark of motivation.[2]

"You play to win the game." Athletic competition is built on this foundational principle. It is the very nature of sport and competition. Individuals and teams sacrifice and strain as they measure themselves against one another to find out who will win. Coaches and athletes experience joy and exhilaration when the desired outcome is achieved or disappointment and hurt when it is not. Even fans participate in their own way and experience strong emotions after every victory or defeat. Joy, fun, and a sense of accomplishment are at least potential benefits from sports. It is, after all, a game. For well over a century, American society has wrestled with the value and place of competitive athletics within the goals and mission of institutions of higher education. Christian faith and the message of the gospel informs a uniquely Christian understanding of competition that neither dismisses the pursuit of victory nor fails to set boundaries in that pursuit. Christian universities committed to the integration of faith and learning must also be committed to the integration of faith and competition.

The Role of the Athletics Department and Learning in Higher Education

In the United States, most institutions of higher education have incorporated athletic competition into the college experience. Students at the university train and compete against students at other universities. Coaches are paid by the university; sometimes scholarships are awarded to students. Facilities, promotions, equipment, and support staff are all paid for by the university to assist in athletic competition. Recent Supreme Court decisions and changes in the NCAA bylaws have meant that under new name, image, and likeness (NIL) provisions, universities or their donors are now able to pay student-athletes, and students are now allowed to profit off of their name, image, and likeness. The extent

[2] The Jets won their next four games, and seven of their next nine games to make the playoffs where they defeated the Indianapolis Colts to advance to the AFC Divisional round before falling to the Oakland Raiders.

to which NIL money is involved varies by student, sport, and institution, but in some cases the payments are quite sizeable. The financial investments in coaches, staff, facilities, and the extent to which potential booster money is directed toward these things or toward student-athletes themselves varies widely by institution. For some that compete at the highest levels of collegiate competition, the dollars spent are rather large indeed. After all, "you play to win the game," right? This amount of financial investment indicates that the university sees their athletic programs as a significant benefit to the institution. However, rarely if ever do universities include athletics explicitly in their mission statement. Mission statements often center around the academic role of the institution, and athletics appear to many as a unique aspect of higher education. Sometimes referred to as the "front porch" for a college, on the surface athletic competitions may seem to have very little to do with the academic purpose of higher education. Athletics are often the most visible and well-known part of a university to the community at large, so they serve as a marketing and advancement opportunity. Athletic competition can also add to student life, school spirit, and a sense of community in ways that help student enrollment and retention. Is there more athletics can offer; more that relates directly to the student learning experience and the mission of the institution?

Institutions of higher education exist to train and prepare students for civic, public, and corporate duty.[3] The purpose from the founding of the first institutions of higher education in the United States was for colleges and universities to develop a more skilled, disciplined, and wiser population that would then transform society. In the American colonies, King George petitioned wealthy Englishmen to fund colleges in the colonies because, "a college advances learning; it combats ignorance and barbarism... it is an instructor in loyalty, in citizenship, in the dictates of conscience and faith."[4] This implies more than just job specific technical training. Even today, most university mission state-

[3] Sara Boatman, "The Leadership Audit: A Process to Enhance the Development of Student Leadership," *NASPA Journal* 37, no. 1 (Fall 1999): 325–36; cf. Rudolph.

[4] Ibid., 13.

ments in some way reflect these same goals in various different forms. Likewise, Jesus has called His followers to a lifestyle of character and duty, including mentoring and discipling others along a journey of faith in Him and obedience to His teaching.[5] The apostle Paul pictured the life of faith as one that involves the "renewing of the mind" toward a changed lifestyle.[6] For King George, Jesus, and Paul, there is a learning that goes deeper than knowledge around a topic. True learning changes the whole person. Christian colleges even more than their secular counterparts recognize as their mission an education that shapes the heart and instructs the mind. The growth of the whole person is in view, and this in light of eternity.

While the academic and athletic pursuits of a university may at first glance appear to be distinct, or at best parallel, there is more to consider. If the greater mission of higher education is to prepare students for civic duty and to instruct them in all areas of life, including the spiritual aspect of their life, it seems more may be needed than mere classroom instruction. Athletics departments have the unique potential to both support academic achievement for student-athletes and aid in the character development of students in ways that cannot be achieved in the classroom alone. Within the athletic context, the university staff (coach, administrators, trainers, etc.) has a unique ability to observe, correct, and train student-athletes as whole people whose choices and actions produce immediate and observable results. Where a classroom is theoretical, athletics is practical. A classroom instructor shapes a student's thoughts, a coach shapes their actions. A classroom may use books, a sport may use a ball. The classroom and the athletic arena together are tools to shape the whole person.

It is a common quip that sports build character. However, conflicting research on this idea has challenged the extent to which these goals are being achieved in most universities today. Beller and Stoll found that the longer students participate in athletics, the lower they test on

[5] Matt. 5:48; 28:19–20.

[6] Romans 12–16.

measures of moral reasoning.[7] In addition, student-athletes have been shown to perform more poorly on measures of academic success than their non-athlete counterparts.[8] Yet, the NCAA claims that graduation rates, academic performance, and retention remain higher among college athletes than their peers.[9] So, does participation in college sports build character or not? The research at least indicates that there may be other factors involved. The opportunity is there, but are all colleges taking advantage of this great mentoring, whole person development opportunity?

The opportunity is there for athletics to support the mission of higher education, not only to use athletics for marketing and fundraising, but also to develop the whole person in ways that support and build on the learning that happens in the classroom. Billy Graham claimed, "A coach will impact more people in one year than the average person will in an entire lifetime."[10] For the Christian, that impact is part of the mission of discipleship and has eternal value. It is more than merely the temporary joy of an athletic victory—of playing to win the game. Christian faith and the message of the gospel informs a uniquely Christian understanding of competition that neither dismisses the pursuit of victory nor fails to set boundaries in that pursuit.

The Role of the Christian Faith and Winning in Athletic Competition

Perhaps the role for Christian institutions to use college athletics as a tool for mentoring student-athletes toward their whole person development is self-evident. However, some Christians may argue that

---

[7] Jennifer M. Beller and Sharon K. Stoll, "Moral Reasoning of High School Student Athletes and General Students: An Empirical Study versus Personal Testimony," Pediatric Exercise Science 7 (November 1995): 352–63.

[8] Edwin W. Eckard, "NCAA Athlete Graduation Rates: Less Than Meets the Eye," *Journal of Sport Management* 24, no. 1 (January 2010): 45–58.

[9] Michelle B. Hosick, "DI College Athletes Reach 90% Graduation Rate," Media Center, NCAA, November 17, 2020, https://www.ncaa.org/news/2020/11/17/di-college-athletes-reach-90-graduation-rate.aspx.

[10] Shelley Pearson, "To the Coach and Then Through the Coach," *Fellowship of Christian Athletes*, March 17, 2021, https://www.minnesotafca.org/to-through-coach.

athletic competition has no eternal value and is therefore superfluous at best, and distracting at worst, to the faith-based mission of a Christian college. This dualistic understanding separates sacred and non-sacred spaces within human experience in ways that are contrary to the thinking of the biblical authors. In fact, the whole of this book is an effort to demonstrate that Christian faith and practice permeates every area of life and is not merely regulated to certain "sacred" activities.

A Christian college seeking to integrate Christian faith into their athletics department has both an opportunity and a calling to be unique in its role of character formation. This is something that a Christian university has access to that a secular institution cannot in the same way. The Christian place of higher education where there is a real integration of faith into every arena has not given up on the "old fashioned" idea of moral instruction, right and wrong, and a divine standard of wise living. These are not "upper story" ideas that cannot be touched by academic learning to the Christian. The Christian maintains the idea of Truth and Goodness in a way that is not merely Machiavellian or democratic. The Christian accepts a design—a divine law, a *telos* or ultimate end—that is the standard for all of life. That standard does not change once one leaves the pews and enters the world of the marketplace or the arena of competition. An athletics department therefore, can be involved with students in an activity, a doing, that presents real case studies for mentoring students toward civic, public, and corporate duty. In athletics, unlike many other areas of a university, faculty and staff engage with students in an experience where decisions must be made regarding right and wrong, truth and error, wisdom and foolishness. If Christ has asked His followers to disciple other followers into obedience of everything that Jesus commanded, surely this means more than theological discussions in the classroom. Theology must be applied. Hands on experiences, of which athletics is one, are opportunities for faith to be applied. Competition unites athletes around a goal (to win), but along the way the journey toward that goal involves thousands of behaviors that flow out of a person. In shaping behavior, a coach does more than direct the physical body, they direct the heart.

What are the qualities of a Christ-follower that are being shaped in the athletics departments of Christian colleges? How does an athletics department support the mission of an institution to train young men and women in godliness? What are the unique roles, opportunities, and resources for athletic departments who are also working in a context where the goal is to win the game?

A well-known idea drawn from Scripture and articulated in the Westminster Catechism and elsewhere is that the "chief end" or the *telos,* of every human is to "glorify God, and fully to enjoy Him forever."[11] If human design is to glorify God, and as Paul says we are to do all things for the glory of God, then that must apply to every human endeavor.[12] Often Christian athletes or sports groups will talk about playing their sport "to glorify God," but what does this mean?

Brian Smith, in his excellent work, *The Christian Athlete*, provides a helpful definition of what it means to glorify God. Smith says that glorifying God means "thinking and acting in a way that pleases Him and draws attention to who He is."[13] The Christian coach and student-athlete must then consider what that looks like in the athletic arena. While none of the biblical authors were athletic competitors, there are a number of examples from Scripture that are helpful in considering what this might look like.

A first principle is that the glory God deserves is not to be taken for ourselves. In Acts 12, King Herod is celebrated (worshiped) by a crowd, and compared to a god, not a man (vs. 22). The very next verse says, "Immediately, because Herod did not give praise to God, an angel of the Lord struck him down, and he was eaten by worms and died" (Acts 12:23 [NIV]). Herod took glory meant only for God from the crowd. Just two chapters later in the book of Acts, a crowd saw the apostle Paul heal a crippled man, and they called Paul and Barnabas gods (Zeus and

11 "What is the Chief and Highest End of Man?" The Westminster Larger Catechism, Ligonier, accessed November 27, 2023, https://www.ligonier.org/learn/articles/westminster-larger-catechism.

12 1 Cor. 10:31.

13 Brian Smith, *The Christian Athlete: Glorifying God in Sports* (Colorado Springs, CO: David C Cook, 2022), 24.

Hermes). Thankfully, Paul and Barnabas reacted very differently than Herod. They "tore their clothes and rushed out into the crowd, shouting: 'Friends, why are you doing this? We too are only human, like you" (Acts 14:14–15 [NIV]). Accepting worship and glory, and not giving the glory to God is no small thing.

Athletics does not just involve the coaches and players on the field. Athletics is prized in American society and culture. Good athletes are often treated with an elevation that at times can feel much like worship. This is no small thing in God's eyes, and the way it affects our own hearts is a temptation that those in the arena must battle. Every good and perfect gift is from God (James 1:17)—including the ability to run fast, jump high, or hit a ball far. Often there are "fans" participating in the athletic event. There is a camaraderie and involvement from others in the student body, from parents, from the community that often come to cheer on (or jeer at) the competitors. There is a joy in seeing an individual or a group excel at a high level due to their skill and training. However, human nature can sometimes go beyond admiration to worship or glory. Christian coaches and administrators must help their students to recognize that only God is worthy of worship, and fan participation may never be used or abused for our own glory. Sometimes athletes may deflect the praise of others with a simple, "I want to thank God for giving me the ability…" or a finger pointing to the sky. However, these small gestures may or may not reflect a heart attitude that is consistent with their intended message. Playing in such a way that glorifies God goes far beyond a simple phrase or gesture.

These spiritual gestures of deflection come most often after a victory or a big play. A home run is hit, a three-pointer made, a touchdown caught, a big spike in volleyball, a breaking through the finish line tape. In interviews after a big victory, an athlete will interrupt the reporter to throw in a quick comment to deflect and "give glory to God." This may be helpful at a time when all attention and eyes are on the student athlete (remember Herod). In the athlete's own heart, and before a watching crowd, this is an opportunity to redirect the attention to God. This sounds a lot like the stories of Herod and Paul in Acts. However, public pronouncements of faith in special moments must also be supported by a lifestyle and reputation that also honors God. Remember Brian Smith's definition of what it means to glorify God. It is more than just drawing attention to Him. Many are turned off by the way they perceive the use of God in those special moments, especially if it comes across as backhanded self-promotion, rather than representing true gratitude. In addition, these comments or gestures may also come from a heart that views God as an ombudsman, or a deity to be manipulated. Even at their very best, these examples are not the totality of integrating faith in athletics. Many of these side gestures represent a Christian faith interacting alongside of athletics, not necessarily a faith integrated into the whole. There is more to integrating faith and athletics, but what?

Blackaby and Blackaby noted that Christian leaders are called first and foremost to seek success in God's eyes rather than merely striving after success in the world's eyes.[14] If this is true, then a Christian must commit themselves to their primary calling toward God and measure their success in His eyes, by His standards. The Lord's standards are not the same as the world. To the world, "you play to win the game," but is this God's primary interest? The world measures athletic success through wins and losses, a scoreboard. This may run parallel at times to God's way of measuring success. At other times, the way the world measures may be in conflict with God's judgment. For the Christian, it is ultimately God's opinion that matters. Remember, a human's purpose is to glorify God, and that means, "thinking and acting in a way that *pleases Him*..."[15] According to Paul, it is the Lord who judges, and "who will bring to light the things now hidden in darkness and will disclose the purposes of the heart. Then each one will receive his commendation from God."[16]

If God is primarily interested in our character, and in forming His people into a better reflection of Jesus,[17] then what traits reflect

[14] Henry Blackaby and Richard Blackaby, *Spiritual Leadership: Moving People on to God's Agenda* (Nashville, TN: B&H, 2001),143.

[15] Smith, *The Christian Athlete*, 24.

[16] 1 Cor. 4:5 (ESV).

[17] Rom. 8:29.

God's character that might lead us toward athletic victory? Are there any boundaries to our pursuit of winning? Consider that without any boundaries, the athlete is not submitting to God, but to their sport, and competition may become an idol of his or her heart. This runs counter not only to our culture, but to our inherent sinful human nature. This is where coaches and administrators have the great opportunity of setting a different perspective. Mentoring may very well occur in the pursuit of victory, and in both the achieving or falling short of a "win." In a statement that echoes Paul in 1 Corinthians, Pastor Miguel Lopez of Duncanville's First Baptist Church has previously stated, "Success is not measured by people's recognition of our achievements, but by Jesus' recognition of our faithfulness."[18] The Christian has a different audience, a different perspective, a different motivation, and different goals. God's character and His Word must direct our values and set our boundaries.

What are the values that a Christian athletics department pursues, models, and develops in their student-athletes? One of the classic character traits or values believed to be developed through athletics is a commitment to great effort. Effort, being a good steward, a strong work ethic, are all ways to describe making a good use of one's time, talents, and resources for something rather than burying them in the sand. Jesus' parable of the talents is an example of the divine call toward intentional stewardship. Consider also Paul's charge to the Ephesians to live "making the best use of the time, because the days are evil."[19] A strong work ethic has historically been connected to the Christian faith, even calling it the Christian work ethic or the Protestant work ethic.[20] Athletics has a unique potential in the academic institution to develop a strong work ethic.

---

[18] Miguel Lopez, email message to editor, November 29, 2023.

[19] Eph. 5:16 (ESV).

[20] Timothy J. Keller and Katherine L. Alsdorf, *Every Good Endeavor: Connecting Your Work to God's Work* (New York, NY: Dutton, 2012); Petrus L. Steenkamp, "Protestant Ethic: Contributing Towards a Meaningful Workplace," *Hervormde Teologiese Studies* 69, no. 1 (January 2013):1–11, https://doi.org/10.4102/hts.v69il.1315.

Another character trait elevated in value both in athletics, especially team sports, and in Scripture is selflessness. Jesus called His followers to an upside-down kingdom that elevates selfless servants. Team sports also calls athletes toward selflessness. Often, teammates must work together with others toward a common goal, even laying down their own self-interest at times. Grit, perseverance, selflessness, and effort are valuable character traits for members of any society. Christians should be selfless hard workers, and those are traits that also lead toward competitive greatness. In this way, the values of the Bible support the qualities needed for teams to win.

The Integration of Faith in Athletic Competition

The difference between integration and the surface level gestures mentioned earlier is like the difference between a solution and a mixture. Consider a mixture of different parts, like a bag of trail mix compared to a solution, like a glass of salt water, where different substances are completely dissolved and cannot be easily filtered out. Integration is like the solution. In the mixture, the different parts remain distinct. They may be close to one another, but a new substance is not formed.

At DBU, beginning in 2005, one of the stated goals for the athletics department was to require every coach to be leaders in the disciple-making process of each of their student-athletes. There was a feeling that it was far too easy for coaches to allow Christian faith to interact with their sport, but not to integrate faith into their sport. A sports chaplain, a "character coach," a pre-game devotional or post-game prayer, a Fellowship of Christian Athletes group or other para-church ministry are wonderful ways to bring Christian faith into proximity of sport. But if during practice, during bus rides, during hotel stays, and yes, even during competition itself, a vibrant Christian walk consistent with those occasional messages is not in practice, then integration is not happening. How would this look different from any other team? If some values like hard work and teamwork are common to the Christian and non-Christian alike, is there any difference in the values of eternity and of the world?

It has been noted that hard work and a strong work ethic is a biblical value. However, God's Word also provides some boundaries on human work ethic. The writer of Ecclesiastes points out an appropriate tension on this point. Effort may also become a "striving after the wind" if temporal things are the end goal. Victories and accomplishments are fleeting, not eternal. Some things are of greater and more lasting value.[21] God also has established patterns of rest that provide boundaries to human striving. God created humans for work, and He calls His people away from sloth and toward industriousness, but the concept of rest and Sabbath also reminds us of our dependence on God. Coaches and administrators can help mentor and model for students a proper work-life balance. Christians should work hard, and they should also work with an eternal perspective.

Another biblical value that receives much less attention is the biblical value of suffering. Suffering is a value? Of course, not in the sense of self-flagellation or seeking out suffering. But a Christ follower must be willing to endure through difficulties to pursue righteousness. Christ Himself was the promised "Suffering Servant," a "man of sorrows and acquainted with grief."[22] Jesus promised His followers, "In this world you will have trouble."[23] A Christian ought not to follow the cultural current that seeks to avoid suffering at all costs. The Christ follower instead seeks to follow Jesus in the way of truth, wisdom, love, and righteousness in obedience to the will of God wherever that may lead. In discussing the leadership model of servant leadership, authors Kouzes and Posner encourage every Christian leader to ask themselves two questions, "Who am I serving?" and "Am I willing to suffer?"[24] Additionally, the famous Pastor Charles H. Spurgeon claimed, "there are certain truths and promises in the Bible that have little or no meaning to

---

[21] 1 Tim. 4:8.

[22] Isa. 53:3 (ESV).

[23] John 16:33 (NIV).

[24] James M. Kouzes and Barry Z. Posner, eds., *Christian Reflections on the Leadership Challenge* (San Francisco, CA: Jossey-Bass, 2004), 72.

us unless we have faced affliction."[25] If this willingness to accept suffering as potentially a purpose from the sovereign hand of God, how would this impact our mentoring student-athletes in the field of competition? How does suffering relate to an environment where the goal is to win? If "you play to win the game," then does that imply that the highest value is to succeed in the same way the world evaluates success—winning?

This understanding of power and success is perhaps the most counter-cultural Christian value in the highly competitive world of athletics. Jesus inverted the perception of power in God's kingdom in the Sermon on the Mount.[26] God's blessing, or gracious favor, is not, according to Jesus, offered in the same way to the rich and powerful, the satisfied, the gloating, or the popular. For these, Jesus spoke a warning. Instead, God's blessing was offered to the poor in spirit, those who mourn, the meek, those who hunger and thirst for righteousness, the pure and merciful, the persecuted, and the peacemakers. In fact, the original term used in the English translation "woe to you who laugh now" was a term referring to those who had won, as in a political victory, and has the idea of gloating as the victors.[27] Does this mean Jesus was teaching His followers not to win, or that winning is wrong? At the very least there is a warning in the words of Jesus of a spiritual danger in victory. Perhaps there may be a danger we need to consider if we believe, "you play to win the game."

Another Christian value with great opportunities for growth within the world of athletics would be the virtues of humility and peace. The opposite vice to combat would be pride and anger. These vices may remain hidden in comfortable moments, but the heat of competition has a way of bringing them to the surface. Athletes have been observed

---

[25] Steve Miller, *C. H. Spurgeon on Spiritual Leadership* (Chicago, IL: Moody, 2003), 122.

[26] Matt. 5:1–7:29; Luke 6:17–38.

[27] Timothy J. Keller, "The Upside-Down Kingdom," March 21, 1999, in *Hope for New York*, produced by Gospel in Life, podcast, https://gospelinlife.com/sermon/the-upside-down-kingdom-2/.

(and even celebrated) for having a win-at-all-cost attitude.[28] C. S. Lewis defined the biblical sin of pride as an ultimate evil and notes that it was rooted in a competitive thirst for more.[29] Pride has been described as a feeling of superiority over others. "Pride is the original sin and one of the most dangerous, because it blinds us to our own weaknesses and transgressions... When we feel that we are superior to others, we brim with confidence and a sense of superiority."[30] What is athletic competition, but an effort to prove oneself superior to others? Dr. Shirl Hoffman chronicled the historic difficulty the Christian church has had reconciling its own message with the very essence of sport competition. In response to the potential lessons of sports like hard work, teamwork, discipline, and many character traits supported by Christian values, Hoffman recognized some benefits, but noted how hard it was to balance and justify competition with the underlying tenets of the Christian faith.[31] Theologian and social commentator, Michael Novak stated, "basketball without deception, football without aggression, baseball without cunning and trickery can't be played... they provide an almost deliberate exercise in pushing the psyche to cheat and take advantage, to be ruthless, cruel, deceitful, vengeful, and aggressive."[32] Or consider the message communicated by the Duke basketball sign: The Meek Shall Inherit the Earth, but they're not going to Kansas City (i.e. to the Final Four).[33] How might a Christian coach or student athlete integrate humility into the very act of competition? This is no easy task, and is not

---

[28] Michael Gargano, Jr., "A Study to Determine Whether or not the Principles of Sportsmanship and Ethical Conduct can Coexist with the Competing Principles Associated with Highly Competitive Athletic Programs in NCAA Division I Men's Basketball" (PhD diss., George Washington University, Washington, D. C., 2001), 96, ProQuest Dissertations & Theses Global.

[29] Clive S. Lewis, *Mere Christianity: What One Must Believe to Be a Christian* (New York, NY: Macmillan, 1978), 109.

[30] Gary E. Roberts, *Developing Christian Servant Leadership: Faith-Based Character Growth at Work* (New York, NY: Palgrave Macmillan, 2015), 162.

[31] Shirl J. Hoffman, *Good Game: Christianity and the Culture of Sports* (Waco, TX: Baylor University Press, 2010), 145.

[32] Michael J. Novak, *Joy of Sports* (New York, NY: Basic Books, 1976), 312.

[33] Richard Hoffer, Mark Bechtel, and Stephen Cannella, "No More Mr. Nice Guy," *Sports Illustrated* 104, no. 21 (May 2006): 18.

a problem that is solved merely by a group public prayer or pregame devotional.

We play to win the game, right? But what if a moral dilemma arises where the right thing in God's eyes is not the choice that appears to lead toward winning the game? It is easy to justify or rationalize these decisions and cover them with a veneer of faith, because of the opportunities it creates to share faith. Our earlier definition of what it means to glorify God was, "to do what pleases Him in thought and action, and to draw attention to who He is."[34] Half of this definition does have to do with "drawing attention to God," but note that it is drawing attention to "who He is" not just a generic abstract of God. Even before the public act of "drawing attention" though is doing "what pleases Him in thought and action." God sees what is done in secret, and He knows our motives. To truly lead and live in a way that glorifies God, coaches and athletes must be willing to lose. A "win at all costs" mentality can become a new god, an idol, that drives motives and decisions more than a submission to the wisdom and guidance of our Lord Jesus. Competition can be fun, and all who play desire to excel, to win. "You play to win the game," but if it really came to it, are you willing to lose? Would you make a decision in submission to God, even if it felt like it made winning less likely?

Dave Bliss is a self-professing Christian, and from 1999–2003, he was the head basketball coach at a private Christian institution, Baylor University. However, his time there ended in dramatic fashion when it came to light that he had been involved in illicit tuition payments for players,[35] not disclosing failed drug tests of his players, and lying to investigators. Bliss has detailed his own experience in his book, *Fall to Grace*,[36] and the scandal that ended his time at Baylor has also been de-

[34] Smith, *The Christian Athlete*, 24.

[35] At the time, Baylor was limited in their athletic scholarships due to NCAA regulations regarding transfers.

[36] Dave Bliss, *Fall to Grace: The Climb, Collapse, and Comeback of Coach Dave Bliss* (Indian Trail, NC: Core Media Group, 2015).

tailed in a Showtime documentary *Disgraced*.[37] Coach Bliss has become a pariah in Christian and coaching communities, and God alone can judge the authenticity of his faith. But consider how poor decisions can be made when the driving motivation is to win. The sinful human heart has a powerful ability to rationalize and justify unethical decisions if the motive of winning is higher than the motive of integrity. Coach Bliss's story is a warning to any coach who claims to be a Christian of the danger of compromising ethically in the competitive world of athletics. None of us are without sin, and the gospel puts us all on level ground as sinners, who can only be saved by grace. However, an integrated faith is characterized by integrity, even in the world of competition.

This author cannot point fingers outward when it comes to compromised motives. The tension and temptation have been real in my own experience. There have been players that I have wanted to recruit that would have compromised stated values and standards we had set as an organization. I have had players break team rules in such a way that deserved significant discipline, but a suspension would have required playing a game without multiple starters. I have been tempted to lie or be less than honest when it comes to reporting practice hours or recruiting contacts. These are not just abstract questions for those involved with athletics. The decisions do not happen in a classroom, they happen in what often feel like high pressure situations. I know my success as a coach can be greatly influenced by how these decisions are made. It is very easy to lose a game (or more) based on our choices. That is when I must remind myself that my measurement of success comes not from the scoreboard, but from my Savior. Would it please Him?

All these anecdotes present some of the challenges for the Christian athlete seeking to integrate their faith into athletics. One might conclude that athletics cannot be reconciled with Christian faith, but yet, the Bible is replete with at least neutral assessments and usage of athletic imagery. There is something very similar to athletic competition and the Christian life. Both athletic training and following Christ require

---

[37] *Disgraced*, directed by Pat Kondelis, featuring Dave Bliss (Showtime, 2017), https://www.sho.com/ titles/3445716/disgraced.

discipline, effort, focus, and purpose.[38] Jesus spoke of being good stewards.[39] Proverbs 22:29 recognizes the wisdom in doing things well and with skill. Competition, play, and sports are neutral. How, why, to what end, and in what way sports are played determine the spiritual impact of competition. The same could be said of business, money, or many other human endeavors. The fact that athletics present challenges to our sinful nature merely presents more of an opportunity. In this way, athletic competition is a case study in life. The opportunity to mentor and lead young men and women in a walk of faith through not an easy environment, but a difficult one, creates the platform for real mentoring and discipleship to occur.

A Christian athletic department must integrate Christian faith with all its activities. Merely pointing to the sky after hitting a big shot in basketball, or telling a reporter "I want to give the glory to God" after a big victory as a tacked-on dressing, is not integration. Praying before or after a game, doing a Bible study with the team, may bring faith in proximity to sports and athletics, but this is merely interaction—not integration. Are the issues of pride, anger, power, success, suffering, stewardship, and community met minute by minute in a formative way that leads college students to apply their faith? Is there modeling and accountability and repentance amid a heated battle? Or merely in a pre-game devotional that can be easily set aside in the high-pressure situations?

While the Bible communicates certain black and white boundaries of right and wrong behavior, frequently in the gray areas, the Bible's emphasis is on the heart and motives. Malphurs poses this pressing question for the heart and motives of a leader, "Is your motive as a leader to serve Christ and his church and ultimately to glorify God, or is it to gain for yourself personal prominence, prestige, and power?"[40] What would it look like to compete and lead in a university athletic

[38] 1 Cor. 9:24–29; 2 Tim. 2:5; Phil. 2:16; Gal. 2:2; 5:7; Heb. 12:1–2.

[39] Matt. 25:14–30.

[40] Aubrey Malphurs, *Being Leaders: The Nature of Authentic Christian Leadership* (Grand Rapids, MI: Baker, 2003), 32.

department "to serve Christ and His church and ultimately to glorify God?" These are the questions of integration, and they cannot be easily tacked on with an occasional Christian dressing.

The Motives Behind Integrated Christian Faith in Athletics

The following are examples of what it looks like to have different motives and to fully integrate Christian faith. When the ultimate goal is winning, the temptations to compromise are great. Whenever a difficult decision comes along for a leader, a leader's motivations and goals will help shape and drive those decisions. Consider these real-life situations:

- Should I play this ineligible player?
- Should I suspend these players for breaking our team policies and standards?
- Should I remove this player from the team?
- Should I recruit this student athlete to begin with?
- What should I tell them to expect during the recruiting process?
- Should I ask this professor to reconsider this student's grade or to show them some "grace?"
- Should I do what my competitors are doing for a competitive advantage? Performance Enhancing Drugs (PEDs). Pine tar. Summer practice hours. Recruiting contacts.

If the ultimate motive is to "win," then the answer to these questions will be guided by that priority of what will help one's team win, make the NCAA tournament, etc. If, however, the ultimate motive is to please the Lord, then the answer to these questions will be guided by that priority instead.

Desiring true integration presents its own challenges. It is a hard road. All humans will continue to struggle with sin in one way or another, and it is impossible in this life to live in a way that always reflects the character of God. Can an athlete confess sin, be open and transparent if their disciple/mentor is also their disciplinarian and authority? A coach is an authority that can sometimes shut down debate and deep contemplation. Often student-athletes do not feel comfortable wrestling with doubts or faith questions in front of the same person who determines their playing time. Spending time invested in Christian discipleship can be a time-consuming and potentially distracting investment. Is it a competitive disadvantage?

In conclusion, athletic department staff wishing to truly integrate their faith into the world of collegiate athletics have a unique opportunity. They can support the university's mission by challenging, mentoring, and leading students in a way that develops their whole person. The opportunities to walk through real-life situations outside of the classroom are unique among university faculty. However, merely bringing Christian faith and practice near a sport is not true integration. It is not enough to simply give lip service to a few selected character values, like "hard work" or "teamwork." The temptation to place winning as the top goal and purpose can derail efforts to disciple and mentor students, and to live out Christian faith. Striving to do one's best in an attempt to win is inherent to the nature of sports. The Christian athlete on the one hand must be committed to the pursuit of excellence and victory. However, this striving cannot be compromised in ways that would be displeasing to God. There are boundary lines that a Christian must recognize, so while the Christian plays to win, he or she must also be willing to lose. There is a greater purpose for the Christian and the Christian institution when it comes to athletic departments. God knows our motives, and the heart of every coach, administrator, and athlete. The heart and motives are the real difference when it comes to the gray areas of life. Modeling and mentoring students along the life-long journey of faith in accordance with the overall university mission must be the driving purpose for any institution to truly integrate faith and athletics.

Questions for Reflection

- Should we pray publicly at center court before or after a practice or game? This can be a great opportunity to model a relationship with God, and to publicly draw attention to His character. However, Jesus also called His disciples to pray in secret—not for the admiration of others.[41] Public prayer can also be interpreted by others as a type of self-righteous gloating, especially after a win.

- Should we wear a cross on our uniforms or hang signs around our stadium?
- Should coaches lead Bible studies and/or spiritual formation groups?
- How can/should a coach motivate student-athletes to perform at their highest levels in competitive, aggressive environments?
- How do we make the connections for our student-athletes between training for excellence in sport, and excellence in following Christ?

[41] Matt. 6:5–6.

Chapter 16

Integrating Faith in the Physical Operations of Campus

By Rob Lewis,[1] Mat Richter,[2] and Caleb Kestner[3]

Introduction

Physical operations at Dallas Baptist University incorporates a wide range of disciplines and personnel, but is unified around the same standards of faithfulness and excellence. Our job responsibilities range from landscaping, cleaning, cooking, construction, plumbing, and administrative tasks. We oversee minor remodels and major renovations. We are responsible for changing light bulbs and the construction of new buildings. As a student walks onto the DBU campus, they experience the fruit of physical operations during their entire student career.

This chapter highlights how we incorporate the four-part framework of integrating faith and learning into our day-to-day operations. Our worldview influences how we steward our resources and relationships. Attitudinally, we cultivate honor by managing a positive and Christ-like attitude with one another. We prioritize ethical conduct with our resources, which is above reproach and bestows honor, respect, and dignity on our staff. We display gratitude for the legacy passed down to

[1] Rob Lewis serves as an Assistant Vice President for Administrative Affairs at Dallas Baptist University.

[2] Mat Richter serves as an Assistant Vice President for Administrative Affairs at Dallas Baptist University.

[3] Caleb Kestner serves as Adult Ministries Coordinator at Gateway Church in Dallas, but previously served in the Physical Operations staff at Dallas Baptist University.

us in the foundational elements of our national heritage memorialized on our campus.

Before we dive into the core content of this chapter, we want to present the overall culture of DBU's Physical Operations Department to provide a context for the four-part framework. Ultimately, members of the physical operations department understand their contributions are significant by how they help cultivate spaces for learning and growth. We are driven to provide excellent service in a timely manner. When we achieve our goals, the faculty is free to focus on how they train and develop the next generation of biblical servant leaders.

Our biblical models are found in the story of Exodus. The newly freed Israelites, after crossing the Red Sea into the wilderness, began a journey to learn how to worship God. Moses received the instructions for the tabernacle and the name of two craftsmen—Bezalel and Oholiab. God called these two men out by name and commented how He had prepared them to turn God's blueprints into reality. In Exodus 31:1–38, God introduces Bezalel. He said, "I have filled him with the Spirit of God, with wisdom, with understanding, with knowledge and with all kinds of skills" (31:3 [NIV]). Then, God lists Bezalel's resume and portfolio. When Moses presented Bezalel and Oholiab to the people, he repeated God's commendation, "[God] filled him [Bezalel] with the Spirit of God, with wisdom, with understanding, with knowledge and with all kinds of skills… and he has given both him and Oholiab… the ability to teach others" (Exodus 35:31, 34 [NIV]).

God gifted Bezalel and Oholiab with skills, wisdom, understanding, the ability to teach others, and, most importantly, they were filled with the Spirit of God. The men and women of physical operations are skilled, knowledgeable people with the desire to share their knowledge with others. You will also discover a depth of spirituality as you interact with the people of physical operations. We are more than just operations personnel; we are disciples of Jesus Christ.

Like we said earlier, Physical Operations Office has a wide range of responsibilities but carries the same values across each sub-department. We do not operate independently from the rest of campus, but we maintain good relationships with executive leadership, faculty, students, parents, and outside vendors. Our values aid our relationships with others and are rooted in our biblical worldview. The three dominant values in physical operations are: diligence, stewardship, and servant leadership.

First, we diligently strive for excellence in our work and to reflect the character of God. Hugh Welchel said, "being in the image of God refers not only to who we are but also to what we are created to do. We are called not just to work, but to do certain tasks to achieve a definite goal."[4] Our second value is to practice biblical stewardship, which is to understand the principal Jesus taught in the parable of the shrewd manager. In Luke 16:10, Jesus said, "whoever can be trusted with very little can also be trusted with much, and whoever is dishonest with very little will also be dishonest with much" (NIV). We strive to be trustworthy and faithful by how we manage our buildings, vehicles, budgets, resources, and most importantly, our teams. The third value is to practice biblical servant leadership, which is a major theme of the DBU Mission Statement. We empower, equip, and help our people grow personally and professionally. According to Rob Lewis, one of the co-authors of this chapter, "we are growing people, not just the campus."

As you can see, the physical operations culture and scope of work is different from other departments who contributed to this book. We are a unique department; however, we share the same goal to glorify God and to love others. For the rest of this chapter, we will analyze how we integrate faith and learning through Worldview, Attitudinal, Ethical, and Foundational Approaches.

Part 1—Worldview Integration

The topic of worldview is widely taught in academic settings and is understood to be an underlying motivation for how people respond and interact with the world. Unless we take the time to understand why we believe what we believe, we will simply work based on our unperceived values and beliefs. When we delve deep into our beliefs, then we begin

[4] Whelchel, *How Then Should We Work,* 14–15.

to make informed decisions. We also need to be aware of a departmental worldview that is composed of the unique beliefs of each staff member of physical operations. We have a responsibility to strategically instill a communal worldview within the collective staff of physical operations. There are two core strategies we utilize to incorporate a biblical worldview and three essential beliefs we instill in all of our physical operations personnel.

Strategies to Implement Worldview

The first strategy is to constantly remind each other of Paul's exhortation in Colossians 3:17, 23–24: "And whatever you do, whether in word or deed, do it all in the name of the Lord Jesus, giving thanks to God the Father through him… whatever you do, work at it with all your heart, as working for the Lord, not for human masters, since you know that you will receive an inheritance from the Lord as a reward. It is the Lord Christ you are serving" (NIV). These verses provide three directives. First, "whatever you do" is a broad statement that covers the entire scope of work for every physical operations employee. Second, we are to work heartily or enthusiastically for the Lord. We are not only working for a paycheck, but out of obedience and loyalty to Jesus Christ—to bring Him honor and glory. Third, we have the promise of a reward for our faithfulness. When we see each other having a difficult day, we remind each other how the primary purpose of our jobs is to bring God the glory He deserves.

The second strategy is to incorporate worship, prayer, and Bible study into our regular work rhythms. This is not a requirement for employees, but we do provide opportunities for corporate worship and Bible study. We encourage the older staff to invest in the younger. This looks like one-on-one lunches, small group book studies, and prayer time as a team before the day begins. We desire to emulate the daily fellowship of the early church. We allow space in our days to encourage one another in the hallways, construction sites, attics, flower beds, and auto-shop. God meets us wherever two or more of His children gather together in prayer—and this includes when we are working side-by-side on a project.

Core Beliefs to Our Worldview

The first of the core beliefs is how each human bears the image of God and has an inherent value. This belief affects the way we lead our teams and steward our relationships with outside vendors and contractors. In Genesis 1:27, the Bible states, "so God created mankind in his own image, in the image of God he created them; male and female he created them" (NIV). This belief compels us to treat others with respect, dignity, and honor. Every person, regardless of their place on an organizational chart, is an image bearer of God and we will treat them as a brother or sister in Christ. We recognize people are not tools to be used, but a person to be encouraged and edified. We want to invest in others regardless of their affiliation at DBU and to provide them an outlet for meaningful work.

The second core belief is also found in Genesis 1:28 where God blessed man and said, "'be fruitful and increase in number; fill the earth and subdue it. Rule over the fish in the sea and the birds in the sky and over every living creature that moves on the ground'" (NIV). God wanted Adam to know the plants of the field are for his benefit—the same is true for us. At DBU, we take the cultural mandate seriously by how we steward and maintain the physical components of the campus. For animals, we oversee the care and attention given to the swans and cattle that belong to the school. We take pride in the beauty of the variety of trees, bushes, flowers, and types of grass on our campus. We understand our role to care and tend to the plants and animals is one way to obey God's directive. One staff member, who oversees landscaping, had this to say:

> This is God's campus. This is His creation. I just get the privilege of working on it and I get the privilege of dealing with... His creation and this is what He created. And He created beauty, and if creation is beautiful, He is beautiful, then everything that we do here points to Him.

This staff member embodies our call to care for God's creation as a way to redirect glory and honor to Him.

Our third belief is how every space on our campus can be used to foster community and discipleship. Our facilities are designed intentionally for professional, personal, and spiritual growth. We believe God created people to live in community,[5] and so we try to create physical spaces—dorms/residential facilities, classrooms, eating spaces, walking paths, and more—that help to foster and build this type of Christ-centered community. Throughout the Bible, there are examples of God calling His people to support each other as believers,[6] and He commends the idea of community when He says: "Where two or three gather in my name, there am I with them" (Matthew 18:20 [NIV]). Thus, we see each physical space on campus as a potential place where worship can happen, spiritual discipleship can happen, and students can grow as a community of believers. We see professors discipling students in the dining hall, spontaneous worship nights emerging in the dorm lobbies, coaches sharing God's vision on the practice field, and administrators spiritually mentoring students in the workout room and on our running paths. In all of these interactions, we see that our ability to provide the right spaces allows for these spiritual interactions to take place. Thus, we see that every square inch of our campus is an integral part of our mission to build disciples and transform lives for Christ.

For instance, we prioritize how we maintain the classrooms because we understand this is where the next generation of leaders are being trained. Since professors integrate their faith as they teach their disciplines, these classrooms are not only places where knowledge is gained, but where students grow in their faith. Likewise, we know that students attend DBU to be challenged to grow professionally in a safe, clean environment. When we build new dorms, or renovate existing ones, we believe students will experience personal growth in the community. As their Resident Assistants and upperclassmen mentor them and spiritu-

[5] Gen. 1:26; Ps. 133:1; Rom. 12:45.
[6] Isa. 40:11; Ezekiel 34; John 10; Acts 20:28; 1 Pet. 5:2.

ally disciple them, we know these dormitory facilities create room for Christian community to flourish.

One example of using university spaces to facilitate discipleship is found in the actions of a former Director of University Housing Maintenance. This staffer would often host Bible studies with his team at his on-campus residence and provide them a warm meal. He stated: "I wanted them to see that I really cared for them, that I wanted to know where they were in life and where they wanted to be and help bridge the gap."

The dining hall and coffee shop are another environment on campus where students meet with mentors and professors who intentionally sow spiritual seeds into their life. When we asked him about his favorite place to meet with students on campus, a faculty member noted, "There are so many great spaces across campus to have conversations about life, faith, and ministry." We work hard to provide dining facilities where students are not just fed physically, but spiritually, as well. We know that discipleship happens all the time in these facilities as professors and upperclassmen break bread with new students and help them grow as whole persons in Christ. Even though physical operations personnel are not always physically present when this growth takes place, we believe our labor facilitates their conversations and enables an authentic community to happen.

Our worldview is the bedrock from which our strength as a physical operations team is derived. Our approach is intentional and it takes the effort of all levels of leadership within physical operations to ensure our actions are guided by our worldview. We strive daily to heed the words of the Apostle Paul in Colossians 3 and continually "renew our minds" to the reality of how our daily work has an eternal impact for the Kingdom of God. This truth will become more evident as we discuss the remaining three areas of the four-part framework.

Part 2—Attitudinal Integration

Our Attitudinal Approach is influenced by our belief that we are all made in the image of God. Since every person—regardless of ethnicity, gender, or age—is an image bearer, we prioritize people over projects. When we emphasize healthy relationships, we are also able to accomplish our tasks with excellence. Our attitude toward one another and our job responsibilities contribute to the overall success of our department. When one suffers—so does the other. There are four attitudes we value: A culture of honor, relational trust, one team mentality, and Christ-like motivation.

First, the culture of honor originates within each person and is inspired from the top of the department to the lowest position. The leaders must extend a sense of honor toward others. We honor our team members through acknowledgement. We recognize the gifts and strengths they bring to the team. We highlight the value our staff and contractors contribute to the projects and extend honor to them. We also empower and equip our team members so they can grow. Paul exhorts the Thessalonians to "encourage one another and build each other up, just as in fact you are doing" (1 Thessalonians 5:11 [NIV]).

Next, we engage in relational trust. We understand trust is a foundational component to how we relate with one another. We build relational capital through humility, honesty, integrity, and consistency. Paul expresses the importance of humility in relationships by the metaphor of the body of Christ. If one part of the body suffers, then all suffer. If another part of the body is honored, then the whole body rejoices (1 Corinthians 12:26). Since we are all one body, then we understand our success as a department is not because any one person is excellent, but the team as a whole is successful together.

We are honest in our communications with each other. Nothing erodes trust like a dishonest person. Paul calls us to renounce dishonesty like we would take off a sweaty shirt. Paul exhorts us to "put off falsehood and speak truthfully to your neighbor," (Ephesians 4:25 [NIV]) and "do not lie to each other, since you have taken off your old self with its practices and have put on the new self, which is being renewed in knowledge in the image of its Creator" (Colossians 3:9–10 [NIV]). Practically, for us, we lead with an openness around job descriptions and payroll raise opportunities. We endeavor to communicate early and often around what we expect of our staff and what they can expect from us.

Integrity and consistency go hand in hand. Integrity imitates Christ when He is described in Hebrews 13:8 as being the same "yesterday and today and forever." Jesus is dependable, consistent, and trustworthy. We desire to be the same. Luckily, God gives us the ability to change so we are not stuck as immature children, but as we mature, there is a need to ensure our words and actions are aligned by how we lead our teams and build relationships. In many ways, we lead by example: when there is trash in the middle of the road, we turn on our flashers, park our vehicle, and pick up the trash. As leaders, we set the standard for excellence and do the job we expect of others. We are consistent by the fruit of the Holy Spirit in our lives. We cannot force fruit to grow, but we can consistently provide healthy environments for fruit to spring forth in our lives. For us, the fruit originates from the power of the Holy Spirit working in and through us and through our relationships with others.

The third attitudinal component is how we promote a "one team" approach to physical operations. We have several sub-departments under the umbrella of Physical Operations and we can easily become territorial over equipment, material, and our time. Obviously, we cannot be overly generous at the expense of our responsibilities, but a one team mentality is needed to truly incorporate the "body of Christ" metaphor Paul introduced in his letters (1 Corinthians 12:12–26). Every part of Physical Operations is needed for the department to thrive as a whole. The practical steps we take to reinforce a "one team" mindset is to give away honor to others and to express gratitude for the unique contributions of each team. When a member of our team makes a mistake, sure there might be a little teasing, but we rally across departments to find solutions. When one department is slammed and needs help, we reallocate equipment or personnel to meet their needs. After we avert the crisis, team members in the office express gratitude.

A fresh example of this attitude was the Homecoming event where we were responsible for building and distributing all of the floats. The Grounds Department stepped in to help when the maintenance and construction team were spread thin and unable to distribute the floats to the parade staging area. The day of the parade, we were missing drivers and grounds stepped in again to drive the floats along the parade route. We can say with confidence the parade was a success because the Grounds Department filled in the gap.

The final attitudinal element is to have a Christ-like motivation. We want to inspire our teams to lead with a servant's heart. Jesus taught His disciples to serve others (Mark 10:42–45)—even their enemies. He said, "I tell you, do not resist an evil person… if anyone forces you to go one mile, go with them two miles" (Matthew 5:39, 41 [NIV]). We want a second mile mentality in all of our team members when they interact with students, faculty, and each other. One of our former employees spoke to this truth stating, "In my first year of work, I really learned to serve the University and the University's vision, the ministries on campus, the people on campus, the faculty, and the staff." A great example of Christ-like motivation is seen when our team hangs a television in a conference room, and we bring a vacuum to clean up the dust and debris. Or for example when the food delivery is short on vegetables, we go to the local grocery store to buy enough for the next meal rush. We are willing to do more than the minimum requirement. We want to go above and beyond to meet others' needs.

As seen above, the truth that we are all image bearers of God is woven into the way our teams are motivated to carry out their day-to-day work along with how they relate to one another and the campus community. This Attitudinal Approach can be seen as the very identity of the Physical Operations Department. It is from this rich identity that our ethics are formed and shaped.

Part 3—Ethical Integration

Our ethics are strongly influenced by our faith and biblical worldview as well as the culture we try to instill in physical operations. The implications of what we believe affect our Ethical Approach to work in three fundamental ways: transparency, follow through, and stewardship. Since there is ample division and scandal pertaining to ethical and moral failures today, we are intentional to set policies and practices in place to protect the reputation of DBU and the people of physical operations. For example, whenever one of our maintenance team members needs to enter a female's living unit, there has to be more than one employee present in the unit together at all times—not only to protect our employees, but also to provide peace and security to the female students.

We are above reproach in several ways but want to highlight two main areas: new staff onboarding and our bidding process with contractors. Both of these are directed by our desire to follow Paul's advice to Titus, "in everything set them an example by doing what is good... show integrity, seriousness and soundness of speech that cannot be condemned, so that those who oppose you may be ashamed because they have nothing bad to say about us" (Titus 2:7–8 [NIV]). Carrying out this advice given by Paul starts for us during the onboarding process for new hires. As mentioned previously, honoring our employees is a main tenet of the culture we foster within Physical Operations. When a potential employee begins the interview process, our leadership team begins to model a culture of honor for our new hires. After a job applicant is selected, new employees move to the onboarding process for their respective role. Our ethical obligation is to ensure our new employees are prepared with the general knowledge and understanding of our facilities, teams, and the daily operations of the department. We strive to present new employees with a realistic expectation of their job duties and how their roles integrate into the whole of Physical Operations. We believe transparent communication of job duties is paramount to the effectiveness of the individual employee and their respective team.

Another step within the onboarding process is safety training. We believe our moral obligation is to train employees on best safety practices for their specific trade. Due to the various work environments and differing degrees of danger, safety training must be customized to the risks associated with each role. For our Moves and Setups team, we conduct safety training on proper lifting techniques, and cover the dangers of slips, trips, and falls. Within the Transportation Department, the technicians receive safety training on two and four post automotive lift safety, the necessity of eye, ear, and hand protection, as well as the use of Material Safety Data Sheets (MSDS) literature. The Maintenance Department undergoes ladder safety training, eye, ear, and hand protection and area working platforms. Safety training not only happens during onboarding but continues throughout the year on a predetermined schedule dictated by the respective Director. It is our ethical duty to arm our employees with the knowledge of how to execute their role safely and effectively.

We strive to be above reproach when we request proposals from contractors for special projects and new construction. One of the ways we do this is to refrain from "shopping numbers." When we request proposals from several different plumbing contractors, we do not use their bids against each other to drive down their prices. We allow them to send an initial quote then, internally, we compare cost and value. Before making our decision, we give the losing contractor another chance to rework their proposal if they are high or are missing parts of the scope of work. We treat them with honor and respect and make sure they do not feel tricked or manipulated into performing work for less.

Our second ethical fundamental is to follow through on our commitments. This includes commitments to pay invoices within a 30-day window. We agree to follow through on project agreements and provide adequate insurance and materials for contractors to fulfill their job. Follow through is not only a focused item when dealing with outside vendors but is also key when working with other departments and organizations on campus. When our Moves and Setups team is given a work order to perform a setup, we agree to complete the request by an agreed upon date and time. It is our duty to ensure we follow through with that agreement and provide the setup on time and with excellence. We also hold our employees, both part- and full-timers, to their commitment to show up each day on time and document their time honestly. One staff member shared a small testimony of how his belief in God affected his Ethical Approach to stewarding time as a physical operations employee stating, "[Having integrity] with my time, my work, not slacking as much as I could have, it's a really big value to God." As he states, having integrity with our time along with our resources is important to our ethical obligation to follow Christ in word and deed.

The final component of our ethical fundamentals is our calling to be good stewards of our environment. Physical Operations has created a robust energy savings plan that has included the upgrade of several hundred lights across campus to high efficiency LED bulbs reducing our carbon footprint significantly. We monitor all of campus building electrical loads through the use of electric meters and custom tailor our HVAC schedules to reduce energy consumption where possible throughout the 24-hour day. We also have a dedicated position to the oversight of our environmental waste. Along with monitoring our energy consumption, our Environmental Safety Manager oversees the waste out of all hazardous chemicals across campus and ensures we are operating within all state and federal guidelines. In all of these processes, we are stewarding the facilities and environment in a manner pleasing to God and in accordance with the governing authorities.

Part 4—Foundational Integration

Almost every element of DBU's location, architecture, statues, plaques, and gardens hold a particular symbolic value. The foundational element of the faith and learning of physical operations is seen primarily by the religious and patriotic heritage of the early years of the American experiment. Our former President, Dr. Gary Cook, expressed the desire to preserve our faith and history in the physical components of our campus so future generations will be reminded of the primacy of our faith and freedom.[7] The primary foundational elements of our campus are the buildings, Scripture, and statues on campus.

Many of the buildings on campus were inspired by historical sources. We have buildings modeled after Independence Hall, buildings at the College of William and Mary, the first Baptist Church in America, Indiana State House, United States Supreme Court building, Monticello, Congress Hall, Carpenter's Hall, Williamsburg Village, and the University of Virginia. We have added many dorms designed after Colonial and Georgian architecture of the 1700s. The foundational significance of these buildings points students to our heritage of freedom in the United States. The architecture instills a sense of beauty, significance, and intentionality for students to reflect on the principles on which our nation was established.[8]

In 1989, DBU adopted Jeremiah 29:11–13 as the theme verse. Since then, this passage can be found across campus on plaques, signs, and engraved in concrete. We recently finished a fitness trail on campus that is a mile long and displays a passage of Scripture every eighth of a mile for students and faculty to read as they stretch their legs between their studies. There is the road to Emmaus, based on Luke 24:13–35, where Jesus met with two disciples after His resurrection. On many of the buildings, there are cast stone "cornerstones" set into the brick with verses. These visual reminders of Scripture are in obedience to the *Shema* (Deuteronomy 6:4–9) where the children of God are called to post Scripture on their homes so they can remember the promises of God. We intentionally place Scripture on every building, statue, road, and garden to point students to the relationship they can have with Christ.

The final foundational aspect of Physical Operations are the statues we have across campus. Each statue carries a unique connotation to students as they walk or drive past. The Divine Servant Statue symbolizes the call to imitate Christ to be a servant to others.[9] The Great

---

[7] Blake Killingsworth, ed., "Christian Symbols at Dallas Baptist University," *Dallas Baptist University Report*, Fall 2014, 3.

[8] J. Blair Blackburn, *A City on a Hill: Dallas Baptist University an Architectural History* (Dallas, TX: Fluency Organization, 2014).

[9] Killingsworth, "Christian Symbols at Dallas Baptist University," 5.

Commission Statue embodies Matthew 28:18–20 to spread the gospel to all the world.[10] On either exit to campus, students see the statues of Jesus holding a fishing net with the words, "Will you follow me?" prominently displayed to challenge their motivation and decisions off campus. The Eternal Life Globe displays the words of John 3:16 in several different languages to emphasize God's desire for all people to know Him. Recently, we built the Three Cross Plaza where one of the crosses leans on the middle cross to represent the faith of the criminal crucified with Jesus. All of these statues are queues for the students to recognize their divine call to trust in Jesus and to follow Him in their respective vocations.

Conclusion

In conclusion, the Physical Operations team strives to glorify God in all it does and says through developing the people served within the department. Whether a student worker, a full-time staff member, or a contractor, Physical Operations seeks to develop our staff so our influence on campus grows and more lives are impacted for the glory of Christ. Though our disciplines are wide-ranging, our staff is unified and committed in faithfulness and excellence.

According to our biblical model, we do not merely say the things we ought to say but instead practice these things day in and day out. It is our goal to pursue excellence while living a life pleasing to God. This cannot be done alone or in a bubble so as a team and ultimately as brothers and sisters in Christ this is accomplished. Just as our mission in the classroom is to produce servant leaders who can integrate their faith and learning through their respective callings, our mission at Physical Operations is the same.

Our biblical worldview guides our view of the world and how we operate at DBU. A hallmark of our worldview is Paul's exhortation in Colossians 3:17, 23–24.

---

[10] Ibid., 6.

> And whatever you do, whether in word or deed, do it all in the name of the Lord Jesus, giving thanks to God the Father through him...whatever you do, work at it with all your heart, as working for the Lord, not for human masters, since you know that you will receive an inheritance from the Lord as a reward. It is the Lord Christ you are serving (NIV).

May we seek to produce more servant leaders such as the staff member who used his on-campus residence to serve others, challenging other students to grow in their faith.

Our attitudinal integration consists of a culture of honor that we instill among our staff. Included is relational trust so we can operate as a team. Emphasis on the team mentality within Physical Operations is an area of major importance as is. A Christ-like motivation to inspire our team members to possess a servant's heart. Let us produce more staff members who catch this Christ-like motivation early and are thus motivated to learn more, seek more, and do more with his strengths.

Our ethical integration framework promotes the idea of living and working above reproach in all that we do and speak. Being above reproach in our work means having proper onboarding procedures for our staff since we work in a high-risk area of campus. It also means we have an obligation to practice being environmentally conscious. This means taking care of our trees, watching our energy consumption, and practicing safe environmental waste handling and disposal procedures.

Our most visible framework, our foundational framework, is our campus. By no mere chance is this the case as Dr. Gary Cook intentionally wrote our vision and mission across the campus. This is practiced to this day and intentionally discussed as part of future building initiatives. Our buildings, spaces, and statues speak for themselves. We are unapologetically a Christ-centered university.

Above all, our hope and desire is through these approaches our staff and students come to know Christ more deeply. Through their learning of diligence, stewardship, and servant leadership, a deeper understanding of Christ will be had so when they go out into the world after their time at DBU or interact with others outside of DBU, they will shine as beacons of light and hope in a dark world.

Chapter 17

Integrating Faith in the Broader Campus Environment: Concluding Thoughts

By David D. Cook[1]

Introduction

This book has detailed some of the many facets of how faith is integrated on the campus of Dallas Baptist University. What one can see is that there are a great many faculty and staff across campus who work hard at integrating their faith into their work—whether it be teaching students in the classroom or in serving them in another area of campus life. These case studies provide a glimpse of what is happening, but there are many other areas of campus, and this final chapter will attempt to tell the story of how staff in those areas integrate faith into the broader learning and living environment on campus.

Abraham Kuyper famously said: "There is not a square inch in the whole domain of our human existence over which Christ, who is Sovereign over all, does not cry, 'Mine!'"[2] If that is true, then every square inch of the DBU campus and every square inch of a student's experience is important to God. During a student's time at DBU, they will engage with academic advisors who will guide them through the

[1] David D. Cook serves as the Dean of Global Studies and Pre-Professional Programs. He also serves as the Senior Legal Counsel to the President and as a Professor of Leadership Studies.

[2] Kuyper, "Sphere Sovereignty," 26.

process of choosing a major; they will register for classes and eventually graduation itself through our Registrar's Office; they will work out payment arrangements with our Cashier's Office; they will engage with Library staff as they perform research and seek truth; some will need help from our Student Success staff; others may interact with our Police and Security; if they are an international student, they will need extra support from our International Affairs Office; and many of these same students will choose to engage in a transformative academic or mission trip during their time at DBU. This chapter will focus on some of these other key areas of the student experience and how these interactions can be pivotal in transforming the lives of those students. As faculty and staff in these areas integrate faith into the work they do, they are seeing each student in the *Imago Dei*, and they have the opportunity to help that student grow spiritually, mentally, physically, and emotionally. In the pages that follow, we will take a brief look at each of these areas of campus life and how faith integration in these areas can make a huge impact on students.

Academic Advising

One of the unique aspects of DBU is the personalized experience students receive during their degree. This can be seen in small class sizes and professors who mentor students, but it can also be seen in how both faculty and staff advisors provide personalized advice as students select their classes and their major. Unlike at larger universities, each student has a designated advisor who checks in on that student regularly during their time at DBU. Sometimes those advisors are faculty members in their chosen discipline; at other times, there are dedicated staff members who help student-athletes or students in a particular college. Every semester, advisors take the initiative to reach out to students who have not yet registered for classes, and this gives them the opportunity to invite them to meet with them personally to talk about classes, what major is right for them, and about their eventual calling and career. Not every student takes advantage of the opportunity given to them to be mentored in this way by their academic advisor, but for those that do, it can make a significant impact on their growth and success.

In talking about this role, one advisor in the College of Humanities and Social Sciences noted:

> As an academic advisor I thought my primary role would be guiding students through the academic policies and procedures of DBU. But I learned very quickly that what students want most from me is personal advice and encouragement. I would feel completely inept at sharing counsel if it were not for the things God has taught me through His Word and through His faithfulness in my own times of trial and triumph. I do not have the advice they are seeking without His wisdom and truth.

Another advisor in the College of Business, in discussing how academic advisors fit into the overall mission of the University, observed:

> The goal of any university is to see students graduate, but our DBU mission takes it further—we want our students to be people who love and serve the Lord and those around them as they finish their education. A large part of my role as an academic advisor is to show students how to look ahead and make good decisions *now* that will impact them in the future. I encourage, guide, and lead them through the process of choosing classes and creating a schedule, but my prayer is that the same decision-making skills we use will lead them to make good choices beyond their time at DBU.

However, this is not always easy. Students may become frustrated when a class they want to take is not available that semester, or when they misread the catalog and miss a class that was required in their major. In those instances, it is important to show students the love of Christ while also still holding them to the academic standards of their major. As one advisor said: "My personal relationship with the Lord and the way He leads me through situations I don't understand has to be translated into the ways I listen and react to students and parents who are having a difficult time; I must approach those circumstances with the same patience, understanding, and grace that is afforded to me."

These academic advisors see themselves as an important part of the mission of DBU, and their role is critical in helping those students succeed. One advisor noted that being a part of this mission was a "privilege." Another said: "I love the sounds outside my office of students and faculty visiting, the advisor next door praying over the phone with an anxious student, and catching a conversation between staff members discussing how to most compassionately deal with a student who must be held to a standard of integrity."

Registrar's Office

Another key office that students interact with each semester as they register for classes is the Registrar's Office. Just as the academic advisors have a role in helping students register for the correct classes for their major, so, too, does the Registrar's Office serve in an important role to help students know what courses are available, how to properly register for those classes, how to add or drop classes, and similar functions. At times, a student may need to withdraw from classes because of serious health challenges or disciplinary issues. And then, of course, every student hopes to graduate someday, and the Registrar's Office is integral in the process of them getting to that ultimate finish line. All of these functions are important for the student as they journey through their academic career, and thus this area, too, falls under the "every square inch" paradigm mentioned above.

The experience at most large universities is that students do not have close relationships with advisors and are treated very much as a mere number when they enter the Registrar's Office. The rules are harsh and there is no room for compassion or even guidance on how to complete the prescribed rules in the proper manner to graduate. But that is certainly not the heart of the DBU Registrar's Office. They see themselves as an integral part of the mission of DBU and desire to treat each student with care, compassion, love, and respect. While their role also means they have to hold students to high standards of excellence, this can be done in a Christ-like way. One member of the Registrar's staff put it this way: "As we attempt to explain to the students their responsibility for fulfilling requirements toward graduation, it helps to remember that God is a God of order and peace as we guide students and advisors to follow the orderly processes."

For many students, the process of selecting classes, picking a major, and then fulfilling the many requirements for that major, can be challenging. As one member of the Registrar's staff noted: "The Registrar's Office strives to treat DBU constituents with a Christ-like mindset each time we respond patiently with a kind tone to multiple, repetitious procedural and policy questions that are asked." Especially in situations where students make an unwise choice in selecting the wrong class that does not fit in their major, or when they have academic difficulties and need to withdraw from classes, or when a major life difficulty arises (e.g., death of a parent, major loss of family income, or health problems for the student), the Registrar's Office becomes a key focal point for that student's experience at DBU. Many times in these situations, students need to make a registration appeal. As one member of the Registrar's staff noted: "When we hear Registration Appeals, we try to show compassion and fairness to the student as the decisions are made, taking into account all the information provided for consideration. Each appeal is unique to the situation, and the goal is to rule in favor of the student whenever possible within the confines of policy and ethical standards." They look at each case with a desire to mix justice and mercy in the right measure (Micah 6:8) so students are treated fairly, honestly, and with care.

In all their interactions, the members of the Registrar's staff seek to be as kind, friendly, and compassionate as they can during a registration process that can be challenging. One of the leaders in the office noted: "I try to foster an office atmosphere where there is open communication and trust, which lends itself to service to DBU, compassion for the students, ethical decision-making, and the potential for organizational growth." By treating their staff, students, and parents with respect, they are able to show the love of Christ to these constituent groups and help that student ultimately succeed in their journey toward graduation.

Cashier's Office

Another key office that all students interact with on campus is the Cashier's Office. The University as a whole seeks to provide education that is affordable, but for many families, sending a child to college can be an extra financial burden. As they navigate the tricky waters of how to pay for their student's college experience, families need guidance and support from groups such as Admissions, Financial Aid, and ultimately, the Cashier's Office.

Of course, dealing with issues of payment can lead to many situations that have the potential for conflict. The staff in the Cashier's Office know that financial issues can be an area of stress for students and their parents, so they seek to provide an environment that is helpful, kind, and compassionate, much like the Registrar's Office. In both instances, students must be held to standards—to meet the academic requirements of the catalog or to then pay for the classes they have registered for—but in both instances, the members of these offices see themselves as supporting students in their journey toward graduation.

As one member of the Cashier's Office noted: "My faith inspires me to view my role as an opportunity to serve others. I see every interaction with students, faculty, and staff as a chance to demonstrate Christ's love through kindness, patience, and a willingness to help. This approach creates a welcoming and supportive environment within the Cashier's Office." She noted that their staff seek to exhibit "Christ-like values" and provide "personalized assistance." "We embrace a servant leadership mindset, going beyond our roles and trying to foster a welcoming environment where students feel valued and respected during their interactions." This is important, because for many students, the stress of finances can be great.

When conflicts do arise, one member of the staff noted: "…my faith guides me to seek resolution with love and a spirit of reconciliation. I emphasize peaceful and constructive communication to address issues and find mutually beneficial solutions." Another staff member mentioned the importance of "showing compassion to students in times of need." As she discussed, "In all of our actions, the Cashier's Office staff aims to reflect the spirit of love, kindness, fairness, and the mindset of Christ in our service to the University community."

This integration of faith also changes the way the supervisors treat their staff in this office. As one supervisor noted: "My faith encourages me to lead by example and I try to prioritize the well-being and growth of my staff and student workers, striving to serve and support them in their personal and professional development." She mentioned that it was important to her to "foster a relationship that is holistic and meets them where they are." As she equips staff to serve students and parents, she noted that "I like to think of myself as [my staff members'] personal cheerleader."

While students may only come into the Cashier's Office a few times each semester, the interactions they have with this office can be critical in their ability to continue in their academic journey. By integrating faith into the way they treat these students, parents, and even their own staff, the leaders of the Cashier's Office have an opportunity to show Christ's love even when dealing with financial issues. Ultimately, as students work hard to find ways to pay for college, they learn to trust God on a different level and when they do finish their academic journey, their graduation is that much more rewarding because of how much they put into that journey—not just academically, but also financially. The Cashier's Office plays a large role in supporting those students as they financially complete that journey.

Library Services

As students dive into their academic journey, a key resource for them is the University's library. The library is not just filled with books, but is filled with staff who want to serve students as they grow academically. As one staff member put it: "God wants us to pursue excellence and that includes excellence in scholarship and information discovery." In seeing themselves as a part of the larger mission of the University, one librarian had this to say:

> I couldn't tell you how many times on our campus I have heard people talk about experiencing something different when they arrived, the presence of God even. I have heard it so many times that I don't think it is hyperbole. It is my desire that people have the same experience when they walk into the library. YES, the library. I want people to have a sense that something important is happening in our corner of the campus and that God must be a part of that.

With this important mission in mind, the library staff seek not just to wait till students come to them, but actively seek ways to connect with students from the moment they arrive on campus. Thus, library staff stay busy at the beginning of each semester going to different classes and doing Research 101 presentations to help students know about the many resources available to them. Over the last few years, they have begun discussion groups on key social issues as a way to invite students into the physical space of the library and see it as a place to ask deeper questions, grapple with issues, and find research resources that can help them answer those bigger life questions.

One library leader noted the Christ-like mentality they try to instill in their workers begins with service. "We are training our workers to smile and look up, to take extra time with our patrons, and to take their tasks seriously for the betterment of those they are serving." Whether it be in serving a doctoral student doing research for their dissertation, a master's student doing research for a term paper, or an undergraduate student doing research for a project, the library staff enter into each interaction with a heart of service.

Likewise, this mindset of service flows over into how they seek to mentor their younger workers and student workers. Leaders in the library hold a prayer meeting every day at 9:30 am for anyone who wants to pray together, and the Director of the Library regularly holds special mentoring lunches for student workers. As they hire librarians, one of the key things they look for is not just technical competence, but a heart for mentoring and service. One library leader recounted the following story:

> We had many positions to fill. Our first priority was a part time person who could run our Circulation Desk. This person would be working closely with a large team of student workers. I wanted to find someone that could be more than a supervisor but could invest in and mentor our student workers. I needed someone with a minister's heart.

Student Success Services

During a student's time, they may also need additional help with academic struggles. Many universities have dedicated staff to provide additional support to struggling students. At DBU, that role holds added significance, for every student is not just a number for retention, but is an individual who was made in the image of God and has inherent worth and dignity. One student success staff member put it this way:

> Many of the students I work with are struggling in some way whether it be due to finances, physical and/or mental health issues, family and relationship problems, or something else and these struggles are affecting their ability to be successful academically. Through my faith in Christ, I believe I am called to love and serve students. Sometimes they just need someone to be on their side, to advocate for them, to push them when needed, and to be a consistent presence in their lives. My morning prayer is often asking God to help me help students.

As this staff member noted: "I work with an amazing group of people in Student Affairs who love Christ and love students." It is that love for Christ and love for students that makes these interactions unique from other universities. Certainly, other universities care for their students; but at DBU, there is a deeper concern to see them reach their fullest potential so they can shine God's light into the world in their chosen vocations. One staff member put it this way:

> Knowing the stress they [students] are under, I want them to feel valued and seen as a beloved child of God for whom Jesus died. No matter the circumstance, I believe I am called to assist them with kindness and respect. My faith in God's sovereignty also helps me to serve as best I can but then to not carry these burdens home and instead to trust the situation and the people involved to the One who is ultimately in control.

Because of this unique love for students, staff in this area see their role in a deeper way than in traditional student success centers. They strive to serve students in hard situations, equip them when they meet roadblocks, and help them grow into followers of Christ who can transform the world. By helping them overcome challenges that arise during their educational journey, the staff help ensure that each student can maximize their God-given potential for the future.

Police and Security

As students enter the college environment to learn and grow, they naturally want that environment to be safe and secure. Most universities have security and/or police forces to help maintain safety, but DBU's police and security department uniquely integrates faith into their everyday duties. One way that this department has chosen to symbolize their faith integration is in the motto that is emblazoned on the side of their patrol vehicles: "Serve and Protect." Many police departments across the nation use a similar motto, but typically the order is: Protect and Serve. When DBU created the police force on campus, the first police chief intentionally chose to have the order of the words changed so his officers would see themselves first and foremost as officers who serve the campus community, even as they do so in a way that actively protects that community, as well.

As one officer put it: "We serve and protect by being the behind-the-scenes workers and doing things that many others won't ever see." Whether it be helping a student change a flat tire, dealing with an incident in an apartment, or handling other violations of DBU policies, the police and security officers see their faith as an important part of their mission. Another officer noted: "The policies and culture of DBU reflect a service-oriented lifestyle, therefore it is on DBU Security and Police to demonstrate that." He emphasized that the officers see themselves as servant leaders on campus, even in difficult situations. As he shared: "Mixing justice and mercy is a critical facet of the manner in which DBU Police and Security manage situations with individuals…I believe officers attempt to find the justice/mercy balance through each individual contact they are in."

This service-first, Christ-like mindset has a deep impact on the student population. One officer put it this way: "Police and Security are, in many instances, the first point of contact for DBU students, staff, and visitors. Therefore, the image they present is extremely influential on the outward appearance of DBU." He stressed that police and security try to exhibit a mindset of humble, Christ-like service with students. As one student noted: "They always make sure the campus is safe… but they also make sure that we know when we need them, they can be there." Another student put it this way:

> They are set on not only keeping us safe, but on our overall wellbeing. Specifically, I have had several instances where DBU police officers have stopped and asked me how I am doing and how classes are going. It is nice to know how much they care about each student individually as well as the campus as a whole.

Yet another student mentioned the prayer meetings the Chief of Police holds with students on campus. These are times where police officers can pray alongside students for their campus as a whole. This student emphasized that the Chief of Police has a deep interest in each and every student: "Without fail, he always asks us about our lives and if there's anything we could use prayer for. This has always stuck out to me. Here he is putting his life on the line to protect us, yet the first thing he asks about is us, not himself." This heart of service and prayer allows the police and security officers to have a level of trust in the campus community that is very important to the work they do. By integrating their faith, serving humbly, and caring for students, they are in a better position to also have the relational trust built up when bad things do happen on campus. A dorm student summarized it well when he said: "Most people I have interacted with are beyond grateful for DBU's integration of faith within Police and Security. Biblically, justice and mercy must coexist, so knowing that is the model for DBU has students comforted knowing they work to do things guided by the Lord's example."

International Affairs

While the Police and Security team protect the campus as a whole, there is another student population on campus that needs extra care and support: our international students. Close to 15 percent of DBU's student population is comprised of international students from around the world, and as they make DBU their home, they need an additional level of compassion, help, and assistance. Thus, DBU has created a dedicated office not just for international admissions, but also for services to this large international student population. These international student services personnel impact the students' lives in a variety of ways: they pick them up from the airport, help them get situated in their housing, provide a variety of shuttles to grocery stores each week, take students on outings to cultural events, plan cultural events, check in on them during crises, and more. This extra care makes all the difference for students who are thousands of miles from home. One international student put it this way: "...I wouldn't have been able to make it without the support, love, and encouragement of the IO [International Office]! They became my family members on campus." Other students talked about the staff as being "warm" and "welcoming." One student mentioned a story of how her flight into Dallas was delayed till Christmas, and how her professor quickly arranged for a family in his church to pick her up and have her stay with them over the holidays. Another student recalled how, during the COVID-19 pandemic, International Office staff called her every week to check in on her well-being and mental health. Yet another student recalled how one of the volunteers at the International

Office had helped her practice her driving and study for the driver's license test during the blazing heat of the Texas summer—he had gone above and beyond to help her gain the independence of having a car.

These stories are some of the many instances of DBU faculty and staff taking extra care for international students. Professors mentor, guide, and pray with students; staff plan special events during the lonely summer months; and volunteers from churches provide rides to outreach events and Sunday morning worship services for these students. One international student said she felt the faculty and staff had truly invested in her as a person. Another said that the servant leadership and love she experienced at DBU had made a huge difference in how she leads in her career: "Now I try to love on people the way I was loved on by DBU." Similarly, another international alumna said: "I felt loved at DBU…that has ignited in me a passion to serve fellow international students."

The faith of faculty, staff, and volunteers who serve international students is a true distinctive at DBU. Faith is interwoven in this process as the Gospel is shared in both word and deed. Recently, one Biology professor who had mentored an international student from his class shared that this student had accepted Christ and had come back to thank the professor who had so patiently met with him to answer his questions about Christianity. Another international student was baptized by the University's president himself after she had a spiritual conversation with him when he stopped to speak with her after one of his runs on campus. This spiritual impact reverberates across nations, as many of these students go back to their home countries and share the Good News with their families and friends. In this way, DBU faculty and staff are making a global impact for Christ. One student from China summed it up well: "These staff are not just teachers, but messengers of Christ's love."

Concluding Thoughts

This book has attempted to detail how faith is integrated in a broad array of departments on the campus of Dallas Baptist University. Whether it be in the classroom, in the lunchroom, in the dorm room, or on the athletic field, students have the opportunity to learn about Christ and how their faith can impact all aspects of their life. We have seen chapters detailing faith integration in the classroom alongside chapters dealing with faith integration in many other parts of campus. This faith integration across the entirety of campus is vital. As one student said: "From the time I started at DBU, I was saturated by professors and staff who cared deeply about spiritual development in tandem with academics." Yet another student put it this way: "Christian values have seeped into aspects of DBU's culture that extend far beyond the classroom walls. I grew in my faith during my undergraduate years because I was surrounded by individuals in my classes, my house, my workplace, and my extracurriculars who genuinely loved Jesus and pushed me to pursue Him more deeply."

This faith integration leaves a lasting legacy for students. One alumnus who is now serving as a CPA stated: "DBU's commitment to developing God-fearing servant leaders has left a major imprint on me. The academic experience I received carried spiritual implications, helping me develop a posture of humility and servitude toward God as He uses my career to advance His kingdom." Yet another alumnus, who is serving as a Congressional aide in Washington, D.C., put it this way:

> DBU gave me the opportunity to watch my professors live their faith through their work every day. They professed their faith boldly, worked hard on our behalf, and grounded everything in love. These qualities and the sacrifices DBU professors were willing to make...afforded me the opportunity to leave DBU a semester early and begin a career in Washington, D.C. I think about that often, and hope that I replicate that generosity to others when the opportunity arises.

This sentiment was echoed by an alumna who is now a school counselor: "But behind just preparing me for my future career, they helped show me how to integrate my faith into my career. I learned not only how to be a teacher and counselor, but how to love and engage with students in a Christlike way." Yet another student who is about to graduate and work in a federal criminal justice agency noted:

> DBU has transformed my desire to work in the criminal justice system from just a job into a deeper calling. Through their education and values-based approach, they've shown me how my role can have a positive impact on individuals and communities. Now, I see it as a mission to bring justice, compassion, and positive change to the field, thanks to DBU's guidance and support.

What a blessing it is to see faith not only being integrated on the DBU campus, but also in the lives of our alumni as they go out into their respective callings and careers! Integrating faith into the learning environment takes a great deal of intentionality and hard work, but it is work that pays everlasting dividends in God's Kingdom. This hard work of integrating faith is summed up well in a set of verses the faculty collectively read aloud at every commencement service over the graduating students:

> For this reason, since the day we heard about you, we have not stopped praying for you. We continually ask God to fill you with the knowledge of his will through all the wisdom and understanding that the Spirit gives, so that you may live a life worthy of the Lord and please him in every way: bearing fruit in every good work, growing in the knowledge of God, being strengthened with all power according to his glorious might so that you may have great endurance and patience, and giving joyful thanks to the Father, who has qualified you to share in the inheritance of his holy people in the kingdom of light.[3]

Our great hope is that the faith integration students experience at DBU becomes a springboard for their own faith integration as they head into

[3] Col. 1:9–12 (NIV).

their future. Over the years, tens of thousands of students have been impacted by this faith-filled environment, and our abiding hope is that those tens of thousands of alumni share the love of Christ and His Good News in a mighty way with the world around them.

Bibliography

Adams, Jay E. *Competent to Counsel.* Grand Rapids, MI: Baker, 1970.

Adams, John. "Thoughts on Government, April 1776." Founders Online. Accessed November 27, 2023, https://founders.archives.gov/documents/Adams/06-04-02-0026-0004.

Aguinis, Herman and Ante Glavas. "What We Know and Don't Know About Corporate Social Responsibility: A Review and Research Agenda." *Journal of Management* 38, no. 4 (March 2012): 932–68.

Alcorn, Randy. *The Treasure Principle.* New York, NY: Multnomah, 2001.

Alford, Helen J. and Michael J. Naughton. "Managing as if Faith Mattered: Christian Social Principles in the Modern Organization." *Theology Today* 60, no. 3 (October 2003): 411–13.

American Psychological Association. "Society for Psychology of Religion and Spirituality." Divisions of APA. Accessed November 27, 2023, https://www.apa.org/about/division/div36.

Anderson, Tawa J., W. Michael Clark, and David Naugle. *An Introduction to Christian Worldview: Pursuing God's Perspective in a Pluralistic World.* Downers Grove, IL: IVP, 2017.

Aoun, Joseph E. *Robot-Proof: Higher Education in the Age of Artificial Intelligence.* Cambridge, MA: MIT Press, 2017.

Aristotle. *The Works of Aristotle.* Vol. 8, *Metaphysics.* Edited and translated by David Ross. Oxford, UK: Clarendon Press, 1963.

Arnott, Dave and Sergiy Saydometov. *Biblical Economic Policy: Ten Scriptural Truths for Fiscal and Monetary Decision-Making.* Sisters, OR: Deep River Books, 2021.

Astin, Alexander W., Helen S. Astin, and Jennifer A. Lindholm. *Cultivating the Spirit: How College Can Enhance Students' Inner Lives.* San Francisco, CA: Jossey-Bass, 2011.

Babcock, Maltbie D. "This Is My Father's World." Hymnary.org. Accessed on August 15, 2022, https://hymnary. org/text/this_is_my_fathers_world_and_to_my.

Balthasar, Hans U. V. *The Glory of the Lord.* Vol. 1, *Seeing the Form.* San Francisco, CA: Ignatius Press, 2009.

Barry, John D., ed. *The Lexham Bible Dictionary.* Bellingham, WA: Lexham Press, 2016.

Bass, Diana B. *A People's History of Christianity: The Other Side of the Story.* Reprint. San Francisco, CA: Harper, 2010.

Bebbington, David. *Patterns in History: A Christian Perspective on Historical Thought.* Grand Rapids, MI: Baker, 1990.

Beers, Jane and Stephen Beers. "Integration of Faith and Learning." In *The Soul of a Christian University: A Field Guide for Educators,* edited by Stephen Beers, 51–74. Abilene, TX: ACU Press, 2008.

Beller, Jennifer M. and Sharon K. Stoll. "Moral Reasoning of High School Student Athletes and General Students: An Empirical Study versus Personal Testimony." Pediatric Exercise Science 7 (November 1995): 352–63.

Best, Harold. *Music Through the Eyes of Faith.* New York, NY: Harper, 2013.

Blackaby, Henry and Richard Blackaby. *Spiritual Leadership: Moving People on to God's Agenda.* Nashville, TN: B&H, 2001.

Blackburn, J. Blair. *A City on a Hill: Dallas Baptist University an Architectural History.* Dallas, TX: Fluency Organization, 2014.

Blanchard, Ken and Phil Hodges. *Lead Like Jesus: Lessons From the Greatest Leadership Role Model of All Time.* Nashville, TN: Thomas Nelson, 2008.

Bliss, Dave. *Fall to Grace: The Climb, Collapse, and Comeback of Coach Dave Bliss*. Indian Trail, NC: Core Media Group, 2015.

Boatman, Sara. "The Leadership Audit: A Process to Enhance the Development of Student Leadership." *NASPA Journal* 37, no. 1 (Fall 1999): 325–36.

Bok, Derek. *The Struggle to Reform Our Colleges*. Princeton, NJ: Princeton University Press, 2017.

Bradley, James E. and Richard A. Muller. *Church History: An Introduction to Research, Reference Works, and Methods*. Grand Rapids, MI: Eerdmans, 1995.

Brann, Eva. *Paradoxes of Education in a Republic*. Chicago, IL: University of Chicago Press, 1979.

Bratt, James D., ed. *Abraham Kuyper: A Centennial Reader*. Grand Rapids, MI: Eerdmans, 1998.

Bryant, Alyssa and Helen Astin. "The Correlates of Spiritual Struggle During the College Years." *Journal of Higher Education* 79, no. 1 (January-February 2008): 1–27.

Burch, Maxie B. *The Evangelical Historians: The Historiography of George Marsden, Nathan Hatch, and Mark Noll*. Lanham, MD: University Press of America, 1996.

Burns, James M. "Afterward." In *The Quest for a General Theory of Leadership*, edited by George Goethals and Georgia L. J. Sorenson, 234–40. Northampton, UK: Edward Elgar, 2006.

———. *Leadership*. New York, NY: Harper, 2010.

Butterfield, Herbert. *Christianity and History*. Glasgow, UK: Fontana Books, 1958.

Cameron, Euan. *Interpreting Christian History: The Challenge of the Churches' Past*. Oxford, UK: Blackwell, 2005.

Capehart-Meningall, Jennifer. "Role of Spirituality and Spiritual Development in Student Life Outside the Classroom," *New Directions for Teaching and Learning*, no. 104 (Winter 2005): 31–36.

Carnegie, Andrew. "Wealth." *The North American Review* 148, no. 391 (June 1889): 653–64.

Carter, John D. "Secular and Sacred Models of Psychology and Religion." *Journal of Psychology and Theology* 5, no. 3 (June 1977): 197–208.

Carter, John D. and Bruce Narramore. *The Integration of Psychology and Theology*. Grand Rapids, MI: Zondervan, 1979.

Ciulla, Joanne B. "What We Learned Along the Way: A Commentary." In *The Quest for a General Theory of Leadership,* edited by George Goethals and Georgia L. J. Sorenson, 221–33. Northampton, UK: Edward Elgar, 2006.

Clouse, Robert. "Herbert Butterfield." In *Historians of the Christian Tradition: Their Methodology and Influence on Western Thought,* edited by Michael Baumen and Martin I. Klauber, 519–30. Nashville, TN: B&H, 1995.

Conference on Faith and History. "Constitution of the Conference on Faith and History." About CFH. Accessed November 28, 2023, https://faithandhistory.org/about-chf/.

Cook, David. "Bonhoeffer as a Prophetic Leader." In *Dietrich Bonhoeffer: Perspectives on Costly Leadership,* edited by Jay Harley, 85–106. Nashville, TN: Randall House, 2021.

———, ed. *Luther on Leadership: Leadership Insights From the Great Reformer.* Eugene, OR: Wipf and Stock, 2017.

Cosgrove, Mark P. *Foundations of Christian Thought: Faith, Learning, and the Christian Worldview*. Grand Rapids, MI: Kregel, 2006.

Crabb, Larry. *Effective Biblical Counseling: A Model for Helping Caring Christians Become Capable Counselors*. Grand Rapids, MI: Zondervan, 1977.

Crouch, Andy. *Culture Making*. Westmont, IL: IVP, 2008.

D'Souza, Karen. "Many High School Seniors Prefer High-Amenity Colleges, Survey Shows." News Update. Ed Source. June 22, 2022, https://edsource.org/updates/many-high-school-seniors-prefer-high-amenity-colleges-survey-shows.

Dallas Baptist University. "Helping Students Find and Fulfill Their Call." Center for Career and Professional Development. Accessed November 27, 2023, https://www.dbu.edu/ccpd/.

———. "A Holistic Education." The Integration of Faith and Learning. Accessed June 19, 2022, www.dbu.edu/about/integrated-faith.html.

———. "A Living Learning Community Preparing Servant Leaders." John and Nita Ford Village. Accessed November 27, 2023, www.dbu.edu/housing/ford-village/.

———. "Mission Statement," About DBU. Accessed November 17, 2023, www.dbu.edu/ about/.

———. "Mission Statement." School of Leadership. Accessed June 14, 2022, https://catalog.dbu.edu/undergrad/leadership/general-info.

———. "Mission Statement." Student Affairs. Accessed November 27, 2023, www.dbu.edu/ student-affairs/.

———. "RELI 1302 (3-3-0) New Testament Survey." Catalog Fall 22 – Summer 23. Accessed June 19, 2022, https://archive-catalog-dbu-22-23.coursedog.com/undergrad/courses/reli.

Damon, William and Margarita A. Mooney. "Every Child Has a Spark: The Tandem of Internal Motivation and Co-Learning." In *The Love of Learning: Seven Dialogues on the Liberal Arts*, edited by Margarita A. Mooney, 19–42. Providence, RI: Cluny, 2021.

Danker, William J. *Profit for the Lord*. Eugene, OR: Wipf and Stock, 1971.

Dawson, Christopher. *The Crisis of Western Education*. London, UK: Sheed and Ward, 1961.

Detweiler, Richard A. *The Evidence Liberal Arts Needs: Lives of Consequence, Inquiry, and Accomplishment*. Cambridge: MIT Press, 2021.

Dockery, David S. and Gregory A. Thornbury. *Shaping a Christian Worldview: The Foundation of Christian Higher Education*. Nashville, TN: B&H, 2002.

Du Bois, William E. B. *The Education of Black People: Ten Critiques, 1906–1960*. Edited by H. Aptheker. Millwood, NY: KTO Press, 1977.

Du Bois, William E. B. *The Education of Black People: Ten Critiques, 1906–1960*. New York, NY: Monthly Review Press, 2001.

Dungy, Gwendolyn J. "Students and Student Affairs: Facing Perennial Challenges in Ever-changing Contexts." *Change* 50, no. 4 (October 2018): 58–62.

Durant, Will and Ariel Durant. *The Lessons of History*. New York, NY: Simon and Schuster, 1968.

Easton, Geoff. "Critical Realism in Case Study Research." *Industrial Marketing Management* 39, no. 1 (January 2010): 118–28.

Eck, Brian E. "Integrating the Integrators: An Organizing Framework for a Multifaceted Process of Integration." *Journal of Psychology and Christianity* 15, no. 2 (Summer 1996): 101–15.

Eckard, Edwin W. "NCAA Athlete Graduation Rates: Less Than Meets the Eye." *Journal of Sport Management* 24, no. 1 (January 2010): 45–58.

Einstein, Albert. "Science and God." *The Forum* 1930-06: Vol 83 Iss 6 (June 1930): 374–75. Accessed March 9, 2024. https://archive.org/details/sim_forum-and-century_1930-06_83_6/page/374/mode/2up.

Elmore, Tim. *Generation Z Unfiltered: Facing Nine Hidden Challenges of the Most Anxious Population*. Atlanta, GA: Growing Leaders, 2019.

Entwistle, David N. *Integrative Approaches to Psychology and Christianity*. Eugene, OR: Cascade Books, 2021.

Erickson, Millard J. *Making Sense of the Trinity, 3 Crucial Questions*. Grand Rapids, MI: Baker, 2000.

Eusebius. *History of the Church: A New Translation*. Translated by Jeremy M. Schott. Oakland, CA: University of California Press, 2019.

Fea, John. *Why Study History? Reflecting on the Importance of the Past*. Grand Rapids, MI: Baker, 2013.

Felten, Peter and Leo Lambert. *Relationship-Rich Education: How Human Connections Drive Success in College*. Baltimore, MD: Johns Hopkins, 2020.

Ferguson, Everett. "The Problem of Eusebius." *Christian History* 72, no. 4 (November 2001): 8–12.

Fischman, Wendy and Howard Gardner. *The Real World of College: What Higher Education Is and What It Can Be*. Cambridge: MIT Press, 2022.

Freedman, David N., Allen C. Myers, and Astrid B. Beck, eds. *Eerdmans Dictionary of the Bible*. Grand Rapids, MI: Eerdmans, 2000.

Fromm, Jeff and Angie Read. *Marketing to Gen Z*. New York, NY: AMACOM, 2018.

Fryling, Robert. *The Leadership Ellipse: Shaping How We Lead by Who We Are*. Downers Grove, IL: IVP, 2009.

Gallup Poll. "Lawyers." Honesty/Ethics in Professions. Accessed November 17, 2023, https://news.gallup.com/poll/1654/honesty-ethics-professions.aspx.

Gargano, Jr., Michael. "A Study to Determine Whether or not the Principles of Sportsmanship and Ethical Conduct can Coexist with the Competing Principles Associated with Highly Competitive Athletic Programs in NCAA Division I Men's Basketball." PhD diss., George Washington University, Washington, D. C., 2001. ProQuest Dissertations & Theses Global.

Garriga, Elisabet and Domènec Melé. "Corporate Social Responsibility Theories: Mapping the Territory." *Journal of Business Ethics* 53, no. 1–2 (August 2004): 51–71.

Goethals, George and Georgia L. J. Sorenson. *The Quest for a General Theory of Leadership*. Northampton, UK: Edward Elgar, 2006.

Goheen, Michael W. and Craig G. Bartholomew. *Living at the Crossroads: An Introduction to Christian Worldview*. Grand Rapids, MI: Baker, 2008.

Graber, Mary. *Debunking Howard Zinn: Exposing the Fake History That Turned a Generation Against America*. Washington, DC: Regnery History, 2020.

Greer, Peter and Chris Horst. *Mission Drift: The Unspoken Crisis Facing Leaders, Charities, and Churches*. Bloomington, MN: Bethany House, 2014.

Gregory of Nazianzus. *On God and Christ: The Five Theological Orations and Two Letters to Cledonius*. Translated by Lionel R. Whickham. Crestwood, NY: St. Vladimir's Seminary Press, 2002.

Gregory, Brad S. *The Unintended Reformation: How a Religious Revolution Secularized Society*. Cambridge, MA: Harvard University Press, 2012.

Grenz, Stanley J. and Jay T. Smith. *Pocket Dictionary of Ethics*. IVP Pocket Reference Series. Downers Grove, IL: IVP, 2003.

Gross, Norman. "Presidential Bar Leaders: Fascinating Facts About America's Lawyer-Presidents." *Bar Leader* 34, no. 3 (January-February 2010): 1–6, https://www.americanbar.org/groups/bar-leadership/publications/bar_leader/2009_10/january_february/presidential/.

Guinness, Os. *The Call*. Nashville, TN: Thomas Nelson, 1997.

Halme, Minna and Juha Laurila. "Philanthropy, Integration or Innovation? Exploring the Financial and Societal Outcomes of Different Types of Corporate Responsibility." *Journal of Business Ethics*, no. 84 (February 2009): 325–39.

Hardy, Sam A. and Gustavo Carlo. "Moral Identity: What Is It, How Does It Develop, and Is It Linked to Moral Action?" *Child Development Perspectives* 5, no. 3 (September 2011): 212–18.

Hart, Darryl G. "History in Search of Meaning: The Conference on Faith and History." In *History and the Christian Historian*, edited by Ronald A. Wells, 68–87. Grand Rapids, MI: Eerdmans, 1998.

Hathaway, William L. and Mark A. Yarhouse. *The Integration of Psychology and Christianity: A Domain-Based Approach*. Downers Grove, IL: IVP, 2021.

Heck, Joel. *Irrigating Deserts: C. S. Lewis on Education*. St. Louis, MO: Concordia Academic Press, 2006.

Henderson, Roger. "Kuyper's Inch." *Pro Rege* 36, no. 3 (March 2008): 12–14.

Hoekema, Anthony A. *Created in God's Image*. Grand Rapids, MI: Eerdmans, 1994.

Hoffer, Richard, Mark Bechtel, and Stephen Cannella. "No More Mr. Nice Guy." *Sports Illustrated* 104, no. 21 (May 2006): 18–19.

Hoffman, Shirl J. *Good Game: Christianity and the Culture of Sports*. Waco, TX: Baylor University Press, 2010.

Holmes, Arthur F. *The Idea of a Christian College*. Grand Rapids, MI: Eerdmans, 1975.

Hosick, Michell B. "DI College Athletes Reach 90% Graduation Rate." Media Center. NCAA. November 17, 2020, https://www.ncaa.org/news/2020/11/17/di-college-athletes-reach-90-graduation-rate.aspx.

Howell, Russell and James Bradley. *Mathematics Through the Eyes of Faith*. Through the Eyes of Faith Series. New York, NY: Harper, 2011.

Janz, Denis. *A People's History of Christianity*. 7 vols. Minneapolis, MN: Fortress Press, 2014.

Jenkins, Philip. *The New Faces of Christianity: Believing the Bible in the Global South*. Oxford, UK: Oxford University Press, 2006.

Joshua Project. "What is the 10/40 Window?" Accessed June 11, 2022, https://joshuaproject.net/resources/articles/ 10_40_window.

Kang, Charles, Frank Germann, and Rajdeep Grewal. "Washing Away Your Sins? Corporate Social Responsibility, Corporate Social Responsibility, and Firm Performance." *Journal of Marketing* 80, no. 2 (March 2016): 59–79.

Keeling, Richard P. and Richard H. Hersh. *We're Losing Our Minds: Rethinking American Higher Education*. New York, NY: Palgrave Macmillan, 2012.

Keller, Timothy J. "The Upside-Down Kingdom." March 21, 1999. In *Hope for New York*. Produced by Gospel in Life, podcast, https://gospelinlife.com/sermon/the-upside-down-kingdom-2/.

Keller, Timothy J. and Katherine L. Alsdorf. *Every Good Endeavor: Connecting Your Work to God's Work*. New York, NY: Dutton, 2012.

Kepler, Johannes. "Thesis XX." In *De fundamentis astrologiae certioribus*. Accessed November 27, 2023, https://apologetics315.com/2013/08/johannes-kepler-on-god-and-science/.

Killingsworth, Blake, ed. "Christian Symbols at Dallas Baptist University." *Dallas Baptist University Report*. Fall 2014.

Kondelis, Pat, director. *Disgraced*. Featuring Dave Bliss. Showtime, 2017.

Kouzes, James M. and Barry Z. Posner, eds. *Christian Reflections on the Leadership Challenge*. San Francisco, CA: Jossey-Bass, 2004.

———. *The Leadership Challenge*. San Francisco, CA: Jossey-Bass, 2017.

Kuh, George D., Jillian Kinzie, John H. Schuh, and Elizabeth J. White. *Student Success in College: Creating Conditions That Matter*. San Francisco, CA: Jossey-Bass, 2010.

Kuyper, Abraham. "Sphere Sovereignty: A Public Address Delivered at the Inauguration of the Free University, October 20, 1880." The Gospel Coalition. Translated by George Kamps, June 2017, https://media.thegospelcoalition.org/wp-content/uploads/2017/06/24130543/SphereSovereignty_English.pdf.

Lai, Patrick. *Business for Transformation*. Pasadena, CA: William Carey Library, 2015.

———. *Tentmaking: The Life and Work of Business as Missions*. Westmont, IL: IVP, 2006.

Lewis, Clive S. *The Abolition of Man or Reflections on Education With Special Reference to the Teaching of English in the Upper Forms of Schools*. New York, NY: Harper, 2001.

———. *Mere Christianity: What One Must Believe to Be a Christian*. New York, NY: Macmillan, 1978.

———. *Miracles: A Preliminary Study*. New York, NY: Harper, 2001.

———. "Preface." In *Saint Athanasius' On the Incarnation*, translated by John Behr, 11–18. Yonkers, NY: St. Vladimirs Seminary Press, 2012.

———. *Surprised by Joy: The Shape of My Early Life*. New York, NY: Harcourt Brace, 1955.

Ligonier. "What is the Chief and Highest End of Man?" The Westminster Larger Catechism. Accessed November 27, 2023, https://www.ligonier.org/learn/articles/westminster-larger-catechism.

Lucas, Christopher J. *American Higher Education: A History*. New York, NY: Palgrave Macmillan, 2006.

MacPhee, Donald A. "The Muse Meets the Master: Clio and Christ." In *A Christian View of History?* edited by George Marsden and Frank Roberts, 75–87. Grand Rapids, MI: Eerdmans, 1975.

Madison, James. "The Structure of the Government Must Furnish the Proper Checks and Balances Between the Different Departments." In *The Federalist* 51. February 1788. Accessed November 27, 2023, https://guides.loc.gov/federalist-papers/text-51-60#s-lg-box-wrapper-25493427.

Malphurs, Aubrey. *Being Leaders: The Nature of Authentic Christian Leadership*. Grand Rapids, MI: Baker, 2003.

Margolis, Joshua D. and James P. Walsh. "Misery Loves Company: Rethinking Social Initiatives by Business." *Administrative Science Quarterly* 48, no. 2 (June 2003): 268–305.

Mariam-Webster's Dictionary. Online.

Maritain, Jacques. *Education at the Crossroads*. New Haven, CT: Yale University Press, 1943.

Marsden, George and John Woodbridge. "Christian History Today." *Christian History* 72, no. 4 (2001): 50–53.

Marsden, George. "What Difference Might Christian Perspectives Make?" In *History and the Christian Historian*, edited by Ronald A. Wells, 11–22. Grand Rapids, MI: Eerdmans, 1998.

McGrath, Alister. "Augustine of Hippo." In *Historians of the Christian Tradition: Their Methodology and Influence on Western Thought*, edited by Michael Bauman and Martin I. Klauber, 79–93. Nashville, TN: B&H, 1995.

———. *Christianity's Dangerous Idea: The Protestant Revolution—A History From the Sixteenth Century to the Twenty-First*. San Francisco, CA: Harper, 2007.

———. *Dawkins' God: Genes, Memes, and the Meaning of Life*. Oxford, UK: Blackwell, 2004.

McIntire, Carl T. "Modern Pioneers: Herbert Butterfield." *Christian History* 72, no. 4 (2001): 45–47.

Middleton, J. Richard. *A New Heaven and New Earth: Reclaiming Biblical Eschatology*. Grand Rapids, MI: Baker, 2014.

Miller, Steve. *C. H. Spurgeon on Spiritual Leadership*. Chicago, IL: Moody, 2003.

Mitchell, Philip I. "Written by the Finger of God: C. S. Lewis and Historical Judgment." *Mythlore: A Journal of J. R. R. Tolkien, C. S. Lewis, Charles Williams, and Mythopoeic Literature* 38, no. 2 (Spring/Summer 2020): 5–24.

Monroe, Philip. "Building Bridges with Biblical Counselors." *Journal of Psychology and Theology* 25, no.1 (January 1997): 28–37.

Moon, Gary W. *Becoming Dallas Willard: The Formation of a Philosopher, Teacher, and Christ Follower*. Downers Grove, IL: IVP, 2018.

Moreland, James P. "Reflections on a Day with My Professor and Friend." In *Eternal Living: Reflections on Dallas Willard's Teaching on Faith and Formation*, edited by Gary Moon, 119–29. Downers Grove, IL: IVP, 2014.

Moreland, James P. and William L. Craig. *Philosophical Foundations for a Christian Worldview*. 2nd edition. Downers Grove, IL: IVP, 2017.

Nash, Bruce and Allan Zullo, eds. *Lawyer's Wit and Wisdom*. Philadelphia, PA: Running Press, 1995.

Nash, Ronald. *Worldviews in Conflict: Choosing Christianity in a World of Ideas*. Grand Rapids, MI: Zondervan, 1992.

Naugle, David. "A Commentary on the Mission Statement of Dallas Baptist University." About DBU. Dallas Baptist University. Accessed June 19, 2022, www.dbu.edu/naugle/ _documents/mission-commentary.pdf.

———. "Worldview and a Christian Worldview." Unpublished manuscript. Dallas Baptist University, 2003. Accessed November 27, 2023, https://www.dbu.edu/naugle/academic-papers/_pdfs/11/worldview-and-a-christian-worldview.pdf.

Neff, Megan A., Mary A. Peterson, Mark R. McMinn, Brooke A. Kuhnhausen, Jeffrey Dunkerley, Theresa C. Tisdale, Brad D. Strawn, Edward B. Davis, Everett L. Worthington, M. Elizabeth Hall, and Jennifer S. Ripley. "Re-imagining integration: Student and Faculty Perspectives on Integration Training at Christian Doctoral Programs." *Journal of Psychology and Theology* 49, no. 1 (January 2021): 67–84.

Nelson, Tom. *Work Matters*. Wheaton, IL: Crossway, 2011.

Niebuhr, H. Richard. *Christ and Culture*. Grand Rapids, MI: Eerdmans, 1951.

Niebuhr, Reinhold. *Beyond Tragedy: Essays on the Christian Interpretation of History*. New York, NY: Scribner, 1937.

———. *Faith and History: A Comparison of Christian and Modern Views of History*. New York, NY: Scribner, 1949.

———. *Man's Nature and His Communities: Essays on the Dynamics and Enigmas of Man's Personal and Social Existence*. New York, NY: Scribner, 1965.

———. *Moral Man and Immoral Society: A Study in Ethics and Politics*. 2nd edition. Louisville, KY: John Knox Press, 2013.

Noll, Mark A. *The Civil War as a Theological Crisis*. Chapel Hill: University of North Carolina Press, 2006.

———. *Jesus Christ and the Life of the Mind*. Grand Rapids, MI: Eerdmans, 2013.

———. *Turning Points: Decisive Moments in the History of Christianity*. 3rd edition. Grand Rapids, MI: Baker, 2012.

Noll, Mark A., George Marsden, and Nathan Hatch. *The Search for Christian America*. Expanded edition. Colorado Springs, CO: Helmers and Howard, 1989.

Noonan, Peggy. "Wisdom of a Non-Idiot Billionaire." *Wall Street Journal*, May 10, 2018, https://www.wsj.com/articles/wisdom-of-a-non-idiot-billionaire-1525992653.

Northouse, Peter. *Leadership: Theory and Practice*. Los Angeles, CA: Sage, 2019.

Novak, Michael J. *Joy of Sports*. New York, NY: Basic Books, 1976.

Orlitzky, Marc, Frank L. Schmidt, and Sara L. Rynes. "Corporate Social and Financial Performance: A Meta-Analysis." *Organization Studies* 24, no. 3 (March 2003): 403–41.

Ostrander, Rick. *Why College Matters to God: A Student's Introduction to the Christian College Experience*. Abilene, TX: ACU Press, 2009.

Packer, James I. *Concise Theology: A Guide to Historic Christian Beliefs*. Wheaton, IL: Tyndale House, 1993.

Parham, Angel A. and Anika Prather. *The Black Intellectual Tradition: Reading Freedom in Classical Literature*. Camp Hill, PA: Classical Academic Press, 2022.

Parks, Sharon D. *Leadership Can Be Taught: A Bold Approach for a Complex World*. Boston, MA: Harvard Business School, 2005.

Pearson, Shelley. "To the Coach and Then Through the Coach." *Fellowship of Christian Athletes*. March 17, 2021, https://www.minnesotafca.org/to-through-coach.

Perry L. Glanzer, Theodore F. Cockle, Elijah G. Jeong, and Britney N. Graber. *Christ-Enlivened Student Affairs: A Guide to Thinking and Practice in the Field*. Abilene, TX: ACU Press, 2020.

Peterson, Eugene H. *Practice Resurrection: A Conversation on Growing Up in Christ*. Grand Rapids, MI: Eerdmans, 2013.

Pew Research Center. "Importance of Religion and Religious Beliefs." U.S. Public Becoming Less Religious. November 3, 2015, http://www.pewforum.org/2015/11/03/chapter-1-importance-of-religion-and-religious-beliefs/.

Plantinga, Jr., Cornelius. *Engaging God's World: A Christian Vision of Faith, Learning, and Living*. Grand Rapids, MI: Eerdmans, 2002.

Porter, Michael E. and Mark R. Kramer. "Strategy and Society: The Link Between Competitive Advantage and Corporate Social Responsibility." *Harvard Business Review* 84, no. 12 (December 2006): 78–92.

Ream, Todd C. and Perry L. Glanzer. *The Idea of a Christian College: A Reexamination for Today's University*. Eugene, OR: Cascade Books, 2013.

Rehman, Zia Ur, Asad Khan, and Asim Rahman. "Corporate Social Responsibility's Influence on Firm Risk and Firm Performance: The Mediating Role of Firm Reputation." *Corporate Social Responsibility and Environmental Management* 27, no. 6 (August 2020): 2991–3005.

Rice, R. Garrett. "Can a Christian Be a Corporate Lawyer? Tracing Corporate Law's Religious Roots and Identifying How We Can Integrate Our Faith and Work." *The Journal of the Legal Profession* 43, no. 2 (Spring 2019): 1–42.

Richards, Jay W. and Ann Bradley. "Goldman Sachs, Greed and Self-Interest." *Washington Times*, March 16, 2012, https://www.washingtontimes.com/news/2012/mar/16/goldman-sachs-greed-and-self-interest.

Roberts, Gary E. *Developing Christian Servant Leadership: Faith-Based Character Growth at Work*. New York, NY: Palgrave Macmillan, 2015.

Robinson, Nick. "Declining Dominance: Lawyers in the U. S. Congress." *The Practice: Lawyers in Politics* 2, no. 1 (November 2015): 1–12, https://thepractice.law.harvard.edu/article/declining-dominance/.

Roth, John D., ed. *Constantine Revisited: Leithart, Yoder, and the Constantinian Debate*. Eugene, OR: Pickwick, 2013.

Rudolph, Frederick. *The American College and University: A History*. Athens, GA: University of Georgia Press, 1990.

Rutherford, Matthew A., Laura Parks-Leduc, David E. Cavazos, and Charles D. White. "Required Course: Investigating the Factors Impacting the Decision to Require Ethics in Undergraduate Business Core Curriculum." *Academy of Management Learning and Education* 11, no. 2 (June 2012): 174–86.

Saint Augustine. "The Advantage of Believing." In *On Christian Belief.* Edited by Boniface Ramsey. Translated by Ray Kearney, 105–148. Vol. I/8, The Works of Saint Augustine: A Translation for the 21st Century. Hyde Park, NY: New City Press, 2005.

———. *Teaching Christianity (De Doctrina Christiana)*. Edited by John E. Rotelle. Translated by Edmund Hill. Vol. I/11, The Works of Saint Augustine: A Translation for the 21st Century. Hyde Park, NY: New City Press, 1996.

———. *The Trinity (De Trinitate)*. Edited by John E. Rotelle. Translated by Edmund Hill. 2nd edition. Vol. I/5, The Works of Saint Augustine: A Translation for the 21st Century. Hyde Park, NY: New City Press, 2017.

Sandage, Steven J. and Jeannine K. Brown. "Relational Integration, Part 1: Differentiated Relationality Between Psychology and Theology." *Journal of Psychology and Theology* 43, no. 3 (September 2015): 165–78.

Sandeen, Arthur and Margaret J. Barr. *Critical Issues for Student Affairs: Challenges and Opportunities*. New York, NY: John Wiley, 2014.

Sanford, Samuel. *Baptist Campus Ministry at Crossroads: A Historical and Philosophical Perspective on Its Diamond Anniversary*. Franklin, TN: Providence House, 1997.

Santrac, Aleksander S. "Towards the Possible Integration of Psychology and Christian Faith: Faculties of Human Personality and the Lordship of Christ." *Die Skriflig* 50, no.1 (May 2016): 1–8, http://dx.doi.org/10.4102/ ids.v50i1.1908.

Schejbal, David. "The Core and the Adult Student." In *The Great Skills Gap: Optimizing Talent for the Future of Work*, edited by Jason Wingard and Christine Farrugia, 129–40. Stanford, CA: Stanford University Press, 2021.

Schlitz, Patrick J. "On Being a Happy, Healthy, and Ethical Member of an Unhappy, Unhealthy and Unethical Profession." *Vanderbilt Law Review* 52, no. 4 (1999): 871–951.

Schutt, Mike. *Redeeming Law: Christian Calling and the Legal Profession*. Downers Grove, IL: IVP, 2007.

Scionka, Simon, director. *Poverty Cure*. Featuring Michael M. Miller. Acton Institute, 2013.

Senge, Peter. *The Fifth Discipline: The Art and Practice of the Learning Organization*. New York, NY: Doubleday, 2006.

Shockley, Donald. *Campus Ministry: The Church Beyond Itself*. Louisville, KY: John Knox Press, 1989.

Smith, Brian. *The Christian Athlete: Glorifying God in Sports*. Colorado Springs, CO: David C Cook, 2022.

Smith, D. Brent. *The People Make the Place: Dynamic Linkages Between Individuals and Organizations*. New York, NY: Psychology Press, 2012.

Smith, James B. *The Good and Beautiful God: Falling in Love With the God Jesus Knows*. Downers Grove, IL: IVP, 2009.

Speck, William A. "Herbert Butterfield: The Legacy of a Christian Historian." In *A Christian View of History?* edited by George Marsden and Frank Roberts, 99–117. Grand Rapids, MI: Eerdmans, 1975.

Spickard, Paul R. and Kevin M. Craig. *A Global History of Christians: How Everyday Believers Experienced Their World.* Grand Rapids, MI: Baker, 2001.

Stark, Rodney. *The Rise of Christianity: How the Obscure, Marginal Jesus Movement Became the Dominant Religious Force in the Western World in Five Centuries.* San Francisco, CA: Harper, 1996.

Starr, Kenneth. "Christian Life in the Law." In *Can a Good Christian Be a Good Lawyer? Homilies, Witnesses, and Reflections*, edited by Timothy Floyd and Thomas Baker, 47–50. Notre Dame, IN: University of Notre Dame Press, 1998.

Steenkamp, Petrus L. "Protestant Ethic: Contributing Towards a Meaningful Workplace." *Hervormde Teologiese Studies* 69, no. 1 (January 2013):1–11, https://doi.org/ 10.4102/hts.v69il.1315.

Steinmetz, David C. *Memory and Mission: Theological Reflections on the Christian Past.* Nashville, TN: Abingdon Press, 1988.

Strawn, Brad D., Earl D. Bland, and Paul S. Flores. "Learning Clinical Integration: A Case Study Approach." *Journal of Psychology and Theology* 46, no. 2 (April 2018): 85–97, https://journals.sagepub.com/ doi/pdf/ 10.1177/0091647118767976.

Sunquist, Scott. *The Unexpected Century: The Reversal and Transformation of Global Christianity, 1900–2000.* Grand Rapids, MI: Baker, 2015.

Tan, Siang-Yang. "Integration and Beyond: Principled, Professional, and Personal." *Journal of Psychology and Christianity* 20, no. 1 (Spring 2001): 18–28.

Taylor, Charles. *A Secular Age.* Cambridge, MA: Harvard University Press, 2018.

Texas Education Agency. "Educators' Code of Ethics." Accessed November 27, 2023, https://tea.texas.gov/texas-educators/investigations/educators-code-of-ethics.

Thelin, John R. *A History of American Higher Education*. 3rd edition. Baltimore, MD: Johns Hopkins, 2019.

Torrance, Thomas F. *The Christian Doctrine of God, One Being Three Persons*. Edinburgh, Scotland: T&T Clark, 1996.

Tosh, John. *The Pursuit of History: Aims, Methods, and New Directions in the Study of History*. 6th edition. New York, NY: Routledge, 2015.

Trueblood, Elton. *The Idea of a College*. New York, NY: Harper, 1959.

Trueman, Carl. *The Rise and Triumph of the Modern Self: Cultural Amnesia, Expressive Individualism, and the Road to Sexual Revolution*. Wheaton, IL: Crossway, 2020.

Tunehag, Mats. "God Means Business: An Introduction to Business as Mission, BAM." Business as Mission. April 2008, https://businessasmission.com/resources/god-means-business.

University of Minnesota. "The Purposes of Punishment." In *Criminal Law*. Minneapolis: University of Minnesota Libraries, 2015. Accessed November 27, 2023, https://open.lib.umn.edu/criminallaw/chapter/1-5-the-purposes-of-punishment/.

Veith, Gene. *God at Work*. Wheaton, IL: Crossway, 2002.

Veysey, Laurence. *The Emergence of the American University*. Chicago, IL: University of Chicago Press, 1965.

Vygotsky, Lee. *Educational Psychology*. Delray Beach, FL: St. Lucie Press, 1992.

Walsh, Brian J. and J. Richard Middleton. *The Transforming Vision: Shaping a Christian World View*. Downers Grover, IL: IVP, 1984.

Washington, Booker T. *Up from Slavery: An Autobiography*. New York, NY: Doubleday, 1901.

Watts, Fraser. "Doing Theology in Dialogue with Psychology." *Journal of Psychology and Theology* 40, no.1 (March 2012): 45–50.

Wells, Ronald. *History Through the Eyes of Faith: Western Civilization and the Kingdom of God*. Grand Rapids, MI: Baker, 1989.

Wheatley, Margaret. *Leadership and the New Science.* Oakland, CA: Berrett-Koehler, 1992.

Whelchel, Hugh. *How Then Should We Work.* Bloomington, IN: WestBow Press, 2012.

Wilkerson, Josh. "A Math Catechism (UPDATED)." God and Math: Thinking Christianly About Math Education, September 10, 2021, https://godandmath.com/2021/09/10/a-math-catechism-updated/.

Willard, Dallas. *The Divine Conspiracy: Rediscovering Our Hidden Life in God.* New York, NY: Harper, 1998.

———. *Knowing Christ Today: Why We Can Trust Spiritual Knowledge.* New York, NY: Harper, 2009.

Willard, Dallas and Gary Black, Jr. *The Divine Conspiracy Continued: Fulfilling God's Kingdom on Earth.* New York, NY: Harper, 2015.

Williams, Rowan. *Why Study the Past? The Quest for the Historical Church.* Grand Rapids, MI: Eerdmans, 2005.

Wilson, Jason. "Integration of Faith and Mathematics from the Perspectives of Truth, Beauty, and Goodness." *Perspectives on Science and Christian Faith* 67, no. 2 (June 2015): 100–10.

Wolff, Christoph and Walter Emery. "Bach, Johann Sebastian." Grove Music Online. Oxford Music Online. Accessed November 28, 2023, https://doi.org/10.1093/gmo/9781561592630.article.6002278195.

Woodiwiss, Ashley. "From Tourists to Pilgrims: Christian Practices and the First-Year Experience." In *Teaching and Christian Practices: Reshaping Faith and Learning*, edited by David I. Smith and James K. A. Smith, 123–39. Grand Rapids, MI: Eerdmans, 2011.

Worthington, Jr., Everett L. "A Blueprint for Intradisciplinary Integration." *Journal of Psychology and Theology* 22, no. 2 (June 1994): 79–86.

Wright, N. Tom. *The New Testament and the People of God.* Minneapolis, MN: Fortress Press, 1992.

———. *Simply Jesus: A New Vision of Who He Is, What He Did, and Why He Matters*. San Francisco, CA: Harper, 2018.

Yale College. *Reports on the Course of Instruction in Yale College: By a Committee of the Corporation, and the Academical Faculty*. New Haven, CT: Hezekiah Howe, 1828.

Zinn, Howard. *A People's History of the United States*. Reissue edition. San Francisco, CA: Harper, 2015.

Zizzo, Daniel J. and Andrew J. Oswald. "Are People Willing to Pay to Reduce Others' Incomes?" *Annales d'Économie et de Statistique*, no. 63/64 (July-December 2001): 39–65.

Zook, George F., ed., *Higher Education for American Democracy: A Report of the President's Commission on Higher Education*. Vol. 1, *Establishing the Goals*. New York, NY: Harper, 1947.